P9-CQC-328

WHY SHOULD
THE DEVIL
HAVE ALL THE
GOOD MUSIC?

WHY SHOULD

THE DEVIL

HAVE ALL THE

GOOD MUSIC?

LARRY NORMAN

AND THE

PERILS OF

CHRISTIAN ROCK

GREGORY ALAN
THORNBURY

CONVERGENT
NEW YORK

Copyright © 2018 by Gregory A. Thornbury

All rights reserved.
Published in the United States by Convergent Books,
an imprint of the Crown Publishing Group, a division of
Penguin Random House LLC, New York.
crownpublishing.com

CONVERGENT BOOKS is a registered trademark and its C colophon is a
trademark of Penguin Random House LLC.

Grateful acknowledgment is made to Sony/ATV Music Publishing LLC
for permission to reprint the following: "Why Don't You Look into Jesus"
© 1973 by Glenwood Music Corp.; "I Don't Believe in Miracles" © 1970 by
Beechwood Music Corporation; and "Why Should the Devil Have All the
Good Music" © 1973 by Glenwood Music Corp. and Straw Bed Music. All
rights administered by Sony/ATV Music Publishing LLC, 424 Church Street,
Suite 1200, Nashville, TN 37219. All rights reserved. Used by permission.

Library of Congress Cataloging-in-Publication Data
is available upon request.

ISBN 978-1-101-90707-8
Ebook ISBN 978-1-101-90708-5

Printed in the United States of America

Book design by Lauren Dong
Jacket design by Jessie Sayward Bright
Jacket photograph by Charles Norman

10 9 8 7 6 5 4 3 2 1

First Edition

For Jonathan Paul Gillette
and to Fehrion, wherever you are

One of the first signs of a saint may well be the fact that other people do not know what to make of him. In fact, they are not sure whether he is crazy or only proud; but it must at least be pride to be haunted by some individual ideal which nobody but God really comprehends. And he has inescapable difficulties in applying all the abstract norms of "perfection" to his own life. He cannot make his life fit in with the books.

—THOMAS MERTON, *NEW SEEDS OF CONTEMPLATION*

———

It is harder to walk on a tightrope than it is to walk in the middle of the street.

—LARRY NORMAN, IN AN INTERVIEW, 1980

CONTENTS

WHY SHOULD

THE DEVIL

HAVE ALL THE

GOOD MUSIC?

PROLOGUE

JESUS AND LARRY NORMAN

A LTHOUGH HE OCCASIONALLY TOURED WITH A FULL BAND— especially at the zenith of his popularity in the late 1970s and '80s—the typical Larry Norman concert began with him wandering slowly out onto a darkened stage lit with a sole spotlight, his cheap nylon-string acoustic guitar hung around his neck. His contract called for a grand piano arranged at a forty-five-degree angle from the stage, with two boom mics on a stand (one for the instrument, one for vocals), and a pitcher of water and a glass. Center stage out front were two boom mics for guitar and vocal, set to the exact same volume level and a flat EQ—a request that proved to be a perennial source of conflict. Two speakers were positioned in front of the mics, delivering what had become Norman's signature live sound within a few months of playing solo: a folk guitar turned up to the point of distortion and vocals wet with reverb.

The concert setup was disciplined and minimalistic, and the act only worked if the audience was relatively quiet. At times, the atmosphere felt carefree and hilarious. At others, deadly serious. Norman would often quit playing if people started clapping during his songs or singing along. His main interest was forcing his audience toward self-examination, so if people were having fun at his concert, Larry thought, they probably weren't thinking hard enough.

On some occasions, Norman seemed so invested in antagonizing his audience that it felt like a fight was going to break out between him and the crowd. Then there were the conflicts provided by inexpert, church-volunteer help. Larry played major rock venues like the Royal Albert Hall and the Hollywood Palladium, but he also played in churches and at venues operated by ministries, where he often found that whoever had booked the show had not thoroughly read the contract. In his early shows, he would notice that between the sound check and the start of his set, the mic levels had been changed. Church sound men almost always preferred vocals to be louder than instruments, believing instruments and musicianship to be less important than the message—but when Norman noticed the discrepancy, he would bring the concert to a grinding halt. Positioning the sound hole of his guitar in front of the vocal mic, he would strum a chord hard, and then immediately lower it to strum the same chord on the guitar mic. Different sound levels. Every time. Breaking the fourth wall, he would directly address the sound man, almost always a church member and volunteer: "Hey, could you set these two mics at the same level like I asked? This is rock 'n' roll, okay? Louder is better." The humiliated guy in the back of the room would comply.

The sound man shtick became a staple of the Larry Norman concert mythology. Norman sometimes made a joke of it: "Hey, could you turn the guitar up on the dial just past where it says 'folk music'?" Other times he griped about the overall volume level in the room. Staring at the PA, he might say, "You know, back in the war, they used to drop these [speakers] on the enemy, you know, because they couldn't hear them coming." Legitimate technical issues with his guitar volume aside, Norman discovered the routine had a serendipitous side benefit of putting the audience on edge. Suddenly, this wasn't fun anymore. Larry would apologize afterward to the unfortunate fellow at the concert mixing board, but the more one knows about Larry, the more one wonders whether he was really sorry.

In addition to yelling at the sound guy, Norman would startle audiences by criticizing institutional religion, and discussing white Christianity's trouble with systemic racism. He mentioned forbidden topics—everything from STDs to contemporary music, film, and art. He was the godfather of Christian rock, but he stated repeatedly in his notebooks and interviews that he felt called to confront Christian culture. This de facto mission statement had varied repercussions. None other than Paul McCartney once reportedly made the remark that Larry Norman could be a star if he'd just shut up about religion.[1]

Whether or not the story is apocryphal, it was a sentiment repeated by *Entertainment Weekly* senior music writer Chris Willman, and is true even if Sir Paul never actually said it. Larry Norman (1947–2008) was a holy fool, often grossly misunderstood, certainly harassed—mostly by fellow Christians—and uniquely constituted to attract controversy. To put it both mildly and crudely, Larry Norman wanted it both ways; he wanted to rock and he wanted to talk about Jesus, he wanted to follow Jesus and to offend other followers of Jesus, for people to enjoy his music but also be discomfited by it. Larry Norman lived a life of fantasy, especially to people who consider themselves faithful believers. He pretty much did as he pleased. He sang about what he felt, made a living doing what he loved, countenanced no authorities over him, and died a cult hero whose followers and family had to clean up the messes he left behind. Like Søren Kierkegaard's self-understanding, he lived up to the moniker "that individual," the person who is convinced that "wherever there is a crowd there is untruth." I have been fascinated by Larry's career for over twenty years now, and am thrilled to have been given access to his personal archives in order to tell this story, because Larry's story is not his alone.

When *Time* magazine profiled the Jesus movement (the non-drug, non–free love religious youth revival of the early 1970s), they wrote that Norman was "probably the top solo artist in the field." From the 1970s onward, this "Father of Christian Rock" inspired a dazzling, eclectic group of secular artists. Singers as diverse as Tennessee Ernie Ford and Sammy Davis Jr. recorded his songs. Dizzy Reed of Guns N' Roses cited him as an inspiration. Black Francis of the Pixies claimed he wanted to be Larry Norman when he grew up, and artists as varied as Damien Jurado, John Mellencamp, and Martin Sheen are fans. And then came the politicians. Larry Norman was invited by Jimmy Carter to perform on the White House South Lawn, and invited again to the White House by President George W. Bush. After his death in 2008, the *Huffington Post* ran a story calling him "The Most Amazing Artist You've Never Heard Of."[2] And last but not least, there's Bono. During his publicity tour in support of "One: The Campaign to Make Poverty History," Bono came to Nashville, Tennessee, to meet with the leading voices in contemporary Christian music (CCM). After being picked up from the airport, the lead singer and justice activist's first question was whether Larry Norman would be in attendance.

Larry had a remarkable gift for finding himself in illustrious company. He rubbed elbows with the writer Michael Crichton (right before the film of *The Andromeda Strain* was coming out), the actress Elizabeth Ashley (just after her divorce from George Peppard), and in his early days singing with the band People! he played on bills with Jimi Hendrix, Janis Joplin, the Grateful Dead, the Byrds, and Jefferson Airplane. He even tried, over the course of their friendship, to bring the actor Dudley Moore to faith in Christ. He was the Forrest Gump of evangelical Christianity.

The foregoing associations are all ones to which Larry would have proudly pointed as part of his legacy. It was the Christian imitators who followed in his wake that he both encouraged at first and eventually despised, because fellow believers made his life miserable. Many would-be Jesus rock artists coveted Larry's notoriety, but as Christian rock got more profitable in the years after Larry's halcyon days, it became less art than sermonizing; your average Christian rock song boiled down to finding creative ways to tell sinners what to do. Larry Norman, in contrast, was incredibly effective at getting crowds to enter into his "message"—how, through God, coming to terms with your secret sins made you more compassionate to the poor, the needy, and the lost. When his imitators were less successful, they resented him bitterly. Even when he was down and out in his lowest moments, Norman possessed a mystique that invited jealousy, intrigue, and envy from fans, critics, and colleagues. He was, in that sense, special.

He did not start out in the Christian music subculture then break out into the mainstream. He traveled the other direction, signing to Capitol Records at the tender age of nineteen and releasing three albums on major record labels while starting his own underground record company in between. Later, he would form his own proper record company with a national distribution deal. His independent label and artists' agency would eventually go down in flames, but for a while it stood as a beacon of hope for many young Christians, some of whom identified with the hippie-ish Jesus movement and some who didn't, who largely just wanted models for how to be effectively different in an American pop-cultural landscape that was increasingly diverse, sophisticated, and raw—yet somehow, underneath it all, depressingly the same as it ever was. For them, Larry Norman, with his long, corn-colored blond hair, black leather jackets, gorgeous model wife, and willingness to irritate concert audiences by testifying about Jesus at length between songs, seemed (quite literally) a godsend. Boxes of fan mail from the '70s bear testimony to this fact, as did Internet bulletin boards and Facebook fan groups when the singer passed away. One British reporter remarked upon seeing Norman for the first time in 1972: "If, like me, you see Christianity as a reluctantly but irrevocably dying mythology, Larry Norman is still worth hearing for his music and himself."[3]

After his concerts, Larry would stand around backstage, sometimes for hours, to talk to people. He generally refused to sign autographs, or to make small talk. But if someone wanted to talk about his or her problems, and ask for prayer, he was in no hurry to leave. At times he seemed more interested in these backstage conversations than the show itself. This was supposed to be the difference between Jesus rock and the secular alternative. One simply got feet tapping and hips moving. The other one opened up the heart, placed a person in a vulnerable position, and gave a chance for the Holy Spirit to sneak through into a person's life—just long enough for them to feel changed, to imagine that life could be different. Somehow, Larry's music managed to do both.

So of course he had to be taken down, the cynical might say, and they might be right. For the story of Larry Norman is most compelling not for his successes but for his dizzying, at times mystifying, lows. Norman's closest friends disparaged him in interviews, rumor-mongered with concert promoters, and shook their heads at his sinful behavior in backstage conversations with fans. The CCM industry reviled him repeatedly in print. Former associates eagerly contributed to a curiously produced documentary titled *Fallen Angel: The Outlaw Larry Norman*, which seemed to relish in stories of Larry as an unscrupulous, libertine, lying narcissist, whose sins included everything from not attending church services regularly to fathering a child (possibly two) out of wedlock, to a tendency to micromanage, to being a complete and utter fraud. It was released one year after Larry died of heart failure at the age of sixty.

If the Christian establishment found Larry controversial, to the nonbeliever he was equally puzzling, continually offering up Jesus as a solution to problems they didn't think were problems. This wasn't why people listened to rock 'n' roll—to be told they were lacking some missing piece of information or vital truth. And although Larry Norman seemed to spark the imagination of those outside of Christ's fold, he constantly ran the risk of driving away people who were interested in the questions, not the answers.

In many ways, the story of Larry Norman helps explain the rise of the Religious Right, the animosities that launched America's "culture wars," and the recent rise of the religiously unaffiliated in the United States and Europe. In the past decade, much has been written about Evangelicals' ever-tenuous relationship with mainstream American culture, and the way in which millennials rejected a Church that spends less time following Jesus than it does fighting for political power. But forty years ago, Larry Norman rejected the notion that being Christian meant walling oneself off from the outside world, all the while pioneering the notion that young people could be close to God without listening to religious authorities or being a faithful attender of any church. In one of his lyrics, he openly disparaged the notion of "building nice little churches," because the young people following Jesus were "having their church out in the streets." His message was that you could be spiritual without being religious, a concept that practically became cliché with Generation X and today's "religious nones," young people who are neither atheists nor materialists and yet refuse to identify with any known religious system. For them, Larry Norman was a grandparent, a forerunner.[4] For the rest of us, he is an example of what might've been.

"Nothing stops me," he told an interviewer in the late '70s. "I feel that God is with me and this is my profession. I am a provocateur. I am a spy sent behind enemy lines. I am part of the resistance, resisting worldliness and helping others find a way out, safe passage through the guarded borders." In 1941 folksinger Woody Guthrie slapped a label on his guitar that read THIS MACHINE KILLS FASCISTS. Over the years I've been listening to it, I've come to see Larry Norman's voice as a machine for killing complacency in religious people, and it is my sincere hope that this book does the same.

This is the story of a once-in-a-generation musician who died without attaining the acclaim he deserved. It's a story of a man who, despite those setbacks, nevertheless left a lasting mark on America's cultural scene. But at its heart, it is a story of someone who believed so purely that he was following Jesus, that in his mind he frequently saw very little difference between what he was seeing and what the Good Lord himself was seeing. (A characteristic that informs the chapter titles of this book.) This is a feature of the religious mind-set. From the time he was little, Larry considered Jesus his best friend, a possibility opened up to him by gospel hymns he had sung as a boy in church. For example:

What a friend we have in Jesus!
All our sins and griefs to bear

What a privilege to carry
Everything to God in prayer.

Do thy friends despise, forsake thee?
Take it to the Lord in prayer!
In his arms he'll take and shield thee
Thou wilt find a solace there.[5]

As Bob Dylan once reminded us, there is no more powerful idea than the notion that "God is on your side." Like the winds of the jet stream, you experience its different effects. If you're flying east, they speed you up. Due west, they slow you down. But other times, you get crosswinds, and those can take you down. Larry Norman believed in Jesus, and thought the Son of God was his best friend. This is the story of how that adventure turned out.

1

JESUS VERSUS SUPERMAN

LARRY'S GRANDMOTHER GAVE HIM A TOY PIANO WHEN HE WAS two years old. He remembers noticing sounds and trying to reproduce them: "the wood crackling in the stove, the boiling of water, the dripping of the faucet. [I] was absorbed in the music that noise made."[1]

Kids at school teased Larry for singing for his classmates on the playground instead of playing sports. A sensitive youngster, he felt alien, and had a hard time seeing himself as a peer in the midst of other children. One day, in order to bolster his courage against a neighborhood bully nicknamed "Caesar," he took his mother's sewing machine and made for himself a Superman costume that he could secretly wear underneath his school clothes. According to Margaret, his mother, "He bought a piece of [blue] fabric, lay down on it, and traced his body onto the pattern."[2] He was ten years old at the time, grasping for strength in his favorite television hero.

But heroes have a way of disappointing their followers' hopes. On June 16, 1959, a then twelve-year-old Larry woke up at his home just a block from Haight-Ashbury in San Francisco, ran down the stairs, greeted Mom, Dad, and little sisters, and downed his bowl of cereal. His usual morning routine included going out to deliver newspapers with his grandfather to the convalescing patients at Southern Pacific Hospital, but this particular day proved different. He picked up the morning edition—incredibly, a moment captured by the family's 8mm camera—and looked down at the headline: SUPERMAN KILLS SELF.[3]

The article had to do with the mysterious death of George Reeves, who famously played "The Man of Steel" on the 1950s television series. But to a child, all of this seemed quite literal, begging the question: how can Superman die? Larry grew up ten inches from the family television set, and *Superman* was his favorite show—it was an invitation to believe in "truth, justice, and the American way." Margaret Norman recalled her son being devastated by the news: "He had to deliver every single paper that day" with Superman's reported suicide as the headline. But by the afternoon, Larry had rallied. He came down to the kitchen to announce to his parents and grandparents the good news. "I'm not Superman," he reassured them. "I'm Batman."

For the rest of his life, Larry Norman would, in fact, play the role of the vigilante pursuing his own notions of justice. In later interviews he would ascribe his productivity to a desire for balance. He wanted to force those who enjoyed a monopoly—be it on an idea, image, or place of grace—to share the space with others, especially if those "others" weren't exactly their kind of people.

In the meantime, he had to survive a misfit childhood. Another of Larry's lifelong obsessions began at the age of five, when, in his later recollection, he "accepted Jesus without benefit of clergy." For a boy who often felt alone both at school and at home, often lost in his thoughts and feelings, Jesus was a solution to loneliness. "My father worked all night at the [Southern Pacific] railroad," he remembered, "and during the day studied at a small college nearby hoping to pull us out of poverty. My mother stayed home with my two sisters and myself hoping to fill in the hole left by the absence of my father.... [So] I liked Jesus immediately."[4] Larry felt the Son of God was the friend he never had, and consequently, "I didn't feel so alone after that, and I loved him."

As for the clergy in his life, they just got in the way, or couldn't appreciate the depth of his enthusiasm. He remembered being spanked for dancing in the aisles in his "hellfire and brimstone" Southern Baptist congregation—First Baptist in Corpus Christi, Texas. Was church the sort of place where Jesus would want to spend time? It did not seem that way to Larry, looking at the stern faces that populated his parents' church. "I felt that church was boring and the street-corner preachers were no more happy than the people they were preaching to."[5]

School was no haven either. Larry experienced intense boredom and loneliness in the classroom. He would take "alternative routes to school . . . a mile away," to avoid getting teased or hit. "They would stomp on my sandwiches, break my thermos, and knock my books into the gutter."[6] He was also cheeky, once telling an elementary school teacher that if he ever needed arithmetic to complete his income taxes, he would hire an accountant. The teacher sent him to the principal's office for the rest of the afternoon.[7]

So unhappy was he with school, Larry faked illness to stay home to listen to the radio: *Red Ryder, The Great Gildersleeve, Mystery Theatre, The Romance of Helen Trent*, and others. He used whatever free time he had in the library and participating in whatever musical or theatrical productions would have him. In third grade, his teacher asked him to choose a story for the class play. He selected "The Tragic Story of Doctor Faustus." When Satan arrived to claim Faustus's soul, Larry fell backward, and his skull hit the riser—creating a terrible sound in the cavernous school gym. When another child rushed over to see if he was "okay," Larry hissed at him because the boy had broken character during this momentous scene.

Larry possessed a taste for the theatrical—to put it mildly. He came by it honestly, through both sides of his family. His maternal grandfather, the rumbustious Burl Stout, came from Irish stock and plied his trade as a vaudeville performer. Burl turned to the stage after being honorably discharged from the US Army during World War I, due to asthma, after serving in the European theater. "As an actor," remembered Larry, "he had 'trod the boards' all over America, performing on the same bills with the likes of Buster Keaton, Smith and Dale, and Bert Lahr."[8] But once Hollywood movies became the main form of popular entertainment in America, vaudeville effectively died. Grandpa Burl and his wife, Lena, took up an itinerant life, moving from Missouri via covered wagon to the cold prairie of Minnesota, before finally settling in Nebraska, where Larry's mother, Margaret, was born in 1925. When President Franklin D. Roosevelt formed Subsistence Homesteading under the provisions of the New Deal in 1933, the Stouts made their way to Baxter County, Arkansas, where they settled—first in a tent, next in a shed, until they built a log cabin of their own.[9]

Larry's paternal side of the family was Native American (Choctaw and Pawnee). Their origin story was just as colorful as the Stouts': as a baby, Larry's great-great-grandfather was abandoned in a shoebox on a doorstep somewhere in Oklahoma, where a family named Norman took him in and raised him. The next male in the Norman line would grow up to be a circuit-riding evangelist, and the evangelist's son—Larry's grandfather Joseph—would settle in Corpus Christi, Texas, near the Gulf of Mexico, where he became the town barber, married a hearty, stout woman named Rubie Hendrex, and took to music. Soon, guitar and harmonica lessons would become part of growing up Norman.

Rubie gave birth to "Joe Billy," a rough-and-tumble boy. "As red and brown as Joseph Porter Norman was, Joe Billy contrasted it by being white-skinned and a 'towhead' with a shock of white hair," Larry wrote, describing his father. He "was a wild, territorial boy by nature, hunting and fishing and gambling for marbles, bottle caps and 'conkers' without much supervision—as though he was answerable to no one." Determined to flee the shame of his father's reputation as the town drunk, "Joe Billy" left Corpus Christi and joined the US Army Air Force (before it was its own independent branch of the military service) as a private first class. Shortly before his platoon was deployed, Joe injured his leg in a swimming accident, and therefore did not ship out with the rest of his band of brothers. The whole platoon died in battle at D-Day a few weeks later. While Joe was convalescing, his commanding officer noticed he was an excellent typist, and he was summarily assigned to the Communications Office, or as Joe said, he "flew desk" for the remainder of the war.

Meanwhile the Stouts had moved west to California to look for work in the shipyards. It was there that a young Margaret Stout met Joe, now stationed at the Santa Rosa Army Air Field, at a USO dance at the Rio Nido summer resort. That first night, Joe brought two other young women to the event and Margaret danced with two other guys. By the second night, however, Joe asked "Marge" to dance, and the two were smitten. They married on November 1, 1945, at the Seventh Avenue Presbyterian Church near Golden Gate Park—a congregation that would become a refuge for hippies and sexual minorities in the '60s and '70s. Joe was honorably discharged from the service in 1946, and the couple rented an apartment near Buena Vista Park. Thinking they could better afford Texas, they moved to Joe's hometown of Corpus Christi. Larry was born, their first child, in 1947. He would later write: "God, thank you that I got [to] be born. Even if it was in Texas."[10]

All across America, 1947 was a year of exploration, freedom, and ongoing testimony of resistance to the high tide of evil and tyranny seen in the war. Howard Hughes flew the massive *Spruce Goose* as a sign of America's explosion in innovation and industry. Jack Kerouac and his friends set out on their journey across America as free spirits, a trip immortalized a decade later with the publication of *On the Road*, the manifesto of the coming counterculture and the Beat Generation. Elsewhere, Jackson Pollock made the first of his drip paintings, and *The Diary of Anne Frank* was published, reminding the world of the courage it had summoned during the horrors of the Second World War.

Joe and Margaret were straightlaced and upstanding Americans. They didn't talk much about family ties to show business. As Larry would later tell interviewers, their experience of being "born again" led them to stop "competition dancing, going to the movies, drinking, and clubbing." Like many evangelicals, they channeled postwar, post-Hiroshima anxiety into what critic Harris Franklin Roll called "a new apocalypticism," meaning of primary concern was not merely when the world would end (soon, it was assumed) but also how one would fare in the brave new afterlife—or as the Rev. Billy Graham put it, "The only question is: Where will you spend eternity?" According to this ethos, it was dangerous to enjoy too much of the things this world had to offer; if indulgence didn't get you sick, diseased, or broke first, you would certainly go to hell.

After their brief stint in Texas, however, Joe and Marge's young family was pulled back to San Francisco. At first they moved in with Larry's grandmother Lena in Haight-Ashbury, but soon Joe's job at the Southern Pacific Railroad afforded them their own place in Elgin Park, on a street between the Mission District and Hayes Valley, where a combination of working-class whites, immigrants, and minorities lived while trying to get a foothold economically and socially.[11] Larry's cousin and best friend, Bryce, and cousin Tina lived with Larry and his sisters, Nancy (b. 1950) and Kristy Beth (b. 1951) for several years, forming a strong household dynamic for a young boy. Another move broke up this cozy circle, however, when Joe's desire to raise the family's standard of living led them to his next job, and their next home, in the quiet suburb of Pacifica. As Larry later put it, "we moved from the ghetto to a slum."[12]

Larry had two interests during this time—books and music. He expressed pride that the local librarian had allowed him to check out more than one book at a time. Winning a thirty-volume set of *The Encyclopaedia Britannica* in a raffle he took, at the age of nine, as some kind of affirmation. With respect to music, he had to be sneakier. Larry got a major revelation when he found, tucked away in his closet, a ukulele that Joe had originally bought but never played. Upon discovering the instrument, Larry began sneaking into his parents' bedroom (a forbidden zone for the Norman children) and experimenting with sounds and melodies. Joe caught Larry with the ukulele one day—but instead of getting mad, he asked Larry to play him a song. When the young boy walked out of the room that day with the instrument tucked underneath his arm, he felt like a god.[13]

Despite such brief moments of encouragement, Larry would struggle with his relationship with his father. Larry felt that Joe never understood him on an emotional level. In an essay he wrote during his freshman—and only—year in college, Larry recalled an exemplary exchange between him and his father:

> Our conversations are always incongruous. I will ask him a question on one level and he will answer it on another level. We realize that we're talking about the same thing, but we never understand the other's point of view.
>
> For example, I will comment, "You know, people are so different," and he would retort, "That is true. You see, the origin of all races is endemic to the blood lines of three different people: Ham, Shem, and Japheth. As it is written in the Scriptures..."
>
> "No, Dad," I interrupt. "What I mean is people are different from us. I don't fit in with the kids at school. I don't think like they do. None of them seem to care about self-improvement, or about other things that count for so much in life. And you don't fit in with your colleagues either. You are a complete ascetic, for one thing. You don't smoke or even drink."
>
> "Son, every society, no matter how primitive, has had its form of alcoholic beverage, and I don't care to indulge in what they..."
>
> "I think I hear Mom calling," I lie, well aware that he is about to enlarge on a theme of constant subculture similarities. I can't talk to my Dad. He knows all of the rules but none of the reasons. We're worlds apart.[14]

For Joe, the world was structured, built upon eternal law and principle. For Larry, the world was fueled by gray areas, intuitions, and analogies, prompting him to say to his more concrete sequential friends over the years: "Metaphors be with you."

Margaret, on the other hand, could do no wrong in Larry's sight. In 2002 she wrote down her memories of Larry's childhood, noting that he was "always a little helper. Even at the age of two he helped momma wash the dishes and taught his momma to sing on tune to 'Jesus Loves Me.' Finally, little Larry took over the job of washing the breakfast dishes. He had a much better way."[15]

Over time, Larry's personality evolved into a composite of both parents. Like his father, he was driven, righteous, intellectual, and somewhat aloof. Like his mother, he was a dreamer and a poet.

His musical interests, however, bore the stamp of his larger-than-life aunt Nina and uncle Frenchie. Aunt Nina, Marge's older sister, grew up in Arkansas and hated everything there with the exception of her neighbor's piano, on which she taught herself to play. She thought she had found her ticket out by getting married and moving to Kansas City, but her deadbeat husband skipped town days before their baby arrived, prompting both Marge and their mother, Lena, to join her in Kansas City and help raise the child. In a surprising turn of events, Nina went straight to work, finding gigs in local nightclubs, and eventually burlesque shows. Nina struck a deal with her mother: take care of my kid while I travel around the country performing, and I'll send lots of money home.

As Nina's notoriety grew, she received top billing under the heading "The Last of the Red Hot Mamas," picking up the mantle from the internationally famous performer Sophie Tucker. She smoked Pall Mall cigarettes, which gave her a deep, sultry singing voice. Among the stories she later entertained the family with was an account of taking Jayne Mansfield's place for a gig in New Orleans on the day Jayne died in a car accident. Larry's sisters remember their aunt escorting them to her bedroom to show them her "dresses" but all that Kristy Beth remembered seeing was her stockings and garters.[16]

Years later, Nina met her love match in Frenchie Manning, a tightrope-walking clown who dressed as a cowboy and simultaneously performed rope tricks. The couple took a special interest in Larry. By the time Larry was eight, Frenchie had taught him the essential chords on the ukulele. Nina then bought Larry his own ukulele, separate from Joe's. He was off to the races, writing his first song,

"Riding in the Saddle," at the age of nine. "Barbara's My Girl" followed soon thereafter. The extended family record collection would be an ongoing inspiration. Although Joe and Margaret favored Big Band crooners like Frank Sinatra and Dean Martin, Grandpa Burl's folk and vaudeville collection proved more fascinating to Larry. Among his favorite records were those of Bill "Bojangles" Robinson and his grandfather's collector's set of "Famous Songs of Bert Williams," Williams being the Bahamian American singer and comedian who, after establishing himself as a top vaudeville performer, became the first black cast member of *Ziegfeld's Follies* in New York City.

Less than a year after coming under Frenchie's tutelage—in 1956—Larry would write his first truly good, recordable song, "Lonely Boy." Other songs followed, including "My Feet Are on the Rock" (from 1958, written on the heels of being spanked for dancing in church), and "Country Church, Country People," written for his grandma Lena, its lyrics narrating a story about the little chapel that the Stout family had attended in Arkansas.

When he was ten, Larry discovered one of the mainstays of midcentury American suburbia—the bookmobile. From the Works Progress Administration to local municipalities, the bookmobile represented access to knowledge for underserved communities, both urban and rural.[17] Here, Larry found books that he couldn't obtain from his elementary school library. He became mesmerized by a hefty volume on basic psychology, which in his mind promised knowledge that the authorities at school had suppressed, and his conspiracy theory deepened further when he tried to check out the book and the librarian told him that he was not old enough. Insatiable for knowledge about the ways of the world, he stole the book: "It took [me] all year to read it. [I] used a dictionary alongside it to look up words [I'd] never seen before."[18]

Initially, Larry could not find anyone interested in his ideas about life and his precocious interest in Freud. But then, all of a sudden, he found one: Coretta, his babysitter, who was a college student and his first crush. Describing her as having "long-willowy legs," and "a passion for horseback riding," he found that if he could entertain Coretta with his stories and antics, she would let him stay up long past his bedtime. She would only hurry him up to his room when the crunch of the gravel under Joe and Margaret's car announced itself coming up the driveway. Giggling at the fast one he had pulled over on the adults, Larry learned an invaluable lesson: appearances were power. Still, he had to keep his nascent ambitions under wraps. In 1959 Larry went into San Francisco to audition for the syndicated CBS television show *Ted Mack's Original Amateur Hour*, but he knew that even if he passed the audition, his parents would never let him travel to New York to perform on the air.[19]

In 1960 the family moved again, this time to San Jose, where Joe finally landed a job teaching high school English for the Fremont Union High School District (where he taught Steve Wozniak in class as a pupil). By the time Larry reached Campbell High School, his artistic interests were in full bloom. He played roles in performances of *Carousel* and *Oklahoma!*, over Joe's protestations. He began to take writing poetry very seriously, and did his best to study both free verse as well as rhythm and meter. By 1963, his junior year, he produced several pieces which placed in the 16th Annual Edwin Markham Poetry Society Contest. His poem about growing up in the city took first place in its category; entitled "The Streets," it earned Norman the distinction of being the youngest person at the time to become a full member of the society:

> *There is something noble about*
>> *the asphalt lawns and the high, wire hedges of a city.*
> *There is something intriguing about*
>> *gutters silted with dirt, and*
>> *old cracking houses with unswept porches, and*
>> *alleys strewn with yellowing newspaper.*
> *I was raised in the slum and the streets taught me to*
>> *swear and smoke*
>> *and spit elegantly through my teeth, and keep my fists up.*

But the street also taught me to look at myself as I really am.
And I feel a bond with the streets because
> *streets are honest. They're unassuming and unpretentious.*
> *They don't try to be anything but streets,*
> *and they're entirely successful.*

While the world is rich with indifference
> *the streets are aware and resigned.*
> *While people wear masks and try to be what they think*
> *they ought to be,*
> *the streets only try to be streets.*[20]

First place came with a special prize: breakfast with British writer William Golding, author of *Lord of the Flies*. Seated next to Golding at the awards ceremony in Saratoga, California, Larry attempted to make small talk, but Golding, presumably there only for a payday and a brief appearance at the event, didn't seem interested in humoring his youthful counterpart. When Larry asked him, "Do you find it difficult to come up with your ideas for writing?" Golding stubbed out his cigarette in his plate of scrambled eggs, stood up, started to leave the table, and said, "Actually, I find it more difficult to control my bladder." A photo of the pair captures the meeting in quintessence.

Meanwhile, Larry's family started to arrive, Aunt Nina waltzing in wearing a big Hawaiian muumuu dress. When Larry was introduced for his award and the emcee announced that the boy would perform two of his poems set to music, Larry spotted his auntie in the audience and decided to play one of his more recent compositions—a scene from Marge and Nina's hardscrabble Arkansas childhood. Larry had been told the story of how the family's copper tub (used for bathing) went missing one day from the porch of their cabin. No one knew where it went or why. One day, Grandma Lena took Old Pete, their mule, up to a little unincorporated town named Three Brothers to "get corn meal and flour with the pension money." As the sun set, Lena found herself lost, off the beaten path on a hillside, and there it was: their copper bathtub being used for a still, in a moonshine operation run by the local pastor. Seventeen-year-old Larry put the story to music, and played it for the poetry society.

WHEN THE MOON SHINES ON THE MOONSHINE

When the moon shines on the moonshine
on the still upon the hill
Then I smell it drifting down through the pines.

'Cause the night time is the right time
for the stuff to get enough
Of the moonlight to make it taste fine.

You can tell it when you smell it;
It'll knock you off your feet,
So you might want to be sitting down.

Get your fill at the still
for a wrinkled dollar bill
You can buy it from the good Parson Brown.

Everybody ought to buy it
you ain't living till you try it
And you'll drink it again and again.

All the nosy revenuers
want to meet up with the brewers
And redeem them from the bright liquid sin.

High up in the mountaintops
far away from all the cops
Granny's cranking it out every day.

And Brother Frank is in the holler
*   selling two jugs for a dollar*
Who says that crime doesn't pay?

At the end of the song, Nina leaped to her feet and shouted, "I taught him everything he knows!" Joe was mortified, as were other family members. But Larry smiled, because the song was for her. The next day Aunt Nina wrote Larry a letter, elaborating on her enthusiasm:

My Dear Nephew:

Congratulations! It was a great honor for me to sit in your audience yesterday! Man, I really dig your poetry. Will you send me a copy of your poem? Also a copy of "Moonshine." I'm sorry I didn't have the time to discuss your poem with you, and someday I will tell you why I jumped out of my seat and looked like an idiot . . . but I was so proud of you.

You will go far with your writing because you know how to write about life as it is. The world needs writers like you who think as you do. You wrote the story of my life in that one little poem.

All my love and best wishes for your future.
Aunt Nina.

P.S. WORDS ARE POWER

Aunt Nina's letter was precisely the kind of encouragement her nephew needed to keep writing. By now, Larry had noticed that when his poetry was set to music, it produced an entirely different level of reaction. He also discovered that his best song ideas arose from dreams. In one such dream, Larry later explained, he was standing before a class of children and teaching them about poetry:

"For instance," I said, taking up a piece of chalk. "Let's just put down a random line and then see what significance we can bring to it which would give it value.

"Doze, he did, among the rocks . . ." I wrote upon the blackboard and then paused, thinking of a line to follow.

What I was remembering in my sleep was the afternoon—in my real life—when I had felt so full of anguish, as a teenage boy, that I had laid down on the ground outside, quite positive that the emotional pain I was feeling was so intense that it would cause me to die. I saw the scene as though it were being filmed from above me. I could see me curled up, laying on the rocks with flowers around me.

This is the movie I saw in my head, in front of the blackboard . . . in my sleep . . . thinking this was really happening in real life.

"Doze, he did, among the rocks . . .
Poseys [sic], little flowered flocks
Of beauty all around his head.
Death and sleep are nightly wed."

I sat up in bed, awakened by the image of death and sleep being symbolically related, in a poetic and dreamscape kind of way.

I grabbed a pen and scribbled the poem down on the white sheet I was sleeping on—and fell back asleep. I was surprised to see, in the morning, that the whole thing was not a dream.

From then on, sheets became a writing partner for me. I often wrote lyrics while asleep and would simply write them down and go back to sleep to see if there were any more lyrics to follow. And at one point in the band, I felt so alone that I laid flat down on the sheet and drew a line around my body, kind of like police chalk marks. So every night when I jumped into bed, there I was, waiting for me—like Peter Pan's shadow.[21]

Writing on bedsheets instead of notebook paper might suggest someone who was OCD. But Larry was not content to be the only one to lose sleep over his song ideas. After acquiring a reel-to-reel tape recorder, he would wake up his sisters to teach them harmony parts through the floor vents, long after Marge had put them into bed. In exchange, Larry promised to play "house" with his sisters, with only one condition: he refused to play the daddy. (Instead he played the role of the family dog.) It was a bargain worth striking. When morning came, he expected his sisters to have their parts memorized so that they could sing them into the recorder. The results were astonishing. The recordings survived, and have been released by the Norman family. Known as *The Living Room Tapes*, the collection represents the remarkable extent to which Larry Norman's powers had developed by age sixteen. The advanced chord progression found on the tapes' "Face the Wind," for example, was written in the key of F and played in the fifth position on the fret board. Its elegant finger-picking style and inventive deployment of major and minor chord melody tradeoffs sound more classically oriented than either blues or rock 'n' roll.[22] Other tunes, such as "Gotta Travel On," feature Nancy and Kristy singing counterpoint harmonies. One can detect the influence of Brian Wilson, and yet the tapes were recorded in 1963, three years before the compositions heard on Wilson's masterpiece, *Pet Sounds.*

Although most of the songs were folk-oriented, written about girls ("Julie" and "Head over Heels") or about faith ("Moses in the Wilderness" and "Country Church, Country People"), a few touched on Larry's growing awareness of the civil rights movement. Larry also versed himself in the protest tradition of traditional folk music, thanks to a Henry Clay Work songbook that had been handed down from his great-grandmother to Grandma Lena. In addition to singing temperance songs like "Come Home, Father," he and his sisters performed their own version of "The Klan"—a terrifying song that would have been unknown or avoided by most white children their age:

The countryside was cold and still
There was a cross upon the hill
This cold cross wore a burning hood
To hide its rotten heart of wood

Father I hear the iron sound
Of hoofbeats on the frozen ground

Down from the hills the riders came
Jesus, it was a crying shame
To see the blood upon their whips
And hear the snarling of their lips

Mother, I feel a stabbing pain
Blood flows down like a summer rain

Now, each one wore a mask of white
To hide his cruel face from sight
and each one sucks a little breath
Out of the empty lungs of death

Sister, lift my bloody head
It's so lonesome to be dead

He who travels with the Klan
He is a monster, not a man
Underneath that white disguise
I have looked into his eyes

Brother, will you stand with me
it's not easy to be free

Songs like "The Klan" convinced Larry that the judgment of God was
falling upon the United States of America in the age of Jim Crow. He

became spellbound by the writings of the Rev. Dr. Martin Luther King in the buildup to the March on Washington in August 1963. He observed in a school essay that the black man has "consistently been denied voting rights, admittance to restaurants, privileges to public dances, movie houses, churches, etc. But he's expected to pay full bus fare. He's drafted, sent to war, and expected to die like a man, if need be. He's taxed. Yes, he's given all the same consideration offered to a white man when his services are in the balance."[23]

Norman began to write his own protest songs, but with a twist. Retribution would come not for his enemies but himself, and "the terrible swift sword" of "The Battle Hymn of the Republic" was meant for people like him. Instead of the proud, white experience that says, "I am invincible," when writing about his responsibility to his black brothers and sisters, a youthful Larry Norman wrote a song called "I Am Afraid to Die":

A man of freedom or a bonded slave
All men are equal in an empty grave
But then I hear those chains of slavery rattling on
I think to myself what has the white man done?

How can a man put another man in a cotton field
For the rest of his life?
Why did slavery have to raise its ugly head
And why in the world did freedom have to die?

I am afraid to die
I am afraid to die[24]

Larry's views on these subjects may have owed more to his father than he was able to perceive at the time. Joe had written a fiery paper at Bible college about the white Church's need to support the nascent civil rights movement, much to the chagrin of his professor and peers. For both Joe and his son, the Church was not living up to the call of Jesus if it didn't pursue Dr. King's vision of "The Beloved Community," a free association of people of faith and goodwill dedicated to the renunciation of, and advancement of justice regarding, three evils: poverty, racism, and militarism.[25] As University of Virginia professor Charles Marsh describes the philosophy in his history of King's movement: "The 'beloved' community phrase has been used by social philosophers to describe the culmination of world history in some kind of universal brotherhood. But King believed in original sin, so he didn't share that understanding of beloved community. He understood beloved community as something that is a gift of God."[26] This was Larry Norman's world view from the age of sixteen forward. And in his own way, Larry Norman would try to bring these principles to the white Christian community.

Larry's poetic imagination, developing musical ability, love for Jesus, and growing awareness of the principles of "The Beloved Community" needed the right outlet to be shared with the world. The first inkling of what that outlet might be had come years earlier when, sitting in the back of Joe's 1948 Chevy, he heard a radio announcer utter the name Elvis Presley. Larry loved new words and strange names, and his interest was further piqued when his father quickly moved to change the radio dial. The very mention of Elvis's name, Larry recalled, "seemed to be a special magic, an exciting energy."[27] Several weeks later, his thirteen-year-old cousin Bonnie Sue came to the house while the mothers and Larry's sisters went out for errands. Bonnie Sue brought with her a 45 single of the Elvis song he'd heard just a bit of. He described what happened next: "The most exciting, and puzzling song I ever heard suddenly blasted out of the cheap, portable record player speakers: 'You ain't nothin' but a hound dog, cryin' all the time.'" Larry sat mesmerized by the bounce of Elvis's vocals and the reverb-drenched twang of Scotty Moore's rockabilly guitar. He looked up. Bonnie Sue took Larry's hand and told him to stand up. Starting the record again, she told him that until he had learned the dance moves she already knew, he wouldn't get lunch.

She was pushing on an open door: "I needed no threat to apply myself" in those circumstances, Larry remembered.[28]

Still, the popularity of Elvis did not make being artsy or musical in high school any easier. The alienation Larry felt as a young child had not left him. "I was bullied by jocks because I was a singer. 'Pansy,' 'Queer,' and other such jeers were common in the changing room as they snapped towels at me and poked me in the ribs. I had also danced a jazz ballet with a professional choreographer named Dina Hubbel and this didn't help my status among the jocks and wannabes."[29] He found himself delighting in the awkward juxtapositions—how his rehearsal for a Christmas ballet and dance forced the "infuriated" jocks to share the gymnasium. As he told one DJ in Hawaii in 1973, "It was my way of getting equilibrium."[30]

If neither his father nor the boys at school would give him "permission" to be an artist, that sanction would have to come from elsewhere. He got that on February 9, 1964—the day that launched countless musical careers. With Joe and Margaret looking on, Larry sat on the floor in front of the television with his sisters to watch the debut of the Beatles in America. John, Paul, George, and Ringo inspired Larry to seek a career as a performer. A 1964 photograph reveals Larry's band, dressed in convincing Beatles suits, boots, and wigs, playing a gig at the Shriner's Children's Hospital in San Francisco. His first proper group was called the Back Country Seven, and included his sister Nancy and high school friend Gene Mason. They played hootenannies and parties throughout the San Jose area.

More important, the Beatles also taught Larry an important lesson about art, one that changed the way he viewed songwriting. As he wrote in 1966, "Before B.C. [the Beatles Came] my lyrics had always been too exacting, too perfect, too definite. I gave the listener no chance to identify with the thoughts because I had already said them completely, totally. I offered no chance for the listener to apply the thought to himself because I over-said everything. I realized that this was the cardinal sin, it said only what I felt, not what others might feel."[31]

Then there was the matter of how to survive Superman, achieve balance, and pursue justice in his craft. In his mind, Larry knew that Elvis had taken the music of the black church and turned it into rock 'n' roll. Now Elvis, the Beatles, and everybody else were getting rich off their own secular version of "gospel." It would become Larry Norman's obsession to steal that music back.

2

JESUS VERSUS L. RON HUBBARD

B Y THE LATE 1960s, EVANGELICAL CHRISTIANITY COULD NOT
have been less attractive to the West Coast cultural scene in
which Larry would make his way. In an era that valued personal fulfillment and self-expression above all, traditional Christian
religion stood for "fixed" values, politically, culturally, and sexually.
It was hidebound, out of step with the times, and square. Even in
California politics, the shift toward conservatism was Goldwater-
style—more secular and less driven by the cozy relationship that
Protestantism and politics had enjoyed in the 1950s. It is forgotten
by many today, for example, that none other than Ronald Reagan
signed the "Therapeutic Abortion Act" as governor of California
in 1967.

Despite these long cultural odds, however, California also seemed
to be a staging area for something of an evangelical comeback. The
back-to-the Bible movement flourished in 1960s California. Fuller
Seminary in Pasadena and Pepperdine University in Malibu burst
onto the scene in higher education; and on television and radio, pul-
piteers like Billy Graham, J. Vernon McGee, and E. V. Hill were attracting thousands of viewers.[1]

The music they produced, however, sounded stuffy, virtually indistinguishable from what you might hear in an everyday church
service. When Cliff Barrows, Billy Graham's music leader, stood onstage and led crowds at their "crusades" in song, he performed like
a slightly more professional version of your typical parish worship

leader—right down to the robed choirs that backed him. Vocalist George Beverly Shea's bass-baritone crooning helped spread the idea that a "worship service" should include "special music"—light entertainment in which the congregation did not participate. But the whole thing was homespun and old-fashioned, right down to Donald Hustad's organ, wheeled into the stadium for the event and miked into the PA.

As the 1970s dawned, however, a reputation for stodgy music became the least of evangelicals' worries. David Frum, the former speechwriter for George W. Bush who coined the term "axis of evil," wrote his diatribe against the 1970s by deeming it "more expressive, more risk averse, more sexual, less literate, less polite, less reticent . . . the most total social transformation (a revolution!) that has not ended yet."[2] Increasingly, the people now making up even traditional congregations did not see themselves as sinners in need of repentance and salvation. Their attitude toward the fate of their eternal souls was: Relax . . . perhaps we will turn to that subject some other time. In the meantime, California meant a lifestyle of just having fun. No city exemplified that more than Los Angeles, home to the sexual revolution and the drug scene, centerpieces of the rapidly emerging counterculture.

"La La Land" provided a contrast to the sort of thoughtful, even ascetic, approach to rock 'n' roll that Larry Norman had been cultivating since his teenage years. But like an iron filing drawn to a magnet, Larry would be inevitably drawn to Tinseltown. He understood that if he wanted to make it big, he had to make inroads into the record industry in L.A. That the city represented a real and present threat to Christianity's perceived relevance in the modern world may have been part of the attraction.

He loved Joe and Margaret, but their idea of success was a stable career—not the life of a musician. As Larry recalled, "My father had yelled at me, 'No son of mine is going to grow up to be Elvis Presley.'"[3] He claimed he was lectured "that God and Rock and Roll could not go together."[4] Perhaps Larry's fear of his father was enough to dissuade him from combining his emerging thoughts about Jesus with flatted fifth and pentatonic blues licks. But whatever the cause, he kept his thoughts about faith out of his notebook of lyrics, instead writing quirky love songs to no one in particular, and pursuing his own social and political observations in de facto secrecy. He dropped out of San Jose State College after a semester; he'd planned to study English but nothing about the atmosphere or pedagogy appealed.

Meanwhile opportunity was knocking. In 1966, he found himself visiting L.A., standing on the corner of Hollywood and Vine, staring up at a circular office building that looked like a stack of vinyl 45s: The world-famous headquarters of Capitol Records. The company had become a temple to teenagers across the country, with the Beatles as its high priests. But despite its reputation, Capitol Records had been a relative latecomer to the rock-'n'-roll scene. They initially built their reputation producing Big Band and jazz acts like Benny Goodman, Les Paul, and Mary Ford, and later Miles Davis's path-breaking album, *Birth of the Cool*. But when EMI in Britain acquired Capitol, the Beatles came with them, then subsequently the Beach Boys, and the record company scrambled to find the sort of new talent that sold records to teenagers. (It was a pivotal time in rock history—The Beach Boys' *Pet Sounds*, the Beatles' *Revolver*, Simon and Garfunkel's *Sounds of Silence*, and the Rolling Stones' *Aftermath* were all released within eight months of one another.) They quickly discovered a new group of acolytes, a band called People!, who hailed from San Jose and looked to Larry Norman as its principal songwriting inspiration.

In most respects, Larry appeared an unlikely leader for a heady San Francisco psychedelic rock band. He wasn't rugged or conventionally handsome, and it probably didn't help that his affect was fey. He looked like a choirboy, albeit one seen fleeing the church with his robe left on the floor in the vestibule. His voice was queer, so much so that studio executives often wouldn't let him take lead vocals on his own songs. But in the early stages of his career, having nothing particularly Christian about his act proved to be a good move, because it got him gigs—including the one that led him to People!

While performing throughout the Bay Area, Larry was invited to be the opening act at a rather strange show in which the headliner was Buckminster Fuller, the celebrated design and systems theorist and innovator of the geodesic dome. The performance order at the show was Norman, followed by a new San Jose group named People!, and then Fuller. John Riolo, People!'s original drummer, recalls watching Norman's performance:

> He was the hardest act the group ever had to follow. He was such a great entertainer and he looked wonderful, was animated, made the audience laugh, told clever stories, clowned around etc., and most of all sang very well. Larry and his beautiful singing could melt your tender heart one moment and burn down the barn the next. His comedy, acting pranks, and obvious show biz wizardry were irresistible to all present.
>
> Geoff [Levin, the band's founding guitarist] made Larry an offer to join the group several days after this chance meeting. Larry Norman wanted [his high-school friend] Gene Mason in the group also since they had grown up together dreaming of becoming singers like the Righteous Brothers and had also honed their skills in a popular local folk group. They were hired as dual lead singers, which would allow People! to cover almost any of the top hits. Gene and Larry could dance, sing, switch off vocal duties, and put on an amazing show.[5]

Larry had made his first step in breaking with both his parents and the Church. At long last, he was in a proper rock-'n'-roll band; he was in the driver's seat for the first time in his life, and he'd brought a friend along for the ride. People! would be the perfect vehicle for him to talk about his beliefs and sense of dislocation from the world, with its rapidly degenerating moral consensus. As a bonus, he was surrounded by a talented group of young musicians. The band allowed him to dabble in the 1960s without becoming part of the counterculture himself. At least, that's what he thought he was doing.

As People! geared up to start touring extensively, John Riolo had to leave the group because he was still a junior in high school. This left the band in need of a drummer. Norman immediately took charge as though he were the leader of the band, now composed of himself and Gene Mason on vocals, brothers Geoff and Robb Levin (guitar and bass, respectively), and Al Ribisi (guitar and organ). Larry found the band's new drummer, Denny Fridkin, in an electronics store. Larry hadn't met Fridkin before; he just walked up to him, intuitively, and made the ask. Recalls Denny: "I just remember being so taken by his physical presence and his aura, you know, with that long blond hair and his loving demeanor. I was a bit stunned, but I think he just said, 'Do you play drums?' I said, 'As a matter of fact, I do. I was just on my way to get my drums at the Greyhound bus station.' So then Larry asked, 'You want to be in my band?'"[6]

My band. He had been in People!, an outfit formed by the Levin brothers, no more than a couple of weeks—but much like Mick Jagger made the mistake of calling Charlie Watts "my drummer," Larry Norman thought of People! as a possession of his to develop, cultivate, and expand. And although the other players were extant before Norman joined the band, no one seems to question the fact that Larry quickly became the group's major creative force.

By this point Larry had written over a hundred songs. He had an ear for the best melodies and expected a certain standard of excellence from his bandmates. "We practiced five hours a day and did shows at night," Larry said. "I just loved it. Music, music, music." The hard work paid off almost immediately. Performing in concert somewhere in the Bay Area in early 1966, Larry remembered: "One night a vice president from Capitol Records heard us in concert. He asked us if we'd like to record on Capitol. We said OK."

Had he tried, Larry couldn't have devised a more effective way to break the fifth commandment, "Honor thy father and thy mother." Inconveniently, Larry actually needed his parents' help to disobey them. He was nineteen years old, still too young to sign a contract without a guardian's approval, since the legal age at that time in

California was twenty-one. Joe and Margaret had to appear in court and assure a judge that they would assent to signing off on Larry's first songwriting contract with Capitol.[7] His parents "were pretty sure that the road to rock led to ruin," Larry remembered, "but they could see that I would have no other life so they decided to give me their permission, but withhold their blessings, and pray that when I had given up this treacherous course that I would be able to salvage some of my humanity and Christianity. As for mixing God with rock music, well, maybe with God all things are possible, but this was not one of them."[8]

Had the Normans known what else was going on in their son's life at the time, they would likely have been mortified. With an L.A. recording contract in hand, People! still were making their way in the Bay Area, where they rubbed shoulders with some of the more notorious members of the hippie music and drug scene. Larry befriended Skip Spence, the drummer for the psychedelic outfit Jefferson Airplane. Outgoing and effervescent, the pair congregated with some friends at the vacant Ark Club in Sausalito, where they jammed all night and slept on the floor.[9] The Ark launched many up-and-coming alternative bands, including obscure groups like Freudian Slips, and breakthrough acts like Big Brother and the Holding Co. Best of all, it all took place on a converted ferry boat at Gate 6. The club rarely paid performers, but since the gigs continued into the wee small hours, remuneration usually came in the form of huevos rancheros made by the vessel's short-order cook as dawn broke over the Bay.[10]

Larry Norman sought out people on the fringe—characters whose artistic merits were high, but whose character might not hold up to the same exacting standards. His attraction to lost souls, to artists who seemed adrift or even unstable, established a pattern that would repeat throughout his life. Larry enjoyed playing the role of big brother, mentor, and, in some cases, supervisor to people who fit Bob Dylan's description of "no direction home." But by seeking out people who were "betwixt and between" episodes in life, Larry unwittingly put his own stability on the line—a penchant that ulti-mately made his life irreversibly complicated.

Skip Spence, for example, proved to be too wild even for Jefferson Airplane, who dismissed him from the group after he went AWOL to Mexico without informing other members of the band. He left to form his own project, Moby Grape, but quickly descended into a cycle of LSD-induced psychotic events, including an attempt to break down his bandmate Don Stevenson's hotel room door in New York with a fire ax. Moby Grape's guitarist Jerry Miller recounted Spence's rapid decline, which included everything from an acid trip with a "black witch," to delusions that he was the Antichrist. Follow-ing the ax incident, the band called the police, and Spence went to jail. The authorities placed him in Bellevue, a psychiatric hospital, under armed guard for six months. He was eventually diagnosed with schizophrenia.

Despite all of the negative publicity about the Moby Grape star, Norman never referred to Spence critically in his recollections of him. Although it's possible that later songs like Norman's "Forget Your Hexagram" (1969) were directed at Spence, or people like him who dabbled in black magic, in 1967 Larry was more than happy to affiliate with people who were "out there."

Larry also rubbed shoulders with artists who questioned Amer-ica's values of power, money, and war. He recounted hanging out at the Ark with Stephen Stills and Neil Young—then performing as Buffalo Springfield. He loved that the band's mode of transportation was a hearse, and that they were game for camaraderie and a good time. Within months, Buffalo Springfield had a hit entitled "For What It's Worth," which became an anthem for the protest against the Vietnam War. Inspired by Neil Young's sound, Larry wrote "Ha Ha World," a song that eventually made its way onto his first solo record. (If you listen closely enough, you can hear traces of Young's "Mr. Soul" in it.)

In between the late-night jam sessions Larry began chronicling the lives of quiet desperation he found in the Bay Area psychedelic scene. He banked these stories, filing them away as fodder for future songs that could explain to kids why Jesus might be an alternative to drugs. Case in point: on January 14, 1967, San Francisco's Golden Gate Park played host to "The Gathering of the Tribes for a Human Be-In": a preview of sorts for the Summer of Love and the event that, more than anything else, introduced the Haight-Ashbury culture to Main Street America. The beat poet Allen Ginsberg took it upon himself to invite congressmen and other Bay Area VIPs to the gathering, and the mainstream media showed up too.[11] Harry Reasoner brought a film crew from CBS to cover the event, and "*Look* magazine rushed its youngest writer, William Hedgepeth . . . to go underground at the scene."[12]

The concert became the right occasion for a protest of California's ban on LSD, passed the previous October. It also embraced the values of the counterculture: sex beyond the conventions of marriage, radical politics, unrestricted drug use, and a general disregard for the values of the middle class—which for the attendees of this first-of-a-kind festival meant blind acceptance of corporate agendas and systemic racism. Timothy Leary got the festivities under way by familiarizing the crowd with the phrase that later made him famous, "Turn on, tune in, drop out," and the event possessed all of the accoutrements that made later large rock concerts infamous, right down to the Hells Angels being retained to keep the peace for a crowd estimated to number as few as 20,000 to as many as 100,000. Promotional posters featuring a guru with the All-Seeing Eye superimposed on his forehead listed the speakers for the event, and promised simply: "All San Francisco Rock Bands." Some of the groups who played toward the end of the bill included Santana, Jefferson Airplane, the Grateful Dead, as well as Big Brother and the Holding Co. (featuring Janis Joplin). People! played closer to the start of the bill.

People!'s exact playlist hasn't survived, and there aren't any reviews that note how they were received by the audience. What matters for this story is that Larry Norman had access to the artists' area, and could study the onstage acts as an observer. Of particular interest to him was Joplin, whom he had opened for in concert before. Standing on the side of the stage during her performance(s), it would have been apparent to Larry that she was a heroin addict. But mainly what caught his attention was her bottle of Southern Comfort at the foot of her microphone stand, the contents of which she poured into a Dixie cup throughout the set. His heart went out to her. It would be the memory of such scenes that would eventually provide the opening image of one of his most enduring songs:

Sippin' whiskey from a paper cup
You drown your sorrows til you can't stand up.
Take a look at what you've done to yourself
Why don't you put the bottle back on the shelf?
Yellow fingers from your cigarettes
Your hands are shakin' while your body sweats.
Why don't you look in to Jesus? He's got the answer.

By the time Larry released the song "Why Don't You Look into Jesus," in 1973, Joplin had been dead for nearly three years, the casualty of a heroin and alcohol overdose.

In the meantime, he and Gene Mason were primarily concentrated on trying to help People! stand out in a very crowded pack—and arguably the best talent of the time. It helped that People! played songs that had elements of jazz and classical music interspersed with the arrangements, not unlike the Doors. They were also skilled and nimble instrumentalists. When the band got an advance copy of *Sgt. Pepper's Lonely Hearts Club Band* in May 1967, they set to memorizing the entire record and performed it for their audience, prompting concertgoers to wonder how they learned the material so fast. But being great mimics wasn't going to get them far.

It helped that Larry and Gene saw their roles not only as singers but actors as well, and the growing theatricality of People!'s concerts earned them a reputation as a little—but not too—weird. Before long, People! concerts included a performance of *The Epic,* a thirteen-minute rock opera Larry wrote in 1966. Inspired by the fantasy genre, and J. R. R. Tolkien's *The Lord of the Rings* in particular, performances of *The Epic* included flashy satin faux-medieval costumes, sword fights, and papier-mâché dragons. The story was a proto-feminist tale about a prince, Alain, who despite his position and wealth suffers from crippling loneliness. He falls in love with a beautiful maiden named Tory, but instead of letting her choose whether or not to love him, he imprisons her in a tower. When a dragon threatens his kingdom, Alain does something selfless for the first time; he confronts the beast, defeats it, and releases Tory. The curtain falls.

The Epic's narrative—*guy does not get girl but rather realizes he's a creep and releases girl into the world*—was ripe for the era. And Larry would soon be offered a leading part in an even more famous production that captured the zeitgeist: the forthcoming Broadway musical *Hair.* Larry's friend Jennifer Warnes also tried out for a part, and got cast in the "lead ingénue role"—a sheep among wolves. Warnes would go on to a diverse career, which included a long-term songwriting collaboration with Leonard Cohen and a number-one hit in *Dirty Dancing*'s "I've Had the Time of My Life."[13]

Hair was the epitome of the progressive mind-set. It featured a racially integrated cast. It openly protested the Vietnam War. It was, for Larry, irresistible—though he hadn't yet read the entire script when he flew home to tell Joe and Margaret about his big break on Broadway. Unimpressed, his father made him a bargain: "If you get your hair cut, I'll buy you a suit, and a pie." Having already disobeyed Joe once by going into rock 'n' roll, he didn't have the heart to do it again. Incredibly, Larry responded to the offer by getting a buzz cut, and Joe henceforth took him to a Marie Callender's restaurant for his pie. (The suit, apparently, was a bonus. Recalling the moment in concert in 2005, Larry deadpanned: "I hate pie.") Still, Joe saw the image before him as a victory. He snapped a photo and drove Larry back to the airport.

Climbing aboard the $17 one-way PSA airlines flight back to Los Angeles, the freshly shorn rock star and actor folded up into his seat in coach, the irony of the situation not lost on him. What would cause Larry to agree to such a bargain? Did he feel somehow guilty? Or was it an episode of self-sabotage and self-pity that led him to comply with his father's request? Whatever the case, the dynamic between Larry and Joe was strained. Taking out a piece of paper and a pen, he wrote the lyrics from his plane seat for a song he would call "I Am Your Servant," a song many future faithful listeners would presume was about a young person's relationship to God, when in fact the "you" in question was Joe Norman.

When Larry got back to Hollywood, he finished reading the rest of the script for *Hair* and lost his enthusiasm for the project altogether. The musical's glorification of drugs and the sexual revolution was too much for him to swallow. At the last minute, he decided to write Hal and Bo James, who had optioned the musical, to apologize and say that he wasn't available for the role. It was a serious sacrifice. "I am broke at the time," he remembered in his diary. "But I feel that God means for me to do something more noble than disrobe nightly and glorify drugs and lawlessness. I go home and cry."[14] He locked his guitar in a closet and didn't write any music for months.

EVEN IN THIS very early stage of his career as an artist, Larry Norman seemed lost in personal mission drift. From the perspective of the industry, however, he was an immensely talented young songwriter who could blossom into a hit maker if he only disciplined himself to do so. Even before People! signed with Capitol Records, they had retained popular San Jose disc jockey Marion Elbridge Herrington, aka "Captain Mikey," to promote the band. Captain Mikey was on his way to becoming a legendary figure in the radio business, a tastemaker who brought early attention to album-oriented rock. Captain Mikey's first order of business was to get People! a hit, and he queried Norman to find out what the band's principal songwriter had in the vault. The answer was: a lot of songs featuring spiritual longing and searching.

Throughout the ups and downs of 1967, Larry wrote songs that never saw the light of day on People! albums. They did, however, later appear on subsequent solo records—some as late as 1981, including: "I've Got to Learn to Live Without You," "Baroquen Spirits," "Soul Survivor," "Hard Luck, Bad News," and "Walking Backwards Down the Stairs," among others. Captain Mikey, however, did not hear a bankable single among them, so he told Norman to go home and write a hit song. There was one problem. As Larry remembered:

> I had no interest in the kind of music that was on the radio. In fact, I had not listened to the radio since 1956 when my Dad forbade me to. I never listened to it . . . until Captain Mikey told me, in the nicest way, that essentially my songs weren't commercial. So I went home to write something and the next day Gene and I presented the song ["Organ Grinder"] to him.
>
> His response? "That's exactly what I meant. That's going to be the first single." Well, that only frustrated me more because I had set out to write the most worthless, shallow song I could think of, and I was shocked when Captain Mikey liked it better than all of my carefully crafted songs.[15]

Although Captain Mikey had some success getting "Organ Grinder" regional airplay, Capitol didn't promote the single, and the same went with its flip side, "Riding High." "Riding High" spoke of making a person spiritually new, and of a satisfaction with the divine that surpassed sex, drugs, and rock 'n' roll. It also represented the first time Larry attempted to write a song that metaphorically referenced, according to Larry, the work of the Holy Spirit in the heavenly realms. The 45 record with two singles flopped.

Larry's heart was not in it. With the band floundering under Norman's songwriting regime, Captain Mikey took matters into his own hands. Hearing People! cover British act the Zombies' "I Love You" in concert, he told them to cut the record as a single, which was subsequently released on February 2, 1968. The band added a long psychedelic instrumental intro to the song that made the single considerably longer than the Zombies' non-charting version. In July of 1968, the song became a hit, topping out at number 14 on the Billboard Hot 100, and becoming an even bigger success worldwide. "I Love You" went number 1 in Japan (twice), Israel, Australia, Italy, South Africa, and the Philippines. The *Bill Gavin Report* ranked the hit in America much higher than what had been reported in *Billboard*, but industry rivalries stemming from feuds between Captain Mikey and other DJs kept the song from charting higher than its ubiquitous airplay would have seemed to indicate. And in any case, "I Love You" sold more copies than many songs that reach number 1.

The success of "I Love You" emboldened Larry to work on building the band's fan base through a series of concerts focused on virtuoso psychedelic performances of classical pieces like Franz Liszt's "Hungarian Rhapsody." If their top-20 hit was the zenith of the band's commercial success, their eclectic stage show was what brought them attention—and possibly influence. The highlight of People!'s stage show—and the entire second side of their first LP— remained *The Epic*, staged with additional actors and even children. In the summer of 1968 they happened to be touring in support of the Who. Could it have been People!'s performance of *The Epic* that inspired Peter Townshend to begin work on *Tommy*? Townshend has denied the connection.[16] Whatever the true story, *Tommy* appeared one year later, in May of 1969.

Influential or not, Larry Norman's theatrical rock band amassed a dedicated following. As long as Larry was the creative force behind their act, People! was critically acclaimed, remaining beloved by a group of collectors long after their demise. One reviewer in *Spotlight* summed up their appeal: "quirky and in many ways far ahead of their time . . . they were pretty much in a category all their own . . . [with] their on-stage theatrics, they were always a joy to watch."[17]

These first flushes of success gave Larry a chance to meet one of his heroes. In the spring of 1968, while visiting the Capitol Building, Larry found himself standing next to Paul McCartney while heading into the elevator. "Hey, I like your music," Macca told him. Remembered Larry: "I didn't even know he had even heard it until later I found out [our record] was already out in Europe. Considering all the things they were writing at the time I was surprised he'd even like it." Stunned, Norman struck up a brief conversation with the Beatle, who invited him to follow him to his next engagement: Paul's meeting at Capitol about the newly formed Apple Records. When Paul walked into the room, Larry recalled that the studio executives crowded in to get autographs. He also found himself standing next to Woody Allen, who was there in support of his recently released comedy record, *The Third Woody Allen Album*.[18] Woody didn't say much.

In July 1968 People!'s LP "I Love You" appeared. Despite the fact that People! was not designed to be a "Christian" band, Larry used his role as the principal songwriter to shoehorn his religious agenda into the group's repertoire. The album's first track is entitled "1000 Years Before Christ," and the closing selection of side one was the proposed title track, "We Need a Whole Lot More of Jesus, and a Lot Less Rock and Roll." Norman claimed repeatedly that this phrase was the album's original name, as is evidenced by a mock-up of the album artwork with that title in advance of the record's release. Understandably, perhaps, Capitol then reversed field so it could be named after their hit single.

For a while, all seemed stellar. People! played bills with Van Morrison, the Dave Clark Five, Buffalo Springfield, the Doors, and played festivals with the Jimi Hendrix Experience, Jefferson Airplane, Led Zeppelin, Muddy Waters, Chuck Berry, and Santana. But not all was happy in the world of People! Due to the nature of how the band got together, People! never became a band of brothers or even a homogenous creative unit. Complicating matters further were growing theological and religious tensions. Geoff and Robb Levin, joined by

Albert Ribisi and eventually Denny Fridkin, started exploring Scientology. As they delved into the teachings of L. Ron Hubbard and began auditing, the band's two lead singers became the odd men out. Gene Mason didn't seem to bother the Levin brothers, but Larry certainly rubbed the pair the wrong way. In an interview in 2007, Robb Levin remembered a campaign to oust Larry from the band, due to his "difficult" personality and "narcissistic" traits.[19] Others speculate that since Larry so roundly rejected their newfound world view, the band designated him what Scientology calls a "suppressive person."[20] According to Larry, the philosophical and theological tension in the band was nothing new, and it only compounded other concerns his bandmates had about him. He recalled in 2005:

> The band started to become interested in transcendental meditation and other philosophies—and finally Scientology. Most of them seem to disdain my Christian beliefs and felt quite proud that they believe in nothing, and therefore were more "evolved" than I was. And it seemed to be the band's opinion that I had no personality, no physical, animal magnetism. It was true, or at least I tried to project that lack of "it." I wanted nothing to do with girls and certainly didn't put out any vibe that encourage[s] girls to be attracted to me.[21]

Larry Norman and his bandmates were destined to part ways. Essentially, Larry saw himself as the Brian Wilson of People! He wrote the songs, guided the production, and envisioned extravagant theatrical bits like *The Epic*, but didn't see the band as a means to an end for a rock 'n' roll lifestyle. His attitude was phlegmatic at best: "For me, [People!] was a good way to practice all of the arrangement concepts I had inside my head, just as I did when I was six and taught my sisters their harmony parts, only now I had an entire band to amplify my harmonic ideas. I always thought the sound of human voices, intertwining in colorful chords and moving parts was so beautiful."

This diffidence contributed to the rap on Larry that he was

arrogant and hard to get along with. Such conclusions likely stemmed from his overweening sense of spiritual and artistic superiority. In his view, Larry remembers that "the band resented me for coming up with so many songs." He continued:

> I'd already been writing my own songs and performing them for over a decade. Some of them had never written a song in their life but looked at it as an opportunity to make extra money. Whoever had a song on the B side of the single made just as much money as they [sic] hit on the A side. But me? I didn't care about the money. I just thought the best song should always be put forth, not the worst songs just because you're written by someone else and because the band wanted to function as a democracy.[22]

People! was coming apart, and Larry didn't seem to care much. He traveled to meet with members of the Sea Org—a group of Hubbard's most dedicated followers—but resisted joining Scientology himself. The process of "auditing," by which a trained Scientologist asks certain questions of an individual about his or her life, in an attempt to uncover traumatic incidents from their past, while the interviewee holds on to two electrodes attached to a machine called an E-meter, became a bone of contention. By Larry's account, the band members were audited one at a time, including Larry, who claimed that a "top Scientologist" was flown in to audit a musical group who they thought could potentially be the "next Beatles." His stance toward his bandmates' enthusiasm for this process was variously nervous and paternal, and he expressed concern for their souls. When Larry refused to cooperate with the fourth stage of his audit, he claimed that his bandmates stopped regular communications with him. Eventually, Captain Mikey was fired too, perhaps to make room for a new manager who was more Scientology-friendly.

The conflict with Larry didn't last much longer. On the evening before the release of their first LP, People! played in Monterey. At the point in *The Epic* when Larry spears the dragon with his microphone stand, a freak accident occurred: the stage separated, and Larry fell through the hole in the floor. When the stage re-closed, his finger got caught between the sections, resulting in a gruesome scene. Larry climbed out but kept performing. "A piece of bone flew off his finger and blood started spurting out all over the place," Denny Fridkin later recalled. "He finished the song with his finger a bleeding mess."[23] Larry took the incident as a sign from Jesus that it was time to move on.

In an interview on his 1971 independent recording *Bootleg*, Larry explained that something mystical happened when he fell through the stage floor. As he was swallowed up and his finger crushed, he was also "baptized in the Holy Spirit." In Pentecostal and Charismatic Christian circles, such a "baptism" refers to an ecstatic second experience of salvation and grace that commissions one for a new era of ministry. Like Jesus coming out of the wilderness after being tempted by the devil, Larry felt called to be more explicit about his faith in the Lord. In a battle between L. Ron Hubbard and Jesus, for Larry Norman, there was no competition. It would signal the first of many times that Larry's idiosyncratic vision of faith and dogged independence would separate him from collaborators.

LARRY INFORMED THE boys that he was quitting the band immediately after the accident. "You can't quit, because you're fired," he was told. Upon hearing the news, Captain Mikey remarked to remaining band members, "You just fired the talent."[24] As for People!, Christian references in the music had to go. By the time the group released their second LP, *Both Sides of People!*, the album cover featured Robb and Geoff Levin proudly displaying their Scientology medallions.

With Larry out of the lineup, People! followed up the success of "I Love You" with the quirky but unmemorable single "Apple Cider," written by Denny Fridkin. The song failed to chart. Although People! went on to perform several times on *American Bandstand* (Larry was with them for at least one show) and *The Tonight Show Starring Johnny Carson*, they were released from Capitol after their second LP garnered neither hits nor critical acclaim. Possibly their last claim to fame was that after the departure of Captain Mikey, the band hired Wally Amos, who was beginning to represent talent such as Diana Ross and Simon and Garfunkel. Departing the music business shortly thereafter, Amos obtained a small business loan for a retail store from Marvin Gaye and Helen Reddy, as his clients said he was better at baking cookies than managing bands. The result was the Famous Amos Cookie Company.

Larry Norman may have been free of People!, and now free faithfully to follow Jesus, but he was also jobless and penniless. For an artist, especially one who so proudly ran away from home, he'd hit rock bottom: he moved back in with his parents. When he received a job offer from the Youth for Christ outreach ministry, he prayed it over, but "felt no peace about it." Then just a few days later, Herb Hendler, vice president and general manager of Beechwood Music, called from Capitol Records and invited Larry to come back to Hollywood to write rock musicals. Hendler was a former executive for RCA Victor whose collaborations included some of the most notable figures in popular music: Perry Como, Rosemary Clooney, Nat King Cole, comedian Bob Newhart, and the Everly Brothers, among others. It should come as no surprise that Larry Norman "felt a lot of peace about Hollywood."[25] It afforded him an opportunity to continue his fantasy of being in the world, but not of it: a disciple of the Risen Christ hidden behind enemy lines, the holy fool in Tinseltown talking about religion. He accepted the job, although he admitted that during the decision-making process "God was silent."

He'd be working for Capitol again but in a more behind-the-scenes capacity. Suddenly, Larry was back in the business. He rented "a tiny, one room, flophouse apartment, with the rent paid on a monthly basis and no lease, water or electric costs required," on Gower Street across from the Hollywood Memorial Cemetery. He survived on a steady diet of orange juice and sardines. Gower Street—or Poverty Row, as it was called during Hollywood's Golden Era—was ground zero for B-movie studios and downscale productions. Still, there was glamor within view. The Hollywood Walk of Fame started on Gower Street and ran west. Paramount Studios sat on the corner of Gower and Melrose, as a cruel tease. Warren Zevon immortalized Gower Street and Hollywood's unrelenting demands on artists in his 1976 song "Desperados Under the Eaves." Even if the "mystics and the statistics" were correct that California was destined to sink into the sea, Zevon lamented, Gower Street's Hollywood Hawaiian Hotel would stay standing, demanding that every last penny of his bill be paid.[26]

Despite the modest reboot, Larry counted his Capitol Records second coming as a personal victory. He was, to some degree, adrift, unsure of his mission. His job consisted of showing up to the Capitol Records Building, clocking in at Beechwood Music Group, and sitting down at the piano to write songs that could ultimately become hits. Mostly, however, he was supposed to crank out tunes for *Alison*, a new rock musical Hendler was producing, based on a book by the same name. The stage production promised to bring star power to one of the nation's first true rock musicals: Kay Cole (formerly of *Bye Bye Birdie* and *A Chorus Line*) in the title role, and Ted Neeley (who would later go on to star in the title role of *Jesus Christ Superstar*).[27]

The media took notice of Hendler's pet project, noting that he was developing a new series of "'homegrown' Broadway musical properties" for Capitol, alongside "co-producer Albert Selden of 'Man of La Mancha.'"[28] Although *Cashbox* cited the official press release, which touted that the music would be sourced from "some thirty songwriters all under contract to Beechwood Music (BMI), a wholly owned subsidiary of Capitol," the truth is that Hendler looked to Larry Norman to do most of the heavy lifting.[29] Of the twenty tunes that wound up in *Alison*, Norman wrote half, and co-wrote several more, including one from People!, two from former bandmate Denny Fridkin, and one from Gene Mason.

Perhaps to mask the disproportionate look of the songwriting chores, Hendler listed Emmett Grogan as a co-writer on a couple of the Norman tracks. Grogan, the notorious British leftist and figure in the San Francisco art scene (he played a prominent role at the "Human Be-In"), had begun an American version of the Diggers, a radical theatrical troupe that challenged the notion of class distinctions, capitalism, and organized religion. By the mid-1960s, Grogan could claim to have coined a key counterculture catchphrase: "Do Your Own Thing." He inspired Abbie Hoffman's progressive movement in the East Village, and touted his friendship with Bob Dylan.[30] What's odd in retrospect, given Larry Norman's penchant for name-dropping, is that he didn't make much of having Grogan as his erstwhile songwriter partner. The likely reason is that Grogan never touched the tunes.[31] For his part, Grogan probably didn't want to broadcast his paid connection to a major corporation. But one wonders whether Grogan's politics and the countercultural radicalism stirred the environment that preceded Larry's own later involvement in the Jesus movement.

For now, though, Larry had to deliver something Broadway might like, for *Alison* was the wedge that would help him fulfill the artistic aspirations that rock 'n' roll failed to deliver. The lead-off track in *Alison* was a Norman composition that gave Hendler what he was looking for—a soundtrack for the zeitgeist. "Love on Haight Street" was a tune about free love in San Francisco with a pun implied in the title:

People come from everywhere to find the love they need
They come for love on Haight Street
And the people come to share that love with everyone they
*   meet*
There's lot's of love on Haight Street
Love, love, love, that's what everybody's lookin' for
Love, love, love, baby we've got it.

In the second song, "Yes, Dad," we hear Larry's hippie character sing:

Yes, Dad, I've taken acid
No, Mom, I am not an addict
Oh wow, life should be happy (how can you be so dramatic)

Yes, Dad, I think that the War's wrong
No, Mom, I am not a Commie
Oh wow, how can we go on (cutting people like salami)?

Yes, Dad, I sleep with girls now
No, Mom, nobody's pregnant
Oh wow, sex is fantastic,
Aren't you glad I'm not a faggot?

This was a far cry from the squeaky-clean Christian persona Larry Norman portrayed in People! His lyrics and content in *Alison* also seem to contradict his earlier, pious dismissal of *Hair*'s content. Neatly, Larry compartmentalized the whole affair. After all, he was a hired gun, paid to capture the spirit of the age, even if that required him to speak out of both sides of his mouth. Plus, he wouldn't actually be starring in the role once the show hit Broadway, like he would have in *Hair*.

And besides, Larry's portrait of the hippie generation was decidedly unflattering. While the hippies pose as advocates of peace, love, and understanding, in *Alison*, they come off as rude, combative, paranoid, sex-obsessed, and bigoted. Indeed, in one of the play's climatic moments, set at a hippie love-in at Golden Gate Park, Webster, Alison's boyfriend, implores her to flee the culture of free love, even if it means losing her. In its own way, *Alison* wound up communicating Larry's Christian suspicion of the counterculture, after all.

Larry settled in at Beechwood, and Hendler kept him busy. By spring, Larry felt "in the clear" at Capitol, and fired off a letter to family and friends on Capitol stationery, proclaiming his growing confidence:

Hi! I'm back again!

I've been living in Hollywood since last July, when I left The People! I moved to Hollywood to write a rock musical called "Alison" and it opens up on Broadway in September. I've also just now finished writing my second rock musical, "A Birthday for Beethoven," which premieres in Goodspeed after "Alison" hits Broadway.

I've missed all of you. I've also missed singing; so I formed a new group called "The Flies" and wrote a song for T.V.'s "Laugh-In" called, "Blow in My Ear and I'll Follow You Anywhere."

If you haven't heard it yet, phone your disc jockey and ask him to play it. It'll be in the stores in about a week (If it isn't there already). I'll be on television, signing songs from my new album, in a couple of months. I'll write you later on, and let you know exactly what nights I'll be on.

I'll be in California until this Summer with "The Flies," then we're going to New York for the opening of "Alison" and we'll be making a movie of "Alison" for underground cinema. (The other two members of "The Flies" have worked in movies for two years and one of them has been on seventeen television series. I'll be writing about them in the next letter.) We'll also be recording our second album of rock music from "Alison" during the filming.

Until this Summer comes, I plan on enjoying California.

Hey, it's good to be back again.

Larry[32]

If by day Larry was happy serving as a cog in the machine of Capitol Records, after hours he increasingly saw himself as an evangelist, witnessing about Jesus to people he met on the street. "I got pinched by transvestites who come up behind me when I am 'walking my beat,' looking for people to witness to. I'm threatened with violence by young men whose eyes are spinning in their heads. I'm accosted by bikers. Nothing stops me," he wrote. As photographer Ave Pildas (also a Capitol employee) remembers of that environment, there were "people tripping down the street, hippies, hookers, drug addicts, and people dressed to the nines in the middle of the day— either left over from the night before or because they were on their way to an audition."[33] Unlike the Christian cliché he heard growing up—that Christians are supposed to be "in the world but not of the world"—it seemed as though Larry Norman had figured out a method to be both in the world, and of it, simultaneously. Among the people Larry met on the street and "won" to Jesus was Susan Perlman, a Jewish girl from Brooklyn. So transformed was she by what she heard, she started a ministry with Moishe Rosen, an organization that came to be known as Jews for Jesus.[34]

After finishing up work on *Alison*, Larry began to wonder whether music would really be an effective way to reach people for Christ, especially when compared to the direct and personal interactions of one-on-one street witnessing. For one thing, he couldn't tell if people went to a concert to do anything but be entertained. How was that a powerful witness for Jesus? One day, Larry decided to test God. Still swirling in his head were his father's warnings about the world of rock. What if rock 'n' roll really did come from the devil? Maybe if Jesus wasn't really in it, the music he was hearing would stop. So he locked up his guitar and tape recorder in a closet; that way it couldn't be a temptation, and he could focus on sharing the gospel with street people. A few weeks later, though, something changed:

> One night I found myself singing in my sleep. I woke myself up with the sound of my voice. I tried to dislodge the song from my mind but could not. Finally in desperation I went to the closet, retrieved the tape recorder and sang into it. That, having been done, made it possible for me to go back to sleep. . . .

It was only later that I began wondering if perhaps God didn't want me to give up music, and that it had only been something that I was trying to stop doing. The Bible says to "test the spirits" to see if they are from God so I decided to write another song and see what it was like. I wrote "I Wish We'd All Been Ready." It seemed quite unlike any song I'd ever written, and different from any song I'd ever heard.[35]

The result from the first tape recorder experiment turned out to be "Sweet Song of Salvation," the tune that would launch Larry Norman's career as the "father of Jesus Rock" and inspire a thousand church youth group sing-alongs.

At the time, Larry didn't like the song God had given him, but it did spark a new trajectory in his songwriting. His lyrics increasingly became message-based, spun on the loom of an idiosyncratic Christian world view. "Ha Ha World" was a surrealistic tune about a man who began to understand the bankruptcy of his own materialistic lifestyle, as was "The Last Supper." Then "Forget Your Hexagram" warned people of the foolishness of living their lives through astrological signs, fortune-tellers, and Ouija boards—all of which were popular in California at the time. Larry felt like he had a special pipeline to heaven for songwriting, as though God were giving him sanctified pop music.

Larry abandoned his decision to give up music, and instead incorporated it into his street witnessing. Now when Larry got off work at Capitol, he'd strap on his guitar and start singing his new songs about the fallenness of the world out on the sidewalk. Out on the corner of Hollywood and Vine, Larry Norman started thinking of himself less as a musician, or even a pop star, but a Christian called to sing about Jesus Christ. He believed people needed to hear messages like the one from his song "I've Searched All Around the World": "You keep the dance halls hummin' but the End of the Age is comin'."

That he adopted the pose of a Jesus-loving oracle in Los Angeles, of all places, is less counterintuitive than it might first seem. L.A. was totally welcoming to different spiritual expressions, possessing little discernment as to which were good and which less so. Everything was "cool," particularly the weirder religions. Fans of Woody Allen will remember the uproarious *Annie Hall* scene set at the Source, the famous "spiritual vegan" restaurant on the Sunset Strip. Fewer know the bizarre story behind the Source family cult, led by "Father Yod," who owned the health-food restaurant while preaching a New Age blend of sex, mysticism, nature worship, and yoga in the Hollywood Hills, where he surrounded himself with beautiful women.[36] If someone like that could win a following in L.A., why not Larry Norman?

BY THE SPRING of 1969, it looked as though *Alison* wasn't going to make it to Broadway, as various producers haggled over the finances. Edward Padula (who had produced *Bye Bye Birdie*) optioned *Alison*, and Hal and Bo James (*Man of La Mancha* and *Hair*) optioned Larry's next musical, entitled *Birthday for Shakespeare*. But all of a sudden, this and the other musical Larry had begun work on, *Lion's Breath*, didn't look like sure bets. Although Larry had completed significant work on *Lion's Breath*, he began to second-guess the cultural impact of musicals. Echoing the influence of someone like Emmett Grogan, he observed: "I began to realize that a Broadway musical is located in one building and one city, but a rock-'n'-roll album can go all over the world into the bedrooms and living rooms of people who can't afford to go to the theater. In essence, Broadway was for the privileged, and rock 'n' roll was for the masses. I turned my mind away from the theater when I realized that God wanted my message to be democratic, not aristocratic."[37]

Still, the occasion of writing for musicals prompted Larry to write an astonishing number of songs, many of which would appear on later records. During this burst of creative energy, Norman wrote

"Lonely by Myself," "Strong Love, Strange Peace," "Sigrid Jane," "The Six o'Clock News" (about Vietnam), "Pardon Me," "I Don't Believe in Miracles," and many more.

Then, just when Larry was considering whether his life would be more ministry-oriented with a musical component, Capitol Records surprised him again in the summer of 1969. Now headed up by Mike Curb, a record executive sympathetic to Christian ideas and art, Capitol asked him if he would like to record a solo album. Larry accepted, upon one condition: Capitol couldn't censor his songs or message, as had happened during his days with People! By "censor," he meant he wanted full license to sing about morality and Jesus. Capitol agreed to the terms, and he got to work, compiling songs, some of which were originally slated for *Lion's Breath*. Finally, Larry Norman would be able to make a statement for Christ like he wanted to do with People! Better yet, American record executives would foot the bill.

No one seemed to be asking Larry if singing about his faith was a good idea in the first place. Record-industry insiders thought he had talent, and maybe that was enough. Larry was driven by his vision to reach a generation that had lost its way, and the thrill of having been given a song by God in his sleep. People would listen to it on the radio, right? What could possibly go wrong?

Without a backing band in place, Capitol brought in some regular studio pros to assist Larry. "The Hollywood Trio"—Hal Blaine on drums, Joe Osborn on bass, and Larry Knechtel on keys—came in to play. Blaine, well known for his work in the legendary "Wrecking Crew," had recently played on sessions with the Beach Boys, Simon and Garfunkel, and the Monkees.[38] Anthony Harris helped with arrangements and orchestrations. Other than Mike Deasy, then known as "The Psychedelic Friar," playing acoustic guitar, Larry handled the rest of the duties on vocals, guitar, and piano.

The session would produce Larry's debut solo record, *Upon This Rock*. Hal Yoergler was listed as executive producer, but Larry took the controls as producer, which proved to be a mistake. Mere days into the session, he went missing from the studio for a couple of days while down with the flu. Once recovered, he returned to find a disaster on his hands. The band and a rookie Beechwood Music employee had continued to produce the sessions, spending down much of the budget with string arrangements and, in Larry's words, "preposterous overdubs" in the tradition of Phil Spector, complete with stiff female vocalists. Worse, Capitol insisted that Larry sing while recuperating, a fact confirmed by his coughing on "Moses in the Wilderness," which was left on the final record. On "The Last Supper," his voice wavers and sounds as if forced through walls of quivering goo. For the album artwork Norman chose to photograph himself chest up, naked, flying through the clouds towards heaven. It was intended to convey that he felt like he had just survived a near-death experience.

Despite the haphazard fashion in which it was recorded, *Upon This Rock* had its quirky, psychedelic charms. "Sweet Song of Salvation"—the song from God—sounded like a generational theme song for young believers, and "Walking Backwards Down the Stairs" expressed the aimlessness of the flower children. Other tracks such as "I Don't Believe in Miracles" conveyed empathy toward people who were skeptical of the supernatural claims of traditional religion, but remained open to something transcendent:

I don't believe in miracles
I know what's real I don't pretend
I don't believe in miracles
Or stories with a happy end
Life is no one's friend

But when we met I felt so free
And suddenly I felt a change come over me
Do you suppose a miracle is happening to me?

Larry nevertheless was horrified at the final product: "When I heard the final mixes at a private playback party, I wanted to cry. And I felt humiliated. All of my beautiful songs sounded so stupid. Where was the restlessness and loneliness I wanted? The alienation and anger? I thought it gave the overall impression of being a children's record. . . . The only studio experiences I ever had were controlled by me and came out the way I wanted them to sound. This was a nightmare."

For its part, Capitol had no idea how to publicize the record. There was no market for this new brand of "Jesus Rock," and yet the album defied any easy categorization as gospel music. Some tracks could be seen as being sung from the perspective of a skeptic. Songs like "Ha Ha World" and "The Last Supper" used avant-garde imagery and apocalyptic language. Record stores didn't know where to place the album: "Christian Psychedelic" was hardly a category.

The album was met with a mixed reception. One reviewer called it "The Sergeant Pepper's of Christian Rock." *Screen Stars* magazine, sporting a cover with the most recent Liz Taylor/Richard Burton scandal, hailed it Album of the Month, edging out Ringo Starr's *Sentimental Journey*. "Talk about new directions!" they raved. "Larry Norman is a combination of many things—lyricist, composer, performer, backwoods preacher, and gentle, sweet poet! His songs, technically speaking are strictly lyric rock, and he's done a very good job of it; but there's more. . . . Some of them sound like they came straight out of a revival meeting. But there are also tender love songs, as romantic as they come. . . . A strange album, but definitely a good one."[39]

The Los Angeles *Herald Examiner* credited *Upon This Rock* with "creating a whole new school of song." Tracy Cabot from the *Citizen News* raved, "This guy is talented, and I don't care if his inspiration comes from his creator, or if all of his talent comes from Genghis Khan. He's great." Other periodicals were not as kind. Al Goldstein's pornographic *Screw* magazine heaped contempt upon the effort, and *Entertainment World* magazine called it "a hunk of hubris," concluding that "God may have given Larry Norman a recording contract, but he never gave him a voice."[40]

What confused Capitol was that while *Upon This Rock* wasn't selling, Larry was playing to sold-out crowds every time he toured. They opted to sublease the record for two years to the Benson Music Corporation and their Impact Records imprint. The record was an instant hit for Benson, selling tens of thousands of copies in the United States, and quickly becoming the soundtrack for the thousands of kids about to be swept up in a revival of religious expression. Although they had no legal sublicensing agreement, Benson distributed the record around the world; in England (it sold 23,000 copies when it was released in 1972), South Africa, and Australia—all without paying royalties to Capitol or Larry Norman. Benson proceeded on this basis for seventeen years until they finally got a cease-and-desist order from Capitol.

The upside was that Larry Norman was now a household name in Christian communities around the world. Early songbooks for the widely popular Young Life Ministry included the songs "Sweet Song of Salvation" and "I Wish We'd All Been Ready." Writing in 2002, Larry reflected, "Looking back thirty-three years, I must say that I'm rather happy that the album sounded so benign instead of embodying the ferocious rock statement I wanted to make." The album, as he put it, "traveled well," and slipped behind the defensive walls that would have kept out his angrier, more discordant version.

Jesus Rock was born. And though the religious establishment still viewed it with suspicion, Larry and his budding spiritual movement were primed to find a strange, new congregation of their own.

3

JESUS VERSUS ORGANIZED RELIGION

I N THE FALL OF 1969, WHEN LARRY NORMAN PERFORMED AT THE Way Inn, a Christian outreach disguised as a restaurant and performance space not unlike Father Yod's "The Source," he set the stage for an ongoing fight he would wage for the rest of his life. Unreleased for many years, a recording of the concert contains rare moments of Larry "thinking out loud" before he had developed a polished and rehearsed stage act.

First, Larry drew a sharp distinction between a person's life in Christ and their relationship to the Church: "I think that the Christian life refers to Jesus Christ," he told the crowd. "If you're a Christian, you're a 'Christ-One.' Not a 'Church-ian.' I don't believe in Church-ianity."

Then he questioned the Church's sincerity. When he asked the hostess at the Way Inn if she could get a cup of water for someone in the audience, he quipped, "Do they charge us for everything here? Or is this not like a church?" Later, after describing the self-professed miracle healing of his finger after the stage accident in his last People! concert, he asked the crowd, "Why should I go to church? They don't have faith. They don't believe in miracles." His thoughts showed a willingness to not only rethink Church practice, but doctrine too:

I was exposed to church when I was little, and so that ruined a lot of things for me. I was brought up in judgment and I was scared. Now, I was from Texas, so that's one strike against me. I won't mention the name, but there's only one kind of church in Texas that I know of, so that's two strikes against me. I almost didn't grow up, because when you grow up you gotta become responsible. You know what you're doing, you know right from wrong. I wasn't sure I wanted to be an adult, if you had to go to hell after you got there. It seemed to me that you had to go through adulthood [only] to get to hell.[1]

Performing before a rapt audience, Larry described a new way of being a Christian: a completely intuitive following of Christ, day by day, decision by decision.

More than concert patter, the Way Inn recording provides insights into what made Larry Norman the established Church's public enemy number one, and why he became something of a guru for young Christians. He wasn't taking pot shots at the average pastor, or even traditional theological beliefs. His Moby Dick was institutional Christianity itself. How, he wondered, could you take Jesus—the most amazing person of all time; God's Son, even!—and make him banal? No small irony, then, that his desire to shake up the religious establishment would largely rest on his mastery of the competitive jungle of the major-label record industry. Larry knew it was hard, even for ardent Christian believers, to argue with success. What he may not have realized, so early in his ascent, is that empires under attack tend to strike back.

Progress in developing his stage act—intimate, spiritual, flirting with irreverence—coincided with professional setback; Capitol dropped Larry in February 1970, two months after *Upon This Rock* was released. Larry found himself in an awkward position. At the exact moment when he was coming into his own voice as a writer, thinker, and musician, he lost institutional support. The music industry had no interest in promoting his new idiosyncratic direction. He could, of course, do what other Christian artists do: accept the support of what would have been his most natural ally, the Church.

Larry stiff-armed any such suggestion, because accepting support would have also included sanction, which meant editorial control. It turned out to be a stroke of genius. The coming generation dreamed of direct access to Jesus without priests, pastors, or other intermediaries. That was the appeal of Larry Norman, and the only way he could really succeed: to drive a wedge between Jesus and the existing institutional Church.

After being dropped by Capitol, Norman continued to send in songs on spec, but without getting paid. To cut down on expenses, he moved into a "little white cottage" at 6007 Carlos Avenue in Hollywood, around the corner from Hollywood Presbyterian Church, a congregation he had been involved with since the summer of 1968. Under the leadership of the congregation's youth minister, Don Williams, the church had started a coffeehouse called the Salt Company as an alternative to the other sorts of New Agey venues frequented by college-age kids. Williams himself had a seminary degree from Princeton, and a PhD from Columbia University, and was recruited to develop a strategy to reach Los Angeles youth by Henrietta Mears, a pioneer in Christian education. Williams gave lectures entitled "The Gospel According to Bob Dylan," in which he explored spiritual themes in Dylan's lyrics. The Salt Company enjoyed success from its very inception, drawing hundreds of teenagers on Friday and Saturday nights, all of whom paid a $1 cover charge—meaning that the hot spot was profitable to boot.[2] In Larry, Williams saw someone who could become a Dylan for the Jesus generation. Larry quickly became a star attraction for the Salt Company, with performances that kept increasing in popularity.

These performances heightened his status as a leading voice in the burgeoning Jesus movement, a moment in time in which young people who chose not to participate in the free love and drug culture sought solidarity by trying to emulate the practices of the early Church and simultaneously standing for peace in a turbulent era. There was no central committee running operations—like politics, the Jesus movement was best expressed locally—but there were personalities and ministries that gave identity and shape to what began as a largely Californian phenomenon, with one pole being in San Francisco and the other in Southern California. Chief amongst these ministry leaders was Pastor Chuck Smith of Orange County, founding pastor of Calvary Chapel in Costa Mesa. Enlisting the talents of a young "hippie" evangelist, Lonnie Frisbee, to help him, Smith started seeing a wave of young people flocking to his congregation. Since so many of them were lost souls, the church bought a house for communal living: the "House of Miracles." Within a short span of time, the house overflowed with tenants, and a growing number of hippies started sleeping in the backyard. The church eventually converted a dilapidated motel in Riverside into an additional residence facility. As converts started turning to Jesus, baptisms, of course, were administered in the swimming pool.

Who exactly were these youthful Jesus people? Although formal sociological data is hard to come by, a composite sketch points to teenagers and college students who felt burned by the empty promises of the hippies and their gurus. It wasn't an impression shared only by people open to Christianity. When George Harrison and his wife, Patty, visited Haight-Ashbury at the end of the Summer of Love in 1967, they expressed their profound disappointment in the scene. Patty recalled: "We were expecting Haight-Ashbury to be special, a creative and artistic place, filled with Beautiful People, but it was horrible—full of ghastly drop-outs, bums and spotty youths, all out of their brains. Everybody looked stoned—even mothers and babies."[3] To countless young people thinking things through several years later, the hippies had failed at their chance to bring peace, love, and understanding to the world. Perhaps Jesus and his followers could do a better job.

Besides the Salt Company, other ministries throughout Los Angeles possessed their own iconic appeal in the Jesus movement. Arthur Blessitt's ministry to drug addicts on the Sunset Strip, which culminated in him carrying a life-size cross across America on foot, gained national attention. What better picture could there be to say, "Hey man, Jesus suffered and died for you," than actually carrying a cross? Blessitt's version of the cross, however, came conveniently equipped with wheels. Elsewhere, Duane Pederson's periodical of news and views, the *Hollywood Free Paper*, gave the hundreds and thousands of new Jesus Freaks an outlet that helped reinforce their quickly evolving beliefs. The conceit of the paper was to counter the revolution-tinged publications of the political left that glorified liberation through rebellion, sex, and drugs, and offer an alternative vision of freedom through faith in Jesus. But following God didn't have to get too heavy either. Catchphrases of popular ad slogans could be changed to spread the good news. Take out "Pepsi," for example, and insert the name of the second person of the Trinity, and you had a poster that read: YOU'VE GOT A LOT TO LIVE, JESUS HAS A LOT TO GIVE.[4]

In September 1970, Duane Pederson asked Larry to write a regular opinion column for the *Hollywood Free Paper*. Norman's column, "As I See It," would appear from 1970 to 1974 and cover a wide range of topics, from spiritual messages in pop music, to politics, to sex and the drug culture, to the Vietnam War, and whether or not Jesus laughed at and appreciated a good joke. Larry had a gift for anticipating what young converts coming to Jesus were thinking about. Referencing the war in Vietnam, he questioned, perhaps naïvely, how there could be world peace until individuals experienced personal peace. In particular, he was eager to show the empty promises of the Summer of Love: "Years later, the children have thrown down their flowers and picked up bombs, and picked up hypodermic syringes, and picked up the clap. And the children that once held up two fingers are now holding up one. 'Up against the wall Mother Goose.'"

But if Larry was pushing his secular contemporaries up against the wall and saying, in essence, "How do you like Jesus now?," he also relished how fundamentalist preachers saw him as a rebel poet, as if the devil himself had invaded Jerusalem. Phoenix radio evangelist Bob Larson created a cottage industry writing books drawing comparisons between rock music and Satanism. In his scathing missive *Rock and the Church*, Larson concluded, "I maintain that the use of Christian rock is a blatant compromise so obvious that only those who are spiritually blind by carnality can accept it."[5] Larson called out Larry Norman and other Christian musicians, and made it clear that there was no compromise between rock music and the straight and narrow. As religious studies scholar David W. Stowe observed, "Formidable antirock crusaders like Bob Larson and David Noebel . . . viewed a Christian rocker like Larry Norman with nearly as much suspicion as Mick Jagger."[6]

Larry loved the suggestion that he was creating unholy fire. He often referenced his enemies in concert at the time: "I just read this book by this guy who knows all about rock-'n'-roll music—Bob Larson. [audible groans from the crowd] No, really. He used to be a rock-'n'-roll star. I think during the fifties he played accordion. [laughter and applause]." Elsewhere, Christian apologist David Noebel wrote a book to scare parents, explaining how rock lyrics would turn your child into a libertine, communist, or worse.[7] Televangelists Jerry Falwell and Jimmy Swaggart called rock "the new pornography." Citing Larry Norman by name, Swaggart called his music "spiritual fornication." Trolls began to follow Norman around, defacing his concert posters. On one from 1972, someone wrote that the show would be "A Come to Jesus Ecumenical Pro Rome Sham," and further noted that "Norman fans are evanjelly compromisers, dummies, and softies."[8] Across Norman's face the words FORKED TONGUE JESUIT LACKEY IN DISGUISE were scrawled. How Larry Norman became the target of anti-Catholic sentiment is anybody's guess, but in reality he served as a blank slate onto which nervous pastors and church leaders ascribed all of their fears.

Larry Norman didn't mind being the focal point of controversy, and, in fact, he courted it. When he later wrote a song about Jesus entitled "The Outlaw," he was confronting the criticisms many people made toward Larry himself.[9] He portrayed himself as an outsider, a spoke in the wheel of establishments everywhere. "I want[ed] to be the lightning rod for a new sensibility," Norman said years later. "But I want to change the Church, not the music industry." He continued in his journal:

> I'm a Christian. In today's entertainment world you don't get any credit for this. It's like telling someone you're a leper. But I can't help it. I'm a Christian because I believe in the death and resurrection . . . the whole thing. [But] the Church doesn't think I'm a Christian, and I can't help that either. I don't feel like belonging to anything or anyone.[10]

Larry saw the whole business of Jesus rock as poetic justice. Rock came from rhythm and blues, and rhythm and blues came from gospel. Elvis didn't make up rock 'n' roll, he heard it first in the black churches of Tupelo, Mississippi. He was getting young Christians to embrace music that white churches had rejected because of their protracted racism. What could be more appropriate? Comfortable white middle-class preachers and laymen having their little empire upended by the musical traditions of the black people that they so despised. "The beloved community" strikes back.

On *Street Level*, a collection of raw demos and his first self-produced record, Norman further read the riot act on a Church he believed was too bourgeois, comfortable, and indifferent to the poor and marginalized. His performances showcased broadside poems like "First Day in Church." Written by British poet Gordon Bailey and oft performed by British actor Nigel Goodwin, the poem was a tour de force of a new sensibility among younger believers. Originally recited at the Berlin Congress on World Evangelism in 1966—a performance that got both Goodwin and Billy Graham in hot water with the audience—Norman chose the piece as an opener for one of his headlining performances at the Hollywood Palladium. Imitating

Goodwin's British accent, he delivered the lines of the final stanzas in a world-weary voice on a note of resignation:

Listen, I only came to church to see if they could offer hope
But everything that happened there was way outside my scope
You know like afterwards, outside, there was a beggar on the
*   grass*
He held his hand out to the people. They'd smile, then they'd
*   pass*

I'm sure he reached for something real, for something more
*   than cash*
He begged them for a little cheer an' they all pretended not to
*   hear*
I get the message loud and clear
Church is middle class.[11]

Around this time, during the hubbub of Larry's Southern California writing and speaking ministry, his little cottage became the scene for a meeting that would change the course of his life and career. He met a talented young singer-songwriter named Randy Stonehill, who had come to Los Angeles to try to break into the music industry. Randy had seen Larry in concert around Easter in 1969 at an outdoor music festival, and there met Larry's sister Nancy. He developed a crush on Nancy, but was also keen to meet her famous brother. Like Larry, Randy was a singer, songwriter, and guitarist, whose flexible and malleable tenor voice could cover a lot of sonic territory.

Randy was not a Christian at the time, and with a history of experimenting with pot under his belt, he hardly seemed a good candidate for the Jesus movement. But Larry took interest in the tall, gangly, and curly-haired young artist, feeling that he could act as a sort of big brother to the young man. Stonehill wrote an enthusiastic letter to Norman from San Jose, dated June 4, 1970, as he was anticipating high school graduation. Principally, he was writing to persuade Larry to let him move into the cottage with his new girlfriend, Debbie, but he also confessed to having been busted with a group of friends with pot at a beach picnic in Santa Cruz. Randy hoped this turn of events wouldn't prevent future professional musical collaboration between him and Larry. He reassured his older friend that since this was his first offense, hopefully he would get only probation—to which he added, by the way, did Larry have a wig that Randy could wear to court? That way he wouldn't have to cut his now impressively long mane of hair.[12] Randy, who confessed he did not have the best relationship with his parents, seemed eager to impress this new "big brother."

Larry invited the young singer to Los Angeles and tasked sister Kristy, whom he had sent a plane ticket so she could visit him in Hollywood, with the job of escorting Randy—though she did not discover this until she arrived at the San Jose airport. Kristy later remembered:

> It was one of those PSA business commuter flights so my seat was sitting backwards facing this kid. But I had brought a book so I ignored him. The kid was Stonehill. Larry had invited him down also. Larry met us at the airport and I soon found out that his apartment was occupied with several other kids who, it turned out, were being supported entirely by Larry. Stonehill left after one or two days and I only recall seeing him one other time, years later when I was visiting Larry and he stopped by Larry's apartment on Doheny in Hollywood. I don't remember ever hearing him sing. Anyway, the rest of us spent the summer in what Larry thought of as an artist colony.[13]

The situation birthed in Larry a dream: maybe he could provide a haven for outcasts like Stonehill and himself. Maybe he could be for others what no one had been for him: a mentor, a father in the faith, and an artistic inspiration. But there was a darker side too: who could Larry re-create in his own image? Stonehill became his first experiment.

Larry Norman and Randy Stonehill were destined to become "frenemies." But in the beginning, they were the Jesus movement's original "bromance." During their early conversations, Larry kept pestering Stonehill about whether he'd "accepted Jesus" yet. Stonehill would say no, and Larry would wait fifteen minutes and then ask again. Then, in August of 1970, Randy excused himself to the bathroom during a particularly heady spiritual conversation with Larry, to gather himself. Years later, he told a reporter, "So there I was. Eighteen years old and in Los Angeles and I just said a simple prayer . . . 'Jesus, if you're real, I want to know. And if you died on the cross and it is significant and if it has some meaning for me that you died for me to complete some spiritual process that I can't do without you, just show me how much you love me. . . . I just need to know, well, the proof is in the pudding.'" He then recalled being surprised by "an overwhelming sense of the Presence of God," which included a physical sensation of shaky knees, an urge to laugh out loud, and a sense of weight being lifted off him. He commemorated the experience in a song that begins, "I got stoned in Norman's kitchen, we was talkin' bout the facts of life," and goes on to describe the moment of conversion. "When that cat started prayin' the spirit fell on me." Larry helped to record the track, and sang backup vocals, complete with tea-pouring sound effects and the "winds of change" blowing in the background.

Randy was an electrifying solo performer who delighted in making his audience laugh. His songs were emotionally tender, touching, if less brainy than Larry's. So smitten was Larry with his friend's talents that he set to work on producing a record and established an underground label, One Way Records, to be a vehicle for the pair's work. He did so more than a year before Calvary Chapel launched

Maranatha! Music to feature such groups as Chuck Girard's Love Song, and the Sweet Comfort Band. Maranatha! released mostly uplifting material that expressed the artist's love for the Lord, but Norman and Stonehill's output would be grittier, newsier, and express more vulnerability. References to thankfulness for God's love would be accompanied by visceral meditations on the experience of being lost. Larry released his *Street Level* raw demo collection and put together a record for Stonehill titled *Born Twice*, the first half of which featured outtakes from a live concert performed just months after Randy's conversion. And what was more, the entire recording was funded by Pat Boone, the squeaky-clean Christian pop and television star.[14] Boone was not only an investor, he was an endorser, and he liked what he heard.

Larry had big plans for Randy's career, and his self-mythologizing skills were employed on Randy's behalf. Jotting down ideas for a follow-up release, Larry wrote in the proposed liner notes: "I've known Randy since before he was born [again]. He used to have a crush on my sister. He came to Hollywood to be a star, until he met a friend of mine in the kitchen. Randy's crazy, but he knows it. I'm irrevocably sane, so we need each other. He helps me stay up, and I help him stay down. We've survived a lot together."

One of the problems that crept up in the making of *Born Twice* was distinguishing which song ideas, lyrics, and music were Stonehill's contributions and which ones Norman's. Songs such as "I Love You" and "Christmastime" would all later appear on Larry's records, without mentioning cowriting credits for Stonehill on the record sleeve. In fact, there were no writing credits at all on subsequent Larry Norman albums. In the case of "I Love You," Randy claimed the melody and idea were entirely his innovation. Larry responded by saying that Randy might have the germ of a song idea, but he would do the heavy lifting in getting the song put to bed. On "Christmastime," Larry simply removed a verse of lyrics Randy had contributed and took sole songwriting credit. Unlike writing duos like Lennon/McCartney and Jagger/Richards, neither officially recognized a songwriting partnership. It was loose, and informal. They were brothers in Christ, right? What could go wrong?

Larry's plans for One Way Records were more grandiose than just releasing albums. He fancied himself as a U.S.-based version of Francis Schaeffer, the famous author and missionary who opened up a retreat center, L'Abri, in the Swiss Alps for seekers, students, and other intellectually curious young people who wanted to talk about the big ideas that shaped world views. Visitors would sometimes stay for months on end, but the environment produced a veritable who's who of leaders for the emerging Evangelical movement, including sociologist Os Guinness and art critic Hans Rookmaaker. In Larry's mind, L'Abri was a Christian commune, and he wanted to set up his own version for artists in Los Angeles. In brainstorming for proposed promotional material, he described One Way "as a shelter for musicians, writers, and singers who want a place to try out their ideas" as well as "photographers, poets, and journalists, who [want] a home base from which to let their art reach out." Upping the ante considerably, Larry concluded, "One Way Records is not just a record company, it's a family."

What he didn't realize is that what those artists primarily wanted was not a commune, or band of brothers, but things of a less esoteric nature: distribution, publishing, rock-'n'-roll tours, and careers. They wanted Larry to make them successful, to help them achieve what he had achieved. And over the years, he would learn a hard lesson: never help anyone with their dream, because when their desires do not become reality, you become the living embodiment of the fact that dreams do not come true.

Larry did not pause to think about the dangers of building an empire, however, because he was on a roll. Through both his writing and music, the impression seemed to be taking shape that Larry Norman was one of the galvanizing forces behind the great awakening of America's youth. It led to one of Larry's best lines in his early concerts: "A reporter came up to me and asked me if I was the leader of the Jesus movement, and I said, 'No. Jesus is.' Then they said, 'Well, someone said that the Jesus movement started in your living room.' To which I responded, 'Well, if it did, I wasn't home at the time.'"

Solidifying the impression of Larry's leadership was his association with what came to be known as the "One Way sign" of the Jesus movement. As early as 1966, Norman had innovated a practice to subvert the "applause" portion of a normal rock concert. Initially he responded to the clapping by simply saying at a low volume, "Praise the Lord." Then it hit him: after each song, he would simply hold up his right hand, with his index finger pointing to heaven. The takeaway: "Only God should get the praise for what's happening here right now." Soon, the kids in the audience stopped clapping and raised their fingers aloft in the One Way sign as well.

This gave off a mystical, even spooky effect. Jesus rock concerts weren't loud; they were quiet. Having witnessed the resonance of the One Way sign, a young artist and acquaintance of Larry's, Lance Bowen, simply drew up a graphic version of what kids were doing physically during the concerts. With his marketing savvy, and insisting that the concept was his intellectual property, Larry seized upon the moment, filing a copyright notice for the One Way symbol on December 2, 1969. Artist: Lance Bowen.[15] The owner of the copyright? Larry's newly created J.C. Love Publishing Company. The symbol became the icon of the Jesus movement, and was reproduced on posters, bumper stickers, and coffee mugs. Critics plagued him for years for having copyrighted the sign, and he later apologized via an interview in the *New Bay Psalter*: "I don't approve of the 'commercialization of Christ,' and I am very sorry if I accidentally contributed impetus to the pop aspects of all of this. I was further disappointed when conservative Christian magazines began to blame me for the commercial tinge of the Jesus movement."[16]

Far from simply being interested in one-on-one conversion approaches, Larry, along with author Hal Lindsey and other evangelists and church leaders, led large "marches for Jesus" in California. In the period documentary *The Son Worshippers*, a strange half-hour film designed to give viewers a sense of the tone and tack of "Jesus people," thousands of people crowd the streets of Sacramento, carrying signs reading YOU'VE GOT A LOT TO LIVE, JESUS HAS A LOT TO GIVE, and other slogans.[17] Staged on February 23, 1971, alongside movement figures such as Duane Pederson, Al Hopson, and Arthur Blessitt, the film shows Larry Norman standing on the steps of the state capitol. "Peace is not the absence of war; it's the presence of happiness," he announces before a crowd of 15,000 marchers. "You radicals want an all-out revolution?" he asks. "You've got it," he exclaims, raising a worn-out Bible aloft over his Segovia guitar. "Real change!" The crowd roared their approval.

A similar march was held on the steps of the Los Angeles City Hall weeks later. This time, Larry wore a leather star-spangled jacket, and took to the stage carrying a gas mask from Vietnam. He hung his gas mask on his microphone stand, picked up his guitar, and sang his recently penned church protest song, "Right Here in America," captured on the 1970 release *Street Level*:

So I ask you, America: where do you stand?
Your people are starving, they're beaten, and they're raped
And they're dying in jail cells, so what are your plans?
I'm not talking to Congress or you politicians
Or Panthers or Muslims or Nixon or Birch
I'm addressing this song to the Church

'Cause I've been in your churches and sat in your pews
And heard sermons on just how much money you'll need for
    the year
And I've heard you make reference to Mexicans, Chinamen,
    Niggers, and Jews
And I gather you wish we would all disappear
And you call yourselves Christians when really you're not
You're living your life as you please

If you're really a Christian then put down yourself
And follow wherever God leads

I'm not talking religion, I'm talking 'bout Jesus
Put all your plans on the shelf
Let's stop marching for peace and start marching for Jesus
And peace will take care of itself[18]

By the spring of 1971, the Jesus movement had spread beyond Southern California. The message that peace and love could be experienced only through Jesus captured the imagination of youth across the country, from Orange County to Greenwich Village, and artists like Larry Norman, Gentle Faith, Love Song, and gospel artist Andraé Crouch were providing the soundtrack to this experience. There were even some high-profile "conversions" like Barry McGuire, whose antiwar song "Eve of Destruction" had gone number one in 1965. Barry had met Arthur Blessitt and, before too long, had prayed to "receive Christ." There were rumors that Turley Richards and Eric Clapton had become "born again," and thanks to the influence of his wife, June Carter Cash, Johnny Cash had also begun to take his faith in Christ seriously. Even Paul Stookey, of Peter, Paul & Mary, had started witnessing to students at University of California at Berkeley. Jesus was now everywhere; so much so that it caught the attention of Henry Luce III and the editors at *Time* magazine. Sometime that May, Larry Norman fielded a request from reporter Tim Tylor to talk about the Jesus movement, and Larry called collect.

As would become his pattern, Larry documented the entire conversation: he plugged his phone into a cassette-tape player, and hit record. Tylor introduced himself by saying that *Time* was doing a piece on "the whole Jesus thing," and that his understanding was that "a lot of it is in L.A. and a lot of it has to do with music, and everybody says that, well, you're the chief—I have yet to see what kind of music you play . . ."

Larry (interrupting): "It's rock."

"Yeah," Tylor continues, "you're the chief Jesus rock guy in and around L.A." He had also been reading "As I See It" in the *Hollywood Free Paper.*

Larry told Tylor about being in People! and how, three years earlier, they wanted to title their record *We Need a Whole Lot More of Jesus and a Lot Less Rock and Roll,* but Capitol—ironically now, given the success of the Jesus movement—turned the title down because they deemed it uncommercial. Now, Larry continued, everybody's interested in Jesus. Now, Larry said, he'd left Capitol, played the Hollywood Palladium and the Hollywood Bowl to packed audiences, and was getting ready to sign with Elektra Records.

But Larry wasn't content to advance his career with a potentially legacy-defining interview with *Time.* Once Tylor had gotten his basic information, Larry turned the tables and began asking the reporter questions of his own: What did Tylor make of the Jesus movement? When Tylor said he was "kind of amazed" by what was happening, Larry pressed him. What was happening was not like "hippiedom," he said, "something picked up on and manufactured by the press." This was a spiritual movement, underground, completely free of the normal engines of pop culture. The kids had actually accepted Jesus into their lives and it was making a huge difference. They were reading the Bible and applying it to the signs of the times. Curious but slightly aloof, Tylor remarked, "Well, it certainly is big," and thanked Larry and said he was looking forward to listening to his records.

When the article appeared on June 21, 1971, it made the cover. The cover of the issue read "The Jesus Revolution," and featured a letter from the publisher, Henry Luce III, remarking on *Time's* own history covering the so-called Jesus Freaks. The magazine's New York–based religion editor, Dick Ostling, covered the story, and called the Jesus movement "amorphous, evasive, going on everywhere and nowhere." The article opened with one of the *Hollywood Free Paper's* favorite ads/posters:

WANTED

JESUS CHRIST

ALIAS: THE MESSIAH, THE SON OF GOD, KING OF KINGS, LORD OF LORDS PRINCE OF PEACE, ETC.

- Notorious leader of an underground liberation movement
- Wanted for the following charges:
  - Practicing medicine, winemaking and food distribution without a license.
  - Interfering with businessmen in the temple.
  - Associating with known criminals, radicals, prostitutes, and street people.
  - Claiming to have the authority to make people into God's children.

APPEARANCE: Typical hippie type—long hair, beard, robe, sandals.

- Hangs around slum areas, few rich friends, often sneaks into the desert.

BEWARE: This man is extremely dangerous. His insidiously inflammatory message is particularly dangerous to young people who haven't been taught to ignore him yet.

WARNING: HE IS STILL AT LARGE

The first "authority" to be quoted on the Jesus Freaks was predictable: "'It's like a glacier,' says 'Jesus Rock' Singer Larry Norman, 24. 'It's growing and there's no stopping it.'" Ostling seemed to understand that while this youth movement challenged conventional wisdom, it was, oddly, orthodox: "The Jesus revolution, in short, is one that denies the virtues of the Secular City and heaps scorn on the message that God was ever dead."[19] The piece called Jesus rock "both professionally and theologically solid," going on in the same breath to name Larry "the top solo artist in the field."

By 1972, the Jesus movement had fully achieved the Billy Graham seal of approval. The world-famous evangelist had already embraced the influx of young "street Christians" into the evangelical fold with the publication of *The Jesus Generation.*[20] The Explo '72 conference at the Cotton Bowl in Dallas, organized by Billy Graham and Campus Crusade for Christ founder Bill Bright, marked a high point for the Jesus movement's public profile. Graham described the event as a "religious Woodstock" that succeeded in "doing an end run around the Church." Contemporary estimates placed attendance between 80,0000 to 100,000. During the final eight-hour concert, the numbers swelled to 150,000. In addition to playing alongside other gospel artists such as Andraé Crouch, and Love Song, Larry Norman shared a bill with Johnny Cash, Kris Kristofferson, and Rita Coolidge. Cash summed up the spirit of the entire enterprise when he told the massive crowd, "I have tried drugs and a little of everything else, and there is nothing in the world more satisfying than having the kingdom of God building inside of you and growing."[21] In terms of pop culture, the Jesus movement had arrived.

Life magazine, which put the Dallas story on its cover, marveled at the good behavior of the young people attending Explo '72. "Dallas police were incredulous that nobody called them pigs and that no arrests were made among the registered delegates. 'I couldn't believe it,' said one special officer assigned to handle Explo security. 'Everything just went like a dream.'"[22] If anything could back up Graham's, Cash's, and Norman's claims that following Jesus was the answer, it was the outpouring of love, peace, and kindness among the throng of teens and twentysomethings photographed holding up the One Way sign. The good times would roll all the way until 1976, which *Newsweek* dubbed "The Year of the Evangelical" after the United States elected its first ever "born again" president: Jimmy Carter.[23]

Neither the media nor many churchgoers had expected a revolution to take place so far outside the confines of institutional religion on one hand, and the American mainstream on the other. In a television interview Larry Norman took pains to explain the difference. When asked by a reporter if he had been religious before his "baptism in the Holy Spirit," he replied, "I was religious, but Jesus isn't a religion. People make up a religion about him, but he's more than a religion."

REPORTER: What do you mean "more"?
NORMAN: He's real. To me religion's not real, it's all based on superstition, guilt, and ritual. Jesus isn't.
REPORTER: Explain that to me.
NORMAN: Well, I don't have to go to church every day. I go to church in my heart. I don't have to kneel or bow, [because] my spirit has been humbled and bowed. I'm not afraid of the preachers or approval of the members of the church. I just have to be right before God. I have to read my Bible to stay informed on who man is and who God is. . . . The whole Bible is real to me. It's accurate. I didn't used to think that way. I was too intellectual, but now my mind is more cleared up than when I thought I was intellectual. Now it all makes sense.[24]

Suddenly it became plausible to Christian young people that following Jesus and listening to their pastor might be two different, and possibly unrelated, behaviors. The "church of the heart" became the de-facto ecclesiology of the Jesus movement. All of this sort of talk was enough to make the phenomenon suspicious at best and dangerous at worst to what at that time was "the evangelical industrial complex."[25] Conservative pastors started to produce defensive literature that took aim at the Jesus movement. One book, *The Jesus Freaks* by Southern Baptist pastor Jess Moody, implied that there was a gossamer-thin difference between these enthusiastic youths and the run-of-the-mill hippie. The translation to the faithful was clear: this is just liberalism in disguise.[26]

As the Jesus movement was reaching its zenith as a cultural phenomenon, bringing Larry's professional life to new heights, his personal life was about to be taken over by the arrival of Pamela Ahlquist. Pamela hailed from Minnesota, where she managed to get a job as a Northwest Airlines flight attendant at the tender age of nineteen. Hailing from a "solid" evangelical family, she was nevertheless, by any estimation, a wild child, described by her parents as a rebellious, free-spirited flirt. Pam had competed in various beauty pageants, and had dabbled in print modeling regionally in Minnesota. The popularity of the Jesus movement, however, drew her out West to see what all the hubbub was about. She drove out to California with her friend Bruce and proceeded immediately to the Sunset Strip, and later, Hollywood Boulevard. There, as she later claimed, she was amazed to see kids her age kick heroin and start following Jesus. Then, while attending a Jesus rock festival sponsored by the *Hollywood Free Paper* at the Palladium she saw a young man with long blond hair and a guitar who held the crowd spellbound. He had them all silently making the One Way sign while singing "I Wish We'd All Been Ready." Wow! she thought. When she returned to Minnesota, her parents liked what they saw: Pamela was finally serious about the Lord. She returned to L.A. by August of 1971 and this time found herself at a Jesus festival on the beach. This time when she saw Larry Norman onstage, she resolved that she would marry him, a fact borne out by a drawing she made in her diary that day.[27] After he got offstage, she set out to find him. Pam drew a cartoon of the episode in her diary, complete with bubble dialogue boxes. There she was, in the crowd watching Larry playing onstage, thinking to herself, "I am going to marry that man!"

For Larry, it wasn't exactly love at first sight, but he was intrigued, and Pam came on strong. The truth was that Larry hadn't had a serious girlfriend since high school—a strange feat for a Capitol Records recording artist and ringleader of an honest-to-God sociological phenomenon. When Larry told Joe and Marge about Pam, they were overjoyed that he had a girlfriend—positive reinforcement for a young man seeking his father's approval. Larry flew to Minnesota to follow up with her, despite confessing to her later that he initially found her to be vain and selfish. Ominously, he wrote to her that "I saw only the great reservoir of sad things."

Within weeks, however, Larry's view of Pam softened, and he professed undying love for her, as well as his desire to be married. He wrote in the voice of one lovesick, and apologized for his initial reaction to her. In a letter posted on October 14, 1971, he wrote: "I love you so sweetly. I taste a wonderful sweetness in my mouth when I think of you.... It prepares me with a desire to make love to you.... God has touched you ... you are unique." The return address on Larry's envelope stationery depicted him standing in front of a microphone, with a thought bubble coming out of his head that read, "C'mon Norman, smile. December 28 [their wedding date] isn't that far off."[28] For several months they exchanged letters—he in Hollywood, she in St. Paul.

Larry even had a "revelation" as to why he had been so hesitant to embrace Pam initially. Ironically, the answer was Joe, who had discouraged premarital sex to the point of scaring Larry away from romantic entanglements:

> It starts with being little and feeling that my father disapproves of sex. So I refused to think sexually—or at least admit it to myself. As I began to get older, I found it necessary to be ugly so no one would like me. If somebody liked me or thought I was handsome, [I thought] it would imply sexual responsibility to [like] them back, ask them on a date, etc.
>
> So I tried to be as ugly and as out of step as possible so that no one would approach me. So no one would require me to have a sexual confrontation (i.e. So my father would never disapprove of me or "punish" me for acknowledging the sexuality.)
>
> Even later, when I was away from home, I was in [People!], and had the freedom to do anything, but was careful only to befriend young girls who did not threaten me with sex or try to

seduce me. That way I could be their friend, and help them, but never merit disapproval from Daddy.

Well, now it is alright for me to stop being ugly and to begin to stop degrading myself and eventually to have confidence in my appearance; and to have sex with you and desire you, and to become a fully grown man.[29]

With Joe's blessing, the nuptials were planned. The announcement of their engagement captured the attention of United Press International (UPI), which ran the following story, which the couple included in their wedding invitation:

ROCK SINGER TO WED

HOLLYWOOD (UPI)—Jesus Rock singer Larry Norman today interrupted a press conference to announce his engagement to airlines hostess and former model, Pamela Ahlquist. Miss Ahlquist was a finalist in the 1971 Miss Minnesota Universe Pageant.

Norman, an influential leader of the Jesus Movement, is also the creator of the ONE WAY sign which is [a] universally recognized symbol of the Movement. He writes a column for several publications and speaks across the country concerning the sudden revival and spiritual reinterest among the American young people. Formerly an artist with Capitol Records, he released three albums and a multimillion single. Now with MGM he plans to sneak preview songs from his upcoming musical on his next album. The musical is entitled "Lion's Breath" and is about the spiritual revolution.

The wedding is planned for December of this year and he and his bride will honeymoon in New York and then go to Europe to do a series of Christian Rock

Concerts. He closed the press conference by saying
that all members of the press were invited to attend
the wedding "unless Jesus returns first."[30]

Was this a cry for help? Did Larry hope Jesus would come back before he got married? They barely knew each other. Larry Norman
was not ready for marriage, and neither was Pamela Ahlquist. Outwardly, they were the perfect picture. The pair graced magazine
covers, a photogenic power couple for the Jesus movement. But behind closed doors, the marriage was troubled from the beginning. A
wedding photo showed Pam looking sweet, with Larry and his kid
brother, Charles (six years old), looking exasperated. Pam had previously been building a modeling career and job with Northwest Airlines. If she was going to be married to Larry, she wanted that to be
her new "career." Her husband, on the other hand, wanted nothing to
do with this proposition. He was an artist who had been performing
as a solo act for many years, and he couldn't see Pam as a collabora-
tor in that respect. Further, their personalities were polar opposites.
Pam was both lighthearted and materialistic: she focused almost in-
cessantly on the fact that they didn't have a lot of money for her to
buy things. Larry was mercurial, acerbic, and moody. Pam desired
to be together all of the time. Larry preferred long stretches of time,
even days, alone. A showdown was inevitable.

One year after their honeymoon in New York, Larry returned to
Gotham City to play both at the legendary Bitter End in Greenwich
Village (the club that helped launch the careers of musicians like Bob
Dylan and Billy Joel, and comedians like Lenny Bruce and Dick Ca-
vett) and at Calvary Baptist Church in Midtown. The disparity in the
venues for those two performances proved that Larry fully intended
to keep feet in both worlds. Culturally speaking, it was a difficult
time to be a young person and a Christian with genuine biblical
convictions at the same time. Who didn't want to be cool and listen
to rock 'n' roll? And yet there was still a lot of preaching against compromise with the world coming from the pulpits in America. Should

religious attitudes change with the times, or should traditions and practices be more rigid? Larry Norman openly talked about the stress religious people were feeling in this age. Speaking onstage at Calvary Baptist, he deepened the impression that there had to be a way for the average person to bypass the confusions of modern religious life: "There's been a lot of controversy in the Church [lately]. The Catholic Church is changing a lot of the rules and people are getting confused. . . . [quoting] 'How come I've had this man around my neck for all these years and he's not a saint anymore?' Stuff like that is confusing. Controversy like, 'Should people dress a certain way to come to church, or can they come as they are?'" But Larry presented an alternative: a relationship with God as a direct, personal encounter. He told the crowd of New Yorkers how the kids he was dealing with felt about Christ: "One day, sometimes with no warning, [Jesus] stood right there in front of us and held out his hands. And we've grabbed them, and he's been so steady that we've been able to walk with him from that moment on."[31]

Unwittingly, Larry Norman and his Jesus movement co-conspirators were creating new expectations for what it meant to be a Christian in the modern world. This promise of an intense, intimate experience with the divine would become something to which traditional churches would have to respond, for both good and ill. From here on out, Christians would start to expect their religious experience to be relevant to modern times. They expected their faith to make sense in the city, in the suburbs, at home where the television was on, and in the face of an increasingly noisy and secular popular culture. Larry Norman was quickly becoming something like a guru to his listeners and followers. "People accuse me of being anti-Church," he told the crowd in New York City. "I'm not anti-Church. I think we *are* the Church, if we love Jesus. It's not the building; it's the people. It's not like God stays in the building waiting for you to come back. It's the people. It's really in us. . . . Jesus loves us all, no matter what religion we are."[32]

4

JESUS VERSUS THE JESUS MOVEMENT

OLLOWING THEIR WHIRLWIND HONEYMOON IN NEW YORK City, the Normans started packing for London. Larry was scheduled to perform thirty-eight concerts in thirty-five days, mostly at colleges and universities across the UK. But first he and his new bride had to settle their differences over marijuana.

Before leaving for the airport in Chicago, Larry was alarmed when he discovered Pam tucking plastic bags of what he initially thought was tea into her luggage. What in the world was she thinking? Larry asked when he discovered what the contents really were. What if they got caught at customs? The media would have a field day running headlines like "Jesus Rock Singer Busted for Pot." Larry made her flush it down the toilet before they headed to O'Hare Airport.[1] It was an inauspicious beginning for their marriage, to say the least.

The welcome wagon that greeted them on the other side of the Atlantic quickly took their mind off their differences. *Buzz* magazine, the newly minted arts-and-culture periodical for Christians in the UK, heralded the arrival of the man they perceived to be at the vanguard of the Jesus movement: "You are already acquainted with the One Way finger pointing sign," *Buzz* breathlessly announced. "Last autumn's Nationwide Festival of Light saw to that. Everyone from Cliff Richard to Malcolm Muggeridge found themselves with a hand raised to the sky and a simple index finger emerging out of a closed fist to point heavenwards."[2] This was a big deal. Cliff Richard was the Elvis Presley of Great Britain, one of the nation's biggest pop stars, with a legion of female fans. Tickets to Larry's concerts sold at a brisk pace, a remarkable fact, given that most fans didn't even own a Larry Norman record yet: *Upon This Rock* was released on Key Records in the UK the same month as the tour began.

Upon landing at Heathrow, Larry was surprised to find himself immediately standing before a gaggle of reporters representing "every paper from the legitimate press to the tabloid-type *Daily Mirror* and *The Sun*."[3] Jesus rock was the hottest commodity in England, and here was Larry's opportunity to bring the British people the spiritual revolution taking place among American youth. It was a reverse British Invasion for Jesus.

At his first show at Lancaster University, the event promoter remarked that he hadn't seen a reaction to an artist quite like this one, including for acts like Pink Floyd and the Who. After a club gig in South London, one reporter commented: "If, like me, you see Christianity as a reluctantly but irrevocably dying mythology, Larry Norman is still worth hearing for his music and himself. His songs, mainly self penned, are inventive blues-based compositions which he brings to life with a vocal range that few other white singers can equal."[4]

Meanwhile, English clergy were not amused. Upon the announcement of Norman's tour, the *West Lothian Courier* in Scotland ran the front-page headline: "No Place for 'Rock' Gospel." Describing him as an "American Gospel 'hot rock' singer," the paper reported that Larry would "not get a unanimous welcome." They quoted local Rev. Donald Gillies as saying, "This kind of thing is making an absurdity of the Christian faith. . . . It is a misleading of the younger generation."[5]

Whipping up publicity further was the enthusiasm of Cliff Richard, one of the most beloved pop stars in England. Richard invited Norman to his mansion to play for British actor Nigel Goodwin and a small group of friends. In footage captured on film, with him playfully wagging his long, golden locks, Larry performed a recently completed song—an open letter to his parents and all who questioned his project—which would become the rallying cry for what would later be the mammoth contemporary Christian music industry:

> *I want the people to know*
> *That he saved my soul*
> *But I still like to listen to the radio*
> *They say rock and roll is wrong*
> *We'll give you one more chance*
> *I say I feel so good I gotta get up and dance*
>
> *I know what's right, I know what's wrong*
> *I don't confuse it*
> *All I'm really trying to say is*
> *Why should the devil have all the good music?*
> *I feel good every day*
> *Because Jesus is the rock and he rolled my blues away.*

It was this tour, more than anything else, that solidified Norman's position as the "Father of Jesus Rock." Repeatedly, concertgoers described the curious way in which shows were conducted: The lights would come up, and an elfin-looking young man with long blond hair would wander out onstage, carrying his guitar case, acting diffident to the crowd. He would unpack his guitar and start tuning it. What seemed like an eternity would elapse before he spoke a word. The effect was strange and electrifying, and kept concertgoers discussing what they'd seen and heard long afterward. Claude Eton, writing for the magazine *Evangelism Today*, hailed Larry's performance in Bristol for its "droll humor" and for the fact that throughout the show, "we felt like slaves to this unpredictable performance."[6]

Larry wanted to be more than just another rock artist: he wanted to get under people's skin. Whether or not he was strategic in doing so, he cultivated an air of mystery that drove some fans toward obsession. For the most part, this worked for him. Audiences would struggle for hours, trying to decipher the meaning of Larry's cryptic lyrics and surrealist images. Unfortunately for Larry, by 1973 they would begin to return the favor—and spin fantastical images of their own about the artist's personal life.

But for the time being, Larry had reason to think he had the wind at his back. He played to sold-out audiences at Manchester University, Coventry University, in Leicester, Bath, and even fielded an interview for the *New Music Express* (*NME*) at the London School of Economics. The tour's highlight included a packed rally in Trafalgar Square, and a show at the 2,500-seat Westminster Hall, which Larry Norman, with several opening acts, also sold out twice on the same day. Sprinkled throughout the tour, he appeared on various BBC programs. John Peel, one of the first disc jockeys on BBC One to play rock music and later the curator of the widely regarded "Peel Sessions," favorably reviewed *Upon This Rock*, furthering the record's standing in the public consciousness.

The year 1972 would signal the beginning of a flood of handwritten mail from fans around the world hoping, somehow, to make a connection with the man whom they now saw as a father figure—or fellow traveler at least—to their spiritual journey. Fans sent him packages with everything from handwritten Bible verses to concert reactions to samples of their hair. Others just wanted to connect. One dear soul writing from Maidstone, Kent, wrote Larry concerned about his delivery: "It worried me to hear your singing on Radio 4 at 7:50 this morning: not the message, for I am in sympathy, though I know no 'Jesus people.' I was worried about your delivery, your shortness of breath. If you have not already had lessons in breath control, would you do me and yourself some kindness and get some? You may suffer from asthma."[7] Many of the letters consisted of intensely personal narratives: kids describing their despair at home, teenage boys going into grisly detail about their attempted suicides, husbands and wives lamenting their struggles in marriage. Very little of this correspondence had much to do with Larry's music. Those who wrote him seemed more interested in contacting a maharishi.

Although publicly his life had reached a fever pitch of notoriety, not all was well with the recently crowned prince and princess of the Jesus movement. Upon arriving in the UK, Pamela announced her intention to join Larry onstage for his performances. She would sing, and they would banter between songs. Her husband wasn't amused. What did she think this was, Sonny and Cher? He was on a mission from God, and this wasn't amateur hour. To Larry, Pam's request to sing with him sprung from impure motives, from vanity and a desire to be noticed. Pam, on the other hand, felt like she had left her modeling career to be Larry Norman's wife, a sacrifice that should come with commensurate benefits.

The fallout was messy. Just three months into the marriage, Pam would claim that Larry wanted a divorce. He claimed nothing could have been further from the truth. Divorce, according to scripture, was verboten except for extenuating circumstances. He simply wanted to put on a professional show musically, and to make a statement for Christ. After the dust cleared, though, and it was decided that Pam would not be joining him onstage, he became more optimistic about their future together. He went back to writing his ardent love notes, telling her that he loved her and missed her and hated it when they were apart. "I miss you," he cooed several months later, "and am in need of your shoulders and voice."[8]

As his star kept climbing, the record companies regained their interest in Larry Norman as a recording artist. Initially Jac Holzman from Elektra Records, upon hearing *Upon This Rock* and noting the media attention that the new "spiritual revolution" among young people was getting, reached out to offer a contract. He promised Paul Rothschild, who had made records with the Doors and Janis Joplin, as a producer. But thanks to some lobbying from Pat Boone, Mike Curb took an interest in Larry after moving from Capitol to MGM Records. A contract was issued and then signed. The album would be released on MGM, and distributed through the Verve label. In England, Larry would release his next album through Polydor Records.

Larry and Pam hung out with as many non-Christian artists as they did Christian ones. Taking a break from the road, the couple, joined by Larry's sister Kristy, took in Peter Cook and Dudley Moore's now legendary *Behind the Fridge* comedy tour. The duo invited the trio backstage. Moore, whose star was ascendant in the 1970s, and whose appearance in the films *10* with Bo Derek in 1979 and *Arthur* in 1981 made him a household name in America, took an instant liking to Larry, and the two became fast friends. In the UK, Larry and Pam felt like stars. But when they got back to Tinseltown, they were just another beautiful couple in a city of beautiful, not to mention famous, people. Larry would make it a point to return to England as much as possible.

Meanwhile, with a new record contract in hand, Larry went for the brass ring and reached out to George Martin, the legendary producer of the Beatles, to gauge his interest in working together. Martin offered his brand-new AIR Studios on Oxford Street in London, where he'd enjoy a prime location and a state-of-the-art Neve mixing console. By the time the sessions were organized, however, Martin had bad news to deliver: he was too far behind on his projects to act as hands-on producer. Nevertheless, he personally recommended that a trio consisting of Jon Miller, Rod Edwards, and Roger Hand— collectively known as Triumvirate Production—produce the record. Miller had been managing the duo of Edwards/Hand, and Martin had produced three records for them already. Triumvirate had already done their research by attending Larry Norman's first Royal Albert Hall show. Miller recalls: "I remember he walked onstage to rapturous applause carrying a guitar case that he unpacked onstage without a word to the audience who were going wild. Arrogant, confident, and very effective."[9]

Larry and Pam flew back to live in the UK for the duration of the recording of Larry's new record. He had decided that it was better to rent an apartment near London than spend a fortune on hotel bills over the course of what he hoped would be several years of recording and touring. They found a small apartment on Park Lane in Carshalton—about a twenty-five-minute train ride from London's Victoria Station—a scenic suburb in the borough of Sutton, in Surrey.

Despite its modest size, the apartment provided a place of relative quiet for Larry to finish the songs for the upcoming record. It was a place of inspiration. Larry remembered: "So, in that room I completed work on 'The Great American Novel,' for instance, and being in England really helped me see America more clearly. It helped me define its defects more cogently, really—I don't know— America's kinda like England, only totally not at all! So I was able to sift through the variables."[10]

Recording commenced in September 1972 for the session listed in the studio log as "I'm Only Visiting This Planet." The Triumvirate team had assembled a live band to play on the record, as Miller's idea was to have working musicians who could plausibly sound like "The Larry Norman Band." The core group included lead guitarist Mickey Keen, bassist John Wetton (from King Crimson and later, Asia), and Keith Smart and Bob Brady from Wizzard (drums, piano). At the time, the band was a collection of relative unknowns. Hand and Edwards contributed piano, vocals, and virtually anything the album needed. Even Pam made it onto the record as the "airline stewardess" on "The Six O'Clock News." During the recording, she was photographed by the London *Daily Express*—fabulous wife of Jesus rocker hits the town. For everyone involved, it was a heady and exciting time.

Randy Stonehill arrived days after Pam and Larry had settled in, hoping to get his own album produced by the Triumvirate. (He did, though it was never released.) Adding to the energy in the room, on the first day of recording at AIR, a bomb scare evacuated the building for part of the day. Yet there was a sense of optimism in the studio, unlike the tense environment that characterized the recording of *Upon This Rock*. The producers and band seemed to like Larry's material, although Miller saw Larry as a typical artist—a pain in the ass. "I do remember Larry dancing a lot and trying to explain to the musicians in word pictures the ideas he had for the songs. It was a very friendly atmosphere; Larry's wife was there for a while and she was very funny," he later recalled.[11] Wetton recalls Larry being a good time and simultaneously a consummate professional. Larry led the band, playing his trademark Flamenco guitar and the baby grand piano. The running documentary tapes of the sessions, released by Larry before he died, suggest a band that was having a blast in the studio. Excitement was in the air. McCartney and Wings were recording the James Bond theme "Live and Let Die" at the same time as *Only Visiting* and they tracked some of the sessions at AIR Studios. Brian Eno had begun his experiments with atmospheric electronic music in an adjacent studio too.[12] Even more remarkably, the enterprise had Billy Graham's implicit blessing; when Larry approached him for career counseling, it was Graham's advice that if Larry wanted to reach the non-Christian world for Jesus, he should first become a commercial success, to get people's attention, and then they would listen when he spoke of Christ.[13]

London seemed to agree with Larry as a creative inspiration. Having already written "Why Should the Devil Have All the Good Music?" he probably didn't need much more material, considering all of the songs he had written for his unreleased Capitol musicals. Being in the UK, however, gave him a different perspective on American life. On the train to the studio one day, he finished off the final words to what would become his most lyrically powerful song, "The Great American Novel." The third verse especially hit a raw nerve, implying that cultural Christianity had been party to oppression, despair, and the nation's spiritual demise:

> You kill a black man at midnight
> Just for talking to your daughter
> Then you make his wife your mistress
> And you leave her without water

And the sheet you wear upon your face
Is the sheet your children sleep on
At every meal you say a prayer
You don't believe but still you keep on

And your money says "in God we trust"
But it's against the law to pray in school
You say we beat the Russians to the moon
And I say you starved your children to do it.[14]

Unlike other Christian leaders, Larry seemed to believe that the easy relationship the Church enjoyed with American culture was more of a problem than a blessing. He somehow seemed to understand that apologetics may actually need to start with apologies: for the Church's racism, ready acceptance of aggression, violence, and war, and for an unwillingness to listen to the concerns of a generation.

Larry envisioned *Only Visiting This Planet* as the opening salvo in a trilogy of records: one about the present, one about the past, and the last about the future. By claiming they would present a comprehensive overview of the human condition, and by combining the albums with compelling photographs and cryptic liner notes, he wanted to cement the impression that there was more happening here than just rock 'n' roll. "I Wish We'd All Been Ready," originally featured on *Upon This Rock* (and so popular Larry thought it merited inclusion on his first two solo releases), was his terrifying apocalyptic tune about the barbaric world to come after Jesus takes the Church up to heaven and everyone else is "left behind," and spelled out what was going on: the need to sort out your relationship to God now, or else. The song's gritty images—"children died, the days grew cold, a piece of bread could buy a bag of gold," not to mention people suddenly dematerializing—gave Christian teenagers nightmares for decades. The song gained further purchase by its inclusion in *A Thief in the Night*, a creepy B film shown in many churches in the 1970s.[15]

In the movie, Jesus comes back to rapture all of the believers out of the world, whereupon a chaotic, violent hellscape emerges. The song also has been featured recently on HBO's secular take on the end times, *The Leftovers*.

Only Visiting went even further than *Upon This Rock* in its critiques of American culture and attempt to reach the spiritually seeking but not yet Christian listener. He wanted the album to begin with a breakup song, "I've Got to Learn to Live Without You," establishing an imagined sympathy with the average person—in this case someone who has lost the love of their life, and now realizes they must move on. The song "The Outlaw" introduced the audience to the person of Christ, not as a religious figure but as a dangerous rebel. "Why Don't You Look into Jesus?"—MGM's choice for the lead-off track— was the bluesy rocker originally inspired by and written for Janis Joplin. "The Six O'Clock News" was written in 1969 as a Vietnam War protest song, but on the album contained a surprising Marshall McLuhan–esque twist: a critique of how the media presented the war to the American people. Journalists feigned neutrality in the course of the horrors of war—but is objectivity concerning death, poverty, and violence a good thing? Even the beloved American space program took heat from Larry in the song "Reader's Digest":

> *The man on the news said,*
> *"China's gonna beat us*
> *We shot all our dreamers*
> *And there's no one left to lead us*
> *We need a solution, we need salvation*
> *Let's send some people to the moon*
> *And gather information!"*
>
> *They brought back a big bag of rocks*
> *Only cost thirteen billion*
> *Must be nice rocks . . .*[16]

Sprinkled in among the political commentary and implicit and not-so-subtle references to Jesus were commentaries about sexuality, and the confusion that comes from waiting for love. Perhaps the most beautiful and perplexing song on *Only Visiting* was the haunting ballad "Pardon Me":

Pardon me
Kissing you like I'm afraid
But I know I'm being played with
And you'll leave me when you get the chance

Off you'll go
In the darkness of the night
Like a bird in freedom's flight
You're thinking only of deliverance

Close your eyes
And pretend that you are me
See how empty it can be
Making love if love's not really there

Watch me go
Watch me walk away alone
As your clothing comes undone
And you pull the ribbons from your hair.[17]

"Pardon Me" purportedly was about opting out of hookup culture, but the song could be read in various ways. Could it have been about Larry's reservations about getting married? His fear of sex? Around this time, Larry scrawled the following note in his diary: "People are born with a sex, but must acquire a gender."[18] Although the comment never appeared on a record, or made its way into a concert, it shows that Larry Norman questioned orthodoxies quietly at the same time he was championing traditional Christian doctrine from the stage. That tension exacerbated over time.

In creative terms, Norman's songwriting held up to the artistic aspirations of his peers. Although there were definitely "preachy" tracks on the record, others, like "Pardon Me" and "The Great American Novel," invited the individual listener's interpretation. There was enough Jesus on the record to make MGM executives scratch their heads, but this was also no milquetoast Christian LP. With *Only Visiting*, Larry Norman finally had a record of which he could be proud: It preached Jesus, but offended Christians and attracted the lost. Perfect.

The album cover showed Larry standing in Times Square, wearing something resembling vintage workwear: faded denim on denim, interrupted only by a belt that resembled the stars on the American flag. The only deviation from the distinctively American/Western clothing was a simple cross hung around his neck. He's standing with his hand on his head, looking dazed and confused. Subtext: "Is this all there is?" The inscription on the gatefold sleeve of the record reinforced the point: "Does man live or just survive? On this sleeping planet . . . Five." In biblical numerology, five is the number of God's grace, six is the number of both man and Satan, and seven is the number of perfection, of God's word. "Does man really live?" The clear answer to his own question was, no. There had to be something more. The back cover places him at Stonehenge. He later explained:

> *Only Visiting This Planet* is the first part of the trilogy, and represents the present. On the front cover, I find myself standing in the middle of New York City, with buildings and traffic pressed around me and my hand on my head kind of saying, What is going on in this life? Is this really Earth?, and the back cover is me visiting the site of a previous civilization with its own monoliths, not skyscrapers, but amazing, architecturally sound structures just the same. The Druids apparently constructed Stonehenge to

help them observe or worship the sun, and their civilization is now as dead as will someday be New York. And I'm just standing there, looking around, wondering what happened to kill off this culture and reduce its entire recorded history to a few standing structures.[19]

The concept was extremely well planned out. Larry's archives show that he had been working on the trilogy concept, and really a career's worth of record concepts, since the beginning of the 1970s. *Only Visiting* was a masterpiece. But would enough people care about Larry Norman's contrarian message to make the album commercially viable? Would Jesus Freaks buy well-made records? Verve, hoping the answer would be yes, threw a record launch party at the Ivar Theater for Hollywood Music Royalty.[20] Larry performed the material from the record, and everything finally seemed to be coming together.

The first reaction Larry solicited was his father's. After playing Joe the album, he hoped that by now Joe would be impressed. No such luck. Joe told his son bluntly, "Well, I think that this proves that you should get out of music. And anyway, nobody likes your music."

Depressed at his father's reaction, Larry waited for other responses, and what he heard upon the record's release was encouraging. The critics gave almost across-the-board kudos. *Billboard* hailed *Only Visiting* as "an album to be reckoned with" and gave it its "special merit pick."[21] *Cashbox* listed Larry among three in the category of "Best New Artist" on January 6, 1973.[22]

In certain markets, *Only Visiting* performed well. One wire service for American DJs reported that "Charlie Walker flashes from Fayetteville, N.C., that a cut on Larry Norman's Verve album, '6 O'Clock News' . . . is 'pulling unbelievable phones.'"[23] In short order, Larry proudly wore the badge of the antihero of evangelicalism, the patron saint of mixing things that weren't supposed to go together. Larry Norman had written a love letter to the world, and signed it with the name of Jesus.

En route back to the United States, Larry and Pam toured Rhodesia and South Africa. In 1972, this caused something of a stir when audiences at his concerts decided to integrate themselves voluntarily. Dutch Afrikaner church leaders scrambled to respond to the phenomenon, picketing the shows and sending audience members to stage walkouts. But this only attracted more media attention.[24] Larry took pride that his music was of service to the progress of the beloved community, even if it was having greater influence internationally than back home.

The Normans returned to Los Angeles to face the challenges of Larry's growing stardom, and the expectations that come with being the leading figure of a new musical movement. Larry had left Randy Stonehill behind in England to do a tour there, in hopes that his friend's career would ignite too. He was discouraged to receive a letter dated October 16, 1972, from the road manager, complaining of the odd juxtaposition of the fact that while Randy was "really blessing" audiences, "keeping pace with Randy's love life" and "exercising" necessary "diplomacy over difficult situations" was proving difficult.[25] This was not what Larry wanted to hear about the exploits of his most famous protégé. A letter from British Christian musician Alwyn Wall, stating that Randy's Christian tour had been canceled due to moral indiscretion with a girl he met along the way, soured Larry further. "I feel as though I've lost a friend," Wall wrote. "We didn't say anything about Randy's girlfriend until we knew about the tour being off. I don't point the finger at Randy's problem. I pray that he'll get sorted out and start singing for Jesus."[26] Mortified, Larry apparently never replied to the letter. Wall was one of his favorite Christian music artists. Larry admired his message and heart for Jesus, and his momentary loss of confidence in Team Norman was a blow.

As if this weren't enough, back at home, Larry had to respond to increasing attacks from the fundamentalist right wing of the Church in America. For example, John R. Rice wrote a scathing article in his extreme-right church periodical, *The Sword of the Lord*, criticizing the leaders of the Jesus movement for their compromise in everything from hair length and modest clothing to accommodating hippie lifestyles to, well, playing the devil's music. Trying to stand up for her man, Pam took it upon herself to reprimand the editors by letter. Rice's retort to her expressed gladness that she "felt free to write" to them, but concluded that she was "not taught in the Word" and was "not a very mature Christian."[27] To fundamentalists like John R. Rice, American culture had gone to hell in a handbasket, and it was to be avoided by solid Christian families at all costs. Other fundamentalist organizations, such as Bill Gothard's Institute for Basic Life Principles, hosted conferences with audiences upward of 20,000 at their zenith. Gothard preached the authority of the father in the home and the submission of wives and children to male authority as pathways to success in life in the midst of a morally debased culture. Jesus rock, and those who played it, had no part in the kingdom of God.

Meanwhile, Larry was having trouble keeping tabs on his manager, Gary Anderson. The two had met in 1970 and together had set up a booking agency called Street Level Productions to complement One Way Records. Anderson hired an associate named Ed Walker, who helped him with concert bookings, publishing agreements, and registering Larry's songs with BMI and ASCAP. Pam complained that Anderson made Larry perform too many concerts, with insufficient time to recuperate in between. Larry, for his part, was more concerned about where all the money was going, and that the business side of things seemed to be lagging in general. Why, for instance, were ideas for UK record re-releases from Larry Norman, Randy Stonehill, Malcolm and Alwyn, and others taking so long to develop? In July of 1972, Larry had written Anderson a lengthy letter outlining record releases, album artwork, a British version of the *Hollywood Free Paper*, and a marketing strategy for Jesus rock in the UK with established partners whom Larry named.[28] No action was taken for months. Products in demand in the UK, such as the songbook *Why Should the Devil Have All of the Good Music?*, were taking too long to get to market, and contracts with British distributors weren't being honored. Additionally, correspondence from British music promoter Cyril Shane gave evidence of artists who wanted to cover Larry's songs on their albums not getting timely or accurate replies from Anderson.[29] The relationship with Anderson got rocky and eventually led to fisticuffs that Larry claimed left bruises on his body.

Larry would end the partnership within the year, setting an uncertain tone: now he would have to manage affairs for himself. In the future, he would badly overcorrect, leading him to micromanage the people who worked with him.

Larry returned to London in November 1972 to promote *Only Visiting*, but ran into an immediate problem: the record wasn't out yet, due to problems at Polydor records. Why hadn't Anderson been on top of this? Larry wrote to Pam, utterly disconsolate and downcast. His tour seemed poorly organized, he hadn't slept for eleven days, and he had lost his appetite. "It's all just a joke," he wrote. "Tell Ed Walker [Gary Anderson's assistant] to —— if he thinks I'm in it for the money. Tell him also that money is little consolation if it robs you of your joy and your health." The "——" is transcribed as it appears in Larry's letter, showing a disinclination to actually say "piss off" or "fuck off," instead tacitly asking Pam to mentally supply the words. Larry went on to assure Pam he missed her, and just wanted to be home.

But he quickly got frustrated trying to discover his wife's whereabouts while on the road. Writing a week before Christmas, he complained, "I have been trying to call you for four days to talk to you, but the lines have been busy 24 hours a day. The operator told me that the 'calls have been booked in advance.'" He confessed that he did not "care a feather or fig for Christmas . . . [but] because you are in my heart it keeps trying to be more."[30] Although Pam would become a voluminous correspondent years later, when it seemed their marriage was on the rocks, in the early days of 1972, Pam seemed too occupied to write back during Larry's time away.

Within a few short months it was clear that *Only Visiting* had failed to register commercially. The original pressing sold about 20,000–30,000 copies for MGM—not awful, but hardly appropriate for someone who enjoyed widespread international attention and played to sold-out audiences across the States and the UK. Larry had a huge underground following, so why wasn't he selling more records? Larry himself later theorized that this was purely a distribution problem; many fans wouldn't look for his albums in a Tower Records or Sam Goody store, and yet his recordings weren't readily available at their local Christian bookstore either.[31] The A&R team at MGM settled on a more careworn thesis: Larry Norman's records were too edgy for the Jesus people and too religious for the run-of-the-mill rock fans who bought MGM artists.

Remarkably, MGM doubled down on their commitment to him. They wanted him back into the studio to record new material as quickly as possible. Larry appreciated the vote of confidence. He was convinced Jesus had given him something to say, and he was going to get out his message, uncompromised, whether anybody wanted to hear it or not.

The chance to record another record for MGM also created a sense of urgency for him. What if he had been sacrificing his artistic abilities on the altar of evangelism? Shouldn't the highest literary expectations attend the work of the Christian? C. S. Lewis had observed that what was needed in culture were not more writings on Christian apologetics per se, but more work done with excellence in which the Christianity was "latent."[32] What if straightforward "preaching" of Jesus could be replaced by such works?[33] As he would later write to Jarrell McCracken, a Christian record executive, about the problem with the genre of so-called gospel records:

> Music is a powerful language, but most Christian music is not art. It is merely propaganda. It never relies on—in fact it seems to be ignorant of—allegory, symbolism, metaphor, inner-rhyme, play-on-word, surrealism, and many of the other poetry born elements of music that have made it the highly celebrated art

form it has become. Propaganda and pamphleteering is boring, and even offensive unless you already subscribe to the message being pushed . . . which is why Christian records only sell to Christians.[34]

Cliff Richard reinforced Billy Graham's earlier recommendation that Larry appeal to the masses when the two spoke in late 1972, when Larry made a return visit to England. When Larry told him that he planned on writing a record that contained mostly "non-religious" songs, Richard urged him on: try to record songs for the "largest possible audience." No one would think for a second that Larry Norman was not a Christian anymore, he concluded. After all, benchmarked against his other recordings, which were more explicitly religious, such a record would be seen as a momentary parenthesis, not a total departure.

Larry set the stage for his temporary hiatus from direct communication with the Christian public during a sold-out concert at the Royal Albert Hall on January 6, 1973. During the show, he recounted the story of a woman who confronted him about the length of his hair. Wasn't there a Bible verse that spoke to that issue, she wanted to know? He responded:

Do you mean "Does not nature itself teach you that if a man has long hair it is a dishonor to him, but if a woman has long hair, it is a glory to her, because it is her covering"? [1 Cor. 11:14] [Woman]: "Yes, that one!" I said, "Nature itself does teach you. A woman can grow her hair down to her waist if she wants to, but a man can't. His hair will only go to his back—at least the men I know. My hair, it really isn't *that* long; it's just that women today cut their hair so short, it makes my hair look long!"[35]

Next, he referenced the letters he would get from pastors, trying to make the case that rock 'n' roll led to mental and physical ruin. He described one such missive that detailed an experiment ("probably run by some theologian, I would presume") in which a dog was hooked up to electrodes and subjected to rock-'n'-roll music for hours until he lost his motor skills, and eventually went mad, at which point they had to kill the dog. "Funny," Larry joked, "they didn't say which band he was listening to." Another such experiment saw flowers wilt in the presence of rock 'n' roll. "So, apparently rock 'n' roll is dangerous and evil, so I thought I'd just pass that along to you. So when you are listening to your rock collection, just make sure you don't expose your dogs and flowers to it."[36] The crowd roared with laughter, but Larry was making a more serious point. He was tired of being subject to the scrutiny of legalists and fundamentalists, particularly when such judgment was born of hypocrisy.

No more would his main career emphasis be spending time playing concerts to Christian audiences as it had before. Seated at the piano at the Royal Albert Hall, he told the hushed crowd something they didn't expect to hear: "Tonight's a really important night for me, because I have something to say publicly that I've been thinking about for a long time. This will be the last concert that I will be giving of this kind." He then proceeded to rehearse his history with People! and how he left the group to follow the Lord and be an evangelist. But he really didn't expect to wind up playing mostly to Christian audiences. Now he wondered if he might be vulnerable to the charge that he was "trying to make money off of Jesus." He expressed his concern that he not turn into another Marjoe [Gortner], the infamous Pentecostal faith healer who made a film exposing his tactics as an Elmer Gantry type. "I'm just a person," Larry explained to the British audience, "I'm not an evangelist. I never was, I wasn't called to be. I'm just a singer. I sing about the way I feel, and I haven't been afraid to sing about exactly how I feel. I didn't use Jesus to get here. There was no Jesus movement when I started except the one that was started two thousand years ago. . . . I think you have to talk to the people who God has called you to talk to."

He then launched into "I've Got to Learn to Live Without You"— the first single off *Only Visiting* in England for Polydor Records. That song, he explained, was just a love song for lonely people. Not every song needed to be about faith or Jesus. But in the moment, the song seemed a double entendre. It was time for him to say goodbye to the Jesus movement and the Christian subculture. In just a few short weeks he would go from being seen as a leader of the Jesus movement to being regarded by the evangelical community as a dangerous and morally compromised heretic.

LARRY SPENT THE better part of the spring of 1973 in London. He entered AIR Studios on July 27, 1973, to record his next record, *So Long Ago the Garden*, once again with the Triumvirate team of Edwards, Hand, and Miller manning the production controls.[37] Norman brought several new songs to the sessions, although many of them never made the cut. According to his original studio folio, tunes like "Holy Kilt and the Magic Bracelet," "Blind Randall," and "Stumbling Block Scandals" were never even recorded. Other gems, like "You're a Butterfly," and "Peacepollutionrevolution," never made their way onto the record.

If *Only Visiting*'s purpose had been to explore modern-day rootlessness, the second installment in Norman's proposed trilogy, *Garden*, was to represent the past, recalling humanity's loss of the Edenic order. Practically speaking, though, *Garden*'s verbiage was frequently cryptic and dark, bordering on the surreal. The first-person narrator on the record is dislocated and anxious. Larry had his own codex by which each song could be deciphered, but this time, he wanted the audience to struggle with the subject matter. The lyrics and mood were twisty.

Of the nine songs on *So Long Ago the Garden*, none contained an overtly religious message. The opening track, "Meet Me at the Airport (Fly, Fly, Fly)," was a bouncy pop song about Norman's honeymoon, with only an oblique reference to Francis Schaeffer's L'Abri in Switzerland. The next two songs, "It's the Same Old Story" and "Lonely by Myself," featured languid lyrics of existential estrangement. By far the most controversial tune was "Be Careful What You Sign," a nightmarish song that begins with the protagonist murdering an innocent victim, and concludes with him committing suicide. It also featured images such as this:

> *We had dinner at eight and women at nine*
> *The party was great till we ran out of wine*
> *There was a knock upon the bedroom door, my knees began to*
> *   shake*
> *And this man came in and melted all the candles on my cake*
> *He said, "I've come here to escort you, it's time for you to go"*
> *He opened up my body and he took away my soul.*

"Baroquen Spirits" seemed to point to the dilemmas of men adjusting to a world in which women were becoming more confident and self-assured than them. In "She's a Dancer," a song he would later admit was about himself, Larry presented a Jungian take on being an artist. He simultaneously felt enraptured by, and yet had to keep at arm's length, "her"—the artist within:

> *She's a dancer and she knows it*
> *Everywhere she goes she shows it*
> *Condescending not pretending*
> *No regretting*
> *Nor forgetting*
> *She's a dancer*
>
> *And on my early morning walks I often find her*
> *I sit pretending that I'm looking at the paper.*[38]

The record closes out with the trippy "Nightmare #71," which depicts John Wayne and Billy Graham handing out breath mints to a heavenly crowd of spectators as a massive earthquake causes California to break away from the rest of the continent. Then something even stranger happens. California floats, but "everything that wasn't sank down into the sea." In the aftermath, a "marionette of Harpo Marx" (controlled by the puppet master Shirley Temple and an undead, zombie version of Guy Kibbee) offers an apocalyptic prophecy for the forthcoming environmental catastrophe:

> *With the continents adrift and the sun about to shift*
> *Will the ice caps drown us all or will we burn?*
> *We've polluted what we own, will we reap what we have sown*
> *Are we headed for the end or can we turn?*[39]

The message in "Nightmare #71" seems to be pretty clear: Hollywood wins. It will control the destiny of the West unless someone intervenes. But who can? Who will? In a sense, Larry was challenging Jesus to come back or at least "do something" to keep the world from sliding further into a selfish abyss. Still, he doesn't mention Jesus on *Garden*. Any such interpretation comes from between the lines.

Garden may have been "far out," but MGM studio executives liked what they heard. Writing on August 16, Derek Church, director of marketing services for MGM, wrote Larry to tell him: "From this initial hearing, there is no doubt in my mind that this album is going to be the one that will break you wide open in America."[40] Other record executives, such as Jeffrey Kruger at Ember Records in England, lamented in writing to Gary Anderson that they didn't pitch Larry for a contract to release *Garden* in the UK: "It would appear that MGM/Verve's luck, is Ember's loss!" All parties were agreed that Larry needed an image makeover, distancing himself from the Jesus Freak persona and embracing a more diffuse "spiritual poet-prophet of the 1970s" angle.

MGM settled on Bob Levinson's public relations firm to run point on the promotion leading up to *Garden*'s release. The first order of business was to set up a showcase at the Starwood Club in Los Angeles and invite rock critics to come witness the reboot. Levinson dashed off a letter to Tim Cahill at *Rolling Stone* to gauge his interest in doing a profile. He portrayed his client as the victim of guilt by association: "The new LP is getting a final mix and (based on what I've heard) should fully dispel the 'Jesus' label. Whether it's you or whomever, perhaps there's time in all this to sit down with Larry to hear his side of the story—what happens to an artist who's trapped by an image, particularly when it's the wrong image. Fact: Larry, by refusing religioso-oriented dates to make the point and plow ahead, has lopped off about 80% of his income potential for this year . . . And them's lots of dollars." Cahill wrote back that he felt that while there might be a potentially interesting story in the mixes, he was strongly biased against doing a favorable piece on a religiously devoted person. Nevertheless, the association with George Martin and AIR Studios piqued his interest, and he indicated that the record might possibly be worthy of, say, a 1,500-word article and review.

An open mind from the media and music fans was what Larry Norman needed if he had any hope of going mainstream. As Levinson described it to Joyce Becker, owner of several entertainment magazines, Larry's identification with the Jesus movement "retarded his progress with general audiences." People felt uneasy about listening to rock 'n' roll from somebody who could be perceived as some sort of a religious leader.

Levinson and Larry dedicated themselves to a rebranding as, in Levinson's words, the "Social Commentator in Song." New press releases described Larry as a prolific, socially conscious songwriter "who produces up to five songs a month. Each one has a message—anti-war, anti-bigotry, anti-hypocrisy, anti-ego. Despite their content, he disavows any suggestions he is a reformer. 'I'm just a singer and writer, not a zealot hoping to change the world,' he smiles. 'If people draw hope and comfort from my songs, fine. But I'm not out to convert anyone. My art is not propaganda.'"

If Larry's songwriting hadn't solidified his break with the message-oriented Jesus movement, his choice of cover art for *Garden* sure did. It depicted him naked down to his nether regions, with a photo of a lion lying in the grass—taken by Larry during his

Rhodesia concert tour—superimposed over his skin. He would later deny that he was nude when the photo was taken ("I was wearing a bodysuit!"), but negatives from his archives prove otherwise. On the actual record, it is difficult to make out what is Larry's pubic hair and what is African landscape grass. The reverse side featured a pair of snakeskin boots, and an apple with a bite out of it, with the cryptic rejoinder: "THE DAY OF MAN . . . TIME'S LAST STROKE TICKS—IT BOTH BEGAN AND ENDS AT SIX."[41] The number six? Wasn't that the number of Satan?

So Long Ago the Garden was set for a November 1973 release. MGM was enthused by early reactions to the record. Oceanside California's *Blade Tribune* gave the record five stars, commenting: "Larry Norman who survived brief pop fame in the middle '60s has stuck to his guns through several failures and now appears to have a winner." The Gary, Indiana, *Post Tribune* raved: "Once you start playing the record, you're committed. . . . Some of the lyrics are incomprehensible to us, but we find pleasure just relaxing and enjoying the sound. It's great!"[42]

Everything was set for *Garden*'s success, save one thing: MGM Records was in financial ruins.[43] They sold themselves to Polygram's Polydor Records. The practical outworking of this resulted in little to no support from the label to promote either Larry himself or *Garden*. Second-tier MGM artists like Larry weren't on Polydor's radar screen, and *Garden* got lost in the shuffle. Only 4,000 vinyl LPs were printed, and most of the promotional efforts for the record dropped.

Larry didn't help his own cause much either. He had alienated Jesus rock fans by recording a difficult, dark, and metaphorical record, and cultivating a new constituency didn't come easily to him. When he returned to the States upon wrapping up recording, the US Department of the Interior invited Larry Norman to play a concert for their employees at the Cellar Door in Washington, DC, and what they got from the stage was a commentary on Watergate and why the American people couldn't trust government in general. "I don't know [why] they're making such a big fuss over Watergate," he mused. "They're always spying on us, why can't they spy on each other?" Regarding politics: "All I know is that somebody's the president, and he's acting for God while He's away." His government hosts weren't amused.

The problem was compounded by the fact that there were relatively few physical copies of the album in existence. Only small numbers of people were in possession of an actual copy. In a pre-Internet age, all that Larry's fans in the Jesus movement heard was that their former hero had gone off the rails—appearing nude on his record cover, abandoning Christianity, singing secular music, and perhaps dabbling in Satanism. To use the language of the Christian subculture, he was "backslidden." Other rumors crept up too: Larry was on drugs, had appeared in a porn film, and had gotten divorced. Jesus movement newspapers began to question whether the pioneer of the One Way sign was now an apostate.

The tremendous backlash of negative opinion from the Christian community that greeted *So Long Ago the Garden* made Larry Norman public enemy number one in the minds of some people. Although he had told the Royal Albert Hall audience that previous January that he was going to retire from doing Christian concerts, it was a different matter altogether to learn that no one would touch you with a ten-foot pole even if you were offering.

Larry bristled at the criticism, claiming that some people "see only the album cover, just as some people judge others outwardly" since they are initially unable to "understand the message on the deeper levels of parable, allegory, and metaphor."[44] Rather than apologizing or ameliorating the public, he doubled down, comparing himself to Martin Luther, "nailing his music on the doors of contemporary society, both secular and religious."[45]

But beneath this show of brazen independence, there was a cash-flow problem. Larry's breakthrough record had just been fumbled by MGM/Polydor, and he had "retired" from Christian music. What to do? Larry fired off a letter to George Martin to see if the so-called Fifth Beatle would now finally agree to produce one of his records, given that he had been unavailable for the previous two outings. Martin replied with a kind note, thanking Larry for his letter and current records. He sympathized with Larry that he had not as of yet found "the right person to produce [his] future albums. However, I regret that my commitments have not lessened since last we met, and it would be foolish of me to promise that I could be available" to work on his next release. He closed the letter with a word of encouragement that Larry deserved the success he was seeking, with hopes that 1974 would be his year.[46]

Larry also had an ulterior motive for taking time off from his normal tour schedule. His marriage was in trouble, and he hoped that more time at home alone with Pam might stabilize it. He wanted things to work out, for both emotional and prudential reasons. He was pretty sure marriage was supposed to be forever, so he had a biblical injunction as motivation to keep the home fires burning. How good he was at doing that, however, would have to be assessed by Pam.

In the meantime, hate mail about Larry's slide into moral compromise poured in. It was as though Larry Norman had gone from a baby-face to a heel in professional wrestling. Susan Perlman, the woman whom he'd led to Christ on the street in New York, wrote to Larry on Jews for Jesus letterhead, saying that she had been hearing rumors that he had denounced Christ. While she couldn't bring herself to believe it was true, could he please write her back to let her know? After all, her origin story and testimony publicity materials referenced Larry Norman's role in her conversion.

Accusations continued to mount to such a point that Larry felt compelled to respond in an open letter, which he sent in various iterations to different promoters and publishers of Christian magazines. It outlined his dismay at the rumors perpetuated within the Christian community about his "spiritual condition."

One rumor is that I am totally backslidden. Another is that I have denied Jesus. Another is that I am on hard drugs. Another

is that I am homosexual and have left my wife. Another is that I
have turned to Satan Worship. . . .

Some of the mail that I receive is accusatory. The writers identify themselves as Christians but the letters are self-righteous
and judgmental instead of loving. Some of the letters are altogether sick and deviated. Some of them are unsigned so there is
no way for me to answer.

Here is my answer to those who have heard these tales of
derision. The rumors are not true. I am not even in spiritual in-
decision. I attend a local church in Hollywood, and fellowship
regularly, and enjoy communion with the body and with Jesus.

It would take some time for Norman to discover the source of the
rumors. Often it appeared to be other figures in the Christian music
scene, eager to throw the father of Jesus rock under the bus, perhaps
in a moment of Oedipal jealousy. One rumormonger who came forward to confess was none other than Keith Green, who enjoyed great
success as one of the more popular—and self-righteous—Christian
music stars of the 1970s. The two had a history together. Larry had
witnessed to Keith before he was converted to Christ, and Keith and
Randy had co-written the beloved Jesus movement anthem "Until
Your Love Broke Through." Writing on December 18, 1975, Keith
sent a letter, admitting that the "rumors were not true," and that
he was sending this apology as a "broken note." He subsequently
thanked Larry for forgiving him.

Addressing the rumors eventually became a staple of the typical
Larry Norman concert, and remained a part of his act until he died.
Playing in Fort Wayne, Indiana, in 1974, he drily observed, "I was
really discouraged to learn about those rumors. Christians spread
them. They were upsetting me, so I started asking around, and I
found out they weren't true [laughter and titters from the crowd].
I stopped doing concerts almost a year and a half ago . . . Maybe
people think that because they haven't seen me, I must have backslidden. Because when you're not visible, people don't know what to

think about you. And if you're out of their sight, then maybe you're out of God's sight, and maybe He can't even find you too."

Thus began a period in which Larry Norman felt obligated to do what every artist hates to do: explain their work and provide line-by-line commentary on it. In order to clear his name, this is precisely what he did with respect to *So Long Ago the Garden*. Writing to one Charles McPheeters, a Jesus music pioneer, and his followers, he complained: "You know, sometimes I wonder if I'm . . . really inept as a poet. Rarely do I ever receive any letters of encouragement, and when I do, it's [too late]." He went on to explain the secret meanings behind *Garden*, pedantically, almost song for song. "I intended to show the distance man had fallen since he disobeyed God in the garden," he wrote. "The album portrays Adam in the garden with the Lion of Judah. The back portrays Satan standing triumphantly over the apple (Again, the apple is not literal, nor are the snakeskin boots)."

Then further, Larry shared his position on Christianity and the arts. "*So Long Ago the Garden* is not a gospel album. But it is a Christian album. All of the songs I write are Christian songs, because I am a Christian. Whether it mentions Christ or not is no stipulation. . . . Is a man any less a Christian because he is a car mechanic instead of an evangelist? . . . When you give a report in school on American history, is it a non-Christian report? . . . Some people are so conditioned that if a song doesn't have some religious clues like 'blood of the lamb' or 'the cross,' they are unsure of its spiritual qualification."

Exasperated, he came right out with it: "I am not an evangelist. I am not afraid to admit it. . . . My songs aren't evangelistic. They don't mean to be." He concluded:

I'm only . . . trying to talk to people who I am equipped to talk to. The people who I understand; people like myself who . . . grew up only to find themselves out of step with a society that chased after money, feared the bomb, toasted the moon, and were ob-sessively religious without being the least bit spiritual. When I grew up I saw hypocrisy everywhere I looked. Society, politics, religion, and in myself, I was frustrated but found no answers. I could not see God even when I looked for him in church. . . . And I have a burden for the people who I can see are like I was, only they haven't found God.

It does not bother me if some people do not like an album . . . But it does alert me if someone thinks I have backslidden, or they get a completely different impression of something I intended to say, because it might confuse them, and I don't want to serve as anyone's stumbling block. And it is with this in mind that I have written to you and to all the brothers and sisters who read your newspaper. You have my permission to print this letter in full.

God bless you all,
Larry Norman

The truth is, Larry Norman never understood the Christian audience to whom he seemed tragically joined at the hip. With the exception of a song or two, and a logo like the One Way sign, he never delivered on what they wanted. Simultaneously, somehow, he was the music industry's and evangelicalism's most awkward gesture. When the former wanted hits, he gave them sensitive alternative music and songs about Jesus. When the latter wanted preachments, he gave them nude photos and surrealistic lyrics. There was never a more beautiful mess in twentieth-century Christianity than Larry Norman in the early '70s. And this was just the beginning.

5

JESUS VERSUS *PLAYBOY*

FEELING ISOLATED AND BEREFT OF ENCOURAGEMENT—personally, artistically, and commercially—Larry reached out to Francis Schaeffer, whom he and Pam had visited at L'Abri, during their honeymoon. It is almost impossible to overstate the influence that Schaeffer had on young Christian intellectuals in the wake of the Jesus movement. Clad in Alpine hiking pants and sporting a goatee, the man whom *Christianity Today* would later eulogize as "our St. Francis" was one of the few respected voices in establishment evangelical circles that had some awareness and appreciation for the arts.[1] According to Schaeffer's son, Frank, Eric Clapton once gave Jimmy Page a copy of *Escape from Reason*, saying that it was the best book he was reading at the moment.[2]

Schaeffer and Larry had shared billing at a festival for Christians and the arts, and when Schaeffer went backstage to tell Larry how much he enjoyed the performance, the singer told him of his struggles to be an artist in the evangelical Christian community. As Larry saw it, his fellow believers could not handle anything that wasn't straight, direct, message-oriented evangelism, leaving him feeling "caught in between" the world and Christ. "It's true . . . I never mention 'the blood of the lamb' in my songs," he wrote, "a definite sign of apostasy I am told."

Schaeffer encouraged Larry to pursue his artistic vision. Larry sent Schaeffer a copy of *Only Visiting This Planet* and *So Long Ago the Garden*, and asked for his reaction. Schaeffer appreciated the reference to L'Abri in "Fly, Fly, Fly," but he also wanted Larry to know that he liked what he heard in the music itself. More important, he expressed sympathy for the tightrope walk Norman had been attempting:

> I am sorry that you have had a hard time with the Christian music world. I understand the walls that have to be smashed and that sometimes it is a lonely walk. I have a son who is an artist and he was trying to do something in the area of art as you are doing in music. He is a Christian and in the art world and very often people wonder why his painting is not "religious." I feel we have a double responsibility. We must say that Christ is the Lord of the whole life and therefore we do not have to make everything into a tract, and yet looking at the wounded world we do have a responsibility that each of us is a "teller" in our own place.[3]

Schaeffer twice invited Larry to come spend time with him in Switzerland. Schaeffer took note of Larry's feeling of isolation as an artist, and admired his ability to reach non-Christians in the entertainment industry. Their correspondence was characterized by warmth and mutual admiration. (Larry would include Schaeffer in his pantheon of inspirations in the ensuing years in his liner notes.)

Writing to Schaeffer in 1975, Larry recounted how he had befriended the actor Dudley Moore in London. Asking for absolute confidentiality about the relationship, he recounted the tension of trying to share Christ with someone over time, and their need to receive Christ, without offending and driving them away. He expressed the profound ambivalence that many Christians feel about the imperative to share their faith: where does my role merely as a friend end, and my responsibilities as an evangelist begin? To the point: Larry told Schaeffer that he had been haunted by a dinner he and Pam had with Moore and the "diminutive actor" Michael Dunn, a Tony-nominated performer who had appeared in everything from Edward

Albee plays on Broadway to episodes of *Get Smart*. An erstwhile convert to Catholicism, Dunn was swept under in a sea of doubt, complicated by severe physical issues that resulted from his dwarfism. Then Michael's story came to an abrupt end: "[Michael] seemed open to listening [about Jesus] but resistant to making a decision so we didn't press him. We all planned to meet again for dinner in a week, but three days later he was dead."[4]

Larry was in a league of people who had everything but nothing, in Christian terms. That Larry was even having conversations about Jesus Christ with celebrities and influencers was seemingly evidence of some divine sanction, if not exactly grace. Yet religion never seemed to "stick" with these people, so what was the problem? Closer to home, the people closest to Larry professed closeness to God, but it was getting harder to discern any difference between the "saved" and the lost, at least in terms of the choices they were making.

Larry took Michael Dunn's sudden death as a prompt to really reach into Dudley Moore's life to address his spiritual condition that eight "years in analysis" hadn't been able to solve:

> One night at 3:00 in the lobby of our hotel, the Holy Spirit really confronted Dudley. We had been talking to him for an hour and suddenly it seemed his moment of salvation. We could all feel it. It was the definite presence of a very loving and very consuming spirit. It pressed on us all so heavily. Dudley felt it and expressed his anguish, trying to say yes to God but not willing to give up his problems—some of which have been lifelong companions— and then the moment passed. Its departure was as definite as the three or four minutes of its presence had been.[5]

Larry was optimistic that Moore would eventually be converted, but the experience rattled him. Moore's interest was eclipsed by confusion as to "who Jesus really is." Would Schaeffer have any books to recommend on this question? he asked.

More deeply, Larry was bothered by the outcome of the Holy Spirit's "intervention" into his friend's life—an overture that was rejected and inefficacious. Dudley Moore never professed Jesus. How could he come so close to God, and yet just walk away? What did it mean for Moore, or any of us for that matter, to "resist the Spirit"?

That feeling of ambivalence characterized how Larry Norman was feeling about pretty much everything in his life in 1974–75. He was in the "perfect Christian marriage," which he was trying to make work, but the reality was really difficult behind the curtain. He had pioneered Jesus rock, but was regarded by a large part of the Christian community as a traitor to the cause and a dangerous influence on "the kids." Some youth pastors considered Larry's mission from God to be the devil's trick. Then there was the problem that none of his albums seemed to sell.

Amidst these setbacks, Larry Norman was coming up with both a theory about his life and career, and a perceived way forward. The theory was that true artists were never commercial—only the imitators who followed, popularizing their concepts for the masses, sold well. So, for example, the Velvet Underground never sold that many records, but they successfully launched 1,000 bands. Larry's proposal was that perhaps with his "musical L'Abri," he could become the Lou Reed for a new Christian community.

He wanted to pioneer a vision for Christianity and the arts, with a new commune of creatives in the music industry devoted to following Jesus. He decided to put his thoughts down on paper in a manifesto of sorts, and sent it to Schaeffer. He wanted to know, didn't Schaeffer experience the same sense of disconnect with his own readers? Did people really understand the profound depths of his books, or did they misconstrue his meanings and come up with loose and poor paraphrases of their own? Could Larry stop by L'Abri for a while on his upcoming European tour to learn more about how Schaeffer created such a legendary Christian community?

Whatever else it accomplished, the letter to Schaeffer became the vision document for what would become Solid Rock Records and the

Street Level Artists Agency. Larry's hope was to reverse the trend of tasteless and "cheesy" Christian records by creating infrastructure to launch talented Christian recording artists into the recording industry. In this way, he would drag the Church kicking and screaming into the present. "For whatever reason," he complained in his manifesto, "Christianity seems to wade in irrelevant waters and remain ten or fifteen years behind the times. Almost none of the Christian music succeeds as art . . . it is merely propaganda masquerading as art . . . Not only is it misconceived as a musical project . . . but it fails to deliver its message . . . [their records] are sold only by Christian bookstores or direct mail. Non Christians do not frequent religious bookstores." Also: "There is such a low credibility factor recommending Christianity; my non-Christian associates have a difficult time understanding why I am a Christian. If only I could erase their knowledge of the Church and Church history for a few minutes and let them see Jesus . . . they might still reject Christianity in the end but at least they would understand the substance of the offer God has made them."

Unlike his previous foray into underground independent LP making—One Way Records—this time he intended to make records for himself and other artists that sounded every bit as good and possessed as much artistic merit as anything coming out of Hollywood. The offices of Solid Rock would be just a stone's throw away from Capitol Records—his former employer—at 7046 Hollywood Boulevard, suite 707. In order to get into the offices, one had to make one's way past the store entrance for the International Love Boutique and Sex Museum, which was on the ground floor of the building. Frederick's of Hollywood, the infamous naughty lingerie store, was a few doors down. Solid Rock's location signaled to the record industry and to the Christian community more broadly that these artists were willing to compete in the "devil's backyard," so to speak, that they were fomenting something beyond some ersatz rock. To Larry, situating Solid Rock in the line of sight of Capitol Records was a way of saying, "We are in the game. We're going to the center of cultural influence in the entertainment industry and demanding that people take Jesus and faith seriously."

Before he could reposition himself as the head of a new art collective, however, Larry had some reputation repair to do with the broader Christian public. Even if he refused to apologize for appearing nude on his last record cover, or for writing "difficult" songs that seemed to intimate suicide (to wit: "I pulled out my Thornton Special, I shot me in the head, I threw me in the alleyway, and I left me for dead" on "Be Careful What You Sign"), maybe he could convince them that the mission motivating all of this was a sincere wish to build bridges to the modern world for Jesus.

The first priority was to take a couple of interviews from Christian reporters: something he had not done for the better part of two years. The first journalist was Robert Thoreaux, who led off with the question, "Where have you been for the last two years? No one seems to know." Larry explained that he had been in England, and that he was building a new record label for Christian musicians. Thoreaux gave Larry the chance to clear his name with respect to rumors that he had abandoned Christianity. When it came to the controversy over the *Garden* album cover, Thoreaux said: "People . . . feel it is too revealing . . . that you can see things." Norman's reply did not help his cause: "You're kidding. Well, the art department would sure be flattered." Although the point of the interview was to rehabilitate his reputation, Larry couldn't help but skewer the whole conceit that Christian rock music was supposed to "witness" to the "unsaved":

THOREAUX: Well, don't you think that it reaches the unsaved now? I know that mostly it finds its way into the hands of Christians but don't you think that Christians need Jesus music too?

LARRY: Oh, sure. They do. But the irony, and try to understand this because it might get complicated . . . the sad irony of almost all Christian music is that it preaches salvation to people that already have it . . . while the people who need the message don't usually hear it. . . . Christian music needs to do what

Paul suggested in Hebrews 6:1 ... stop going over and over the same ground and move on to weightier matters. Christians don't need musical milk year after year ... there needs to be more new ground broken ... more food for thought ... meat that requires a lot of chewing ...

THOREAUX: I see what you mean. Christian music really doesn't reach that many non-Christians, but it certainly is an encouragement to the ears of Christians.

LARRY: The sound of splashing milk is pleasant, you mean? Sure it is.[6]

For the Canadian Christian publication *Lodestone*, Larry responded once again to the charge that, in the words of interviewer Michael Leo Gossett, he took *So Long Ago the Garden* in "a secular direction": "It wasn't a secular album at all. I suppose [people who say that] didn't understand [Jesus's] parables. 'Be Careful What You Sign' is about a man rejecting Jesus and following after riches ... and the lusts of the flesh and at the end of his life finding out that he rejected Jesus and was no different than Judas and that he killed himself when he rejected Jesus. 'Christmas Time' is about the hypocrisy of Christmas as celebrated in America ... That's definitely not a 'secular' song."

For someone on a rehabilitation campaign, Larry didn't really seem apologetic. When Gossett asked about how Larry felt about other Christian artists covering his records, he stiff-armed the query: "I'm not really into the Gospel music scene, I'm outside of it. I don't identify with any of it. I'm not really part of the Jesus Movement." Gossett replied, somewhat taken aback: "That's ironic because a lot of people considered you to be one of the main leaders, if there were any, other than the Lord ..." The question provided the perfect opportunity for Larry to deconstruct the entire Jesus movement in a single breath:

I was trying to explain the Movement from the beginning that it was not really a street movement like most people wanted it to be and advertised it. The press picked up on the fact that heroin addicts come off of heroin painlessly with 30 second withdrawal cures because of Jesus, but I don't think that was the typical person's testimony. . . . The truth was that most of the kids were middle class who had exposure to Jesus in their early years through their churches, walked away from it, and discovered it later in their teenage years. So most of them were short haired, middle class, non-street freaks who just came to Jesus. I can't help it that the press misinterpreted and misreported what was going on. It just wouldn't sell that many newspapers to say, "Hey, guess what's happening in America? A bunch of nice kids are getting nicer!"[7]

Having thrown the Jesus movement and the gospel music industry under the bus, Larry stopped taking interviews and turned his attention to the mission of cultivating artists. But the problem, he soon found, was that the bench of available talent was short. Andraé Crouch was already a legend, but there was only one of him. Phil Keaggy—a virtuoso guitarist and songwriter who had become a Christian during his stint with the band Glass Harp on Decca Records—had, like Larry, gone underground after releasing one religious record.[8] Larry would've signed Phil in a heartbeat, but he already had an offer in hand, and didn't need Larry Norman to make him a star.

Larry's best bet was to reconnect with Randy Stonehill, for whom he had produced the hastily assembled independent release *Born Twice*. Back when Randy joined Pam and Larry in London to record at AIR Studios, he had in fact laid down tracks for an album called *Get Me Out of Hollywood*. But the venture had not been entirely successful. The production team of Rod Edwards, Jon Miller, and Roger Hand had produced it, and though the album was planned for release on the Philips label—a Dutch electronics company that pressed records in the UK from the '50s throughout the '70s—they never did release it.[9] Randy's talents were not in doubt, but at the time, the album was regarded as uneven, bordering on terrible. In Randy's own words, the LP simply became a tax write-off for the company in 1973.[10] It was also barely Christian rock. The album was so devoid of faith content that when British A&R rep Norman Miller, from Chapel Lane Productions, inquired of Jon Miller (no relation to Norman Miller) about possible material taken from Randy's time with him for an upcoming Christian release, the producer drily replied, "As you will see, there is well over two hours' worth of material, so you should have no problem finding an album's worth, if not more. Your only problem might be that there is very little Christian content, and some of the songs are, shall we say, a bit cheeky."[11]

Randy's bid to go secular had fizzled. Throughout his recording career, he would continue seeking a secular recording contract, but for the meantime, he was out of work with no record label prospects on the horizon. Triumvirate had passed on taking up the first of two one-year options that Stonehill owed them.[12]

One obstacle to getting Stonehill over to Solid Rock was the estrangement that resulted from Randy's inappropriate relationship with one of the young women on his UK tour in 1972. Stonehill still shared Larry and Gary Anderson's rebranded "New Generation Artists" booking agency (Anderson wanted his own agency, separate from Larry's), but aside from business dealings, Larry's interest in Randy had largely become a matter of keeping up with the latest happenings in Stonehill's life from a distance. Occasionally, some hints came in the mail, such as one letter from a young woman living on Magnolia Boulevard in North Hollywood written on a notecard addressed to Randy's attention at New Generation/Solid Rock's address in Hollywood. In her missive dated January 7, 1974, she wrote:

You're selfish, hypocritical, and fucked. If you want to get laid, call someone else. If you call me, I'll hang up in your face, and if I ever see you, I'll punch you out.

I'll really <u>hate</u> you, Stonehill. Before, I didn't care, but now you've gone too far. Fuck up someone else's head, but <u>leave me alone</u>.[13]

While the context of the note is unclear, it highlights the challenge Larry faced with Stonehill. Should he be a part of Larry's new label, and join him as the new face of Christian rock? Stonehill seemed to be drifting spiritually, so that was a risk. Furthermore, he hadn't been successful getting a good record out, with *Get Me Out of Hollywood* having imploded on the launching pad. Still, Stonehill could write songs, and he was a great performer. The decision came fast. Yes, Larry would take another chance on Randy, who came promising that he had changed his ways and was really following the Lord now. After all, no one Larry was working with who self-identified as a Christian came close to Randy's ability as a writer.

Larry set about to pick up Stonehill when Randy's obligation to Triumvirate Production concluded in March of 1975. It came at a particularly good time for Randy, who had effectively been out of work during the time he was with Triumvirate. As manager, Gary Anderson explained in letters to prospective labels at the time, Stonehill had canceled trips to England in support of the album that never appeared, "which resulted in him being left without sufficient funds to support himself," and being forced to live at both Anderson's and Larry's houses because of it.[14] Whose fault it was that Stonehill had been reduced to couch surfing was debated by lawyers, but the upshot was that Randy was now free to play Paul McCartney to Larry's John Lennon.[15]

Until he had a full roster of acts, however, Larry would have to bluff his way into convincing a record company to underwrite his dream. But in 1975 he was unlikely to find a willing partner. He had been struck by lightning twice at Capitol, and then MGM/Verve doubled down twice, even absent much evidence of commercial viability. Now that MGM had folded into Polygram, he was in essence starting over.

Then, just when Larry was trying to put together his own record label, he got an unexpected surprise: ABC/Dunhill Records approached him in 1974 and signed him to a new deal. ABC had a solid stable of artists that included Ray Charles, Dusty Springfield, and the James Gang. It would be his fourth record contract with a major music industry conglomerate. Larry submitted recordings done with his sister Kristy in 1969 entitled *Orphans from Eden*, but the album never appeared. Soon thereafter, ABC bought Word Records in Waco, Texas, a Christian record label imprint.[16] Larry saw the opportunity before him; he could get the power of both a secular and gospel company to help get his records to market. He dashed off a manifesto to make his pitch that Word should invest in the records Solid Rock was preparing to produce. Writing to Jarrell McCracken, the founder of Word (1951), he made the case that the gospel music industry needed him. He laid out his grudge against the lack of artistic viability of the Christian music industry, which, in his view, boded ill for the product's ultimate appeal. By contrast, Larry Norman would recruit legitimate artists: "In essence, I look for artists who are professional and have already learned their way around the music business, secularly and Christian-wise." Only such a collective of artists could have an impact on the larger culture. "For example," he argued, "the value of one Andraé Crouch exceeds fifteen Young Life–Campus Crusade type groups (i.e., the type of group that breaks up after a two-year tour of high schools)."[17] Sensing an opportunity, he pressed his argument further:

> If "Jesus Music" was better produced, the songs more carefully chosen, and the artists were authentic and competent as writers, vocalists, musicians, etc., then this allergy that secular radio has to Christian artists would lessen considerably. I know that this is true because I receive radio play on all of my albums, and though I sell to Christian consumers, my sales to non-Christians is always greater.[18]

Was Christian music really as bad as Larry was making it out to be? The answer was: sort of. Mylon LeFevre had put out a Christian rock record shortly after Larry's *Upon This Rock* in 1970. The album single "Gospel Ship" was an old Stamps Quartet gospel number set to twelve-bar blues, but the whole project was still straight-up "I love my Church, love my Lord, and love my mama." Nancy Honeytree was another Christian artist, whose albums featured a light, breezy sound with flutes and strings and song titles such as "Clean Before My Lord" and "Heaven's Gonna Be a Blast!" Other groups like Second Chapter of Acts performed songs with slow tempos, measured vocals, and uplifting messages about their deep and ever-growing "love for the Lord." Petra, a group put together by guitarist Bob Hartman, was more rock-oriented and listenable to open-minded rock fans. Nevertheless, their self-titled 1974 debut record still relied on Christian clichés, with song titles such as "Gonna Fly Away," and "Get Back to the Bible." Despite using some devices heard in regular pop music, most Christian albums from the period were unimaginative, musically, and preached to the choir in their content. And this was as true of the best records put out by Christian record labels as it was for the countless poorly conceived and produced LPs they pumped out.[19]

Larry wanted Solid Rock to change that story with studio excellence, artistic merit, and artistic quality control. He proposed to deliver to ABC/Word four records per year, to be distributed through their channels on the Solid Rock label, at $15,000 per record—not exorbitant by any means for the mid-1970s, but far beyond anything Word would have outlaid for a record at the time. In exchange, Norman promised a turnkey operation for an all-inclusive price, including producer's fees, studio costs, and artwork, plus the rights to the material for the lifetime of the renewable three-year contract with Solid Rock. He signed off underscoring the importance of developing a roster of respected "cultural artists" in the Christian music industry. "It is upon this concept that I have built my career, and upon which all my artists' careers have been hinged."[20] In the vision

WHY SHOULD THE DEVIL HAVE ALL THE GOOD MUSIC? 123

statement for Solid Rock Records that would be printed in the liner notes on early releases, he cited the year 1690 and the example of Isaac Watts, a teenager at the time, complaining to his father of how boring church music was, and who would go on to pen the hymns "We're Marching to Zion," "When I Survey the Wondrous Cross," "Joy to the World," and more than three hundred others. Norman went on to argue that Jesus rock was a part of a continuum that stretched from Martin Luther to William Booth's use of brass band instruments for the Salvation Army Band—a shocking deployment for traditional hymns at that time. But, Larry continued: "William Booth took his band on the street and reached thousands of [people] that had been overlooked by the religious community."[21] Larry got the green light from Word Records executive vice president Stan Moser, and the contracts were signed in 1974.

With ABC/Word signed on, Larry Norman had the best of both worlds: more creative control but a mainstream distribution deal that would help Solid Rock's records break out nationally. In his notebook on the creation of the company, he writes: "Made a deal with WORD to distribute Solid Rock and manufacture it and in exchange for 20% of net wholesale (after manufacturing and jackets have been paid), I pay publishing and everything (up to 50% is still a good agreement)."[22] After working for years on the passenger's side of the record business, Larry was ready to sit behind the wheel.

Every musician who hopes to make a living knows that there's more to the job than recording albums—you have to sell them, and the best way to do that is to build a fan base. The best way to build a fan base is to tour as much as possible. Being on the road means revenue, and potentially more than could be obtained through so-called mechanical royalties of records and tapes being sold. To accomplish his goals, Larry knew that a two-headed beast would be needed. The Street Level Artists Agency would perform management duties, including arranging tours while Solid Rock Records saw to record producing. Although Larry had used the name of Street Level Artists Agency years before at the height of the Jesus movement, he relaunched the concept with his new manager, Philip Mangano, who had replaced Gary Anderson and the New Generation Artists Agency in 1974. Mangano would book shows and tours, and Larry would provide management, production, and artistic direction services to a stable of artists. The enterprise was supposed to be a ministry, and therefore "much more free of financial motives and goals."[23] But all of it was a fiction that existed at this point solely in the mind of Larry David Norman. He really had no idea who this "stable" of artists would be yet.

To solve that problem, he started a development program. If an up-and-coming artist wanted to get a record deal with Larry Norman and be produced by him, they'd have to sign up for a full, uninterrupted year of musical boot camp. Larry would help them hone their songwriting craft, understand recording techniques, and mature into their "sound" before committing anything to vinyl. Originally, he identified two recruits: Steve Camp and Scott Wesley Brown. Camp was in high school at the time, and Brown had recorded a self-titled solo record in 1973. Both artists signed deals. Larry teased Steve Camp with the promise of a double whammy: both secular and Christian deals through ABC. "I did it, Steve," he wrote on July 21, 1975. "I got $15,000 for your albums and that's just your religious albums. How much of a budget ABC Dunhill will give for your commercial albums will be up to how excited you can get them about your music. . . . Everything's really cooking."[24] Both Camp and Brown, however, eventually found "the one-year wait" too long to endure, and opted for other labels with fewer requirements. Larry was crestfallen:

> . . . even though I've spent months putting them through the Solid Rock University, letting them live in the artists' house, paying for their meals, new instruments, their plane flights and phone calls, they ask me to tear up their agreements so they can sign with other labels. I know what they are in for working with these labels and producers, because I know them all too well

so sadly I let them go. They begin working with the old guard who use old ideas, corny production values and archaic mixing techniques. The artists use none of the great songs we planned to use on their first album, probably due in part because the old guard doesn't "get it." Doesn't recognize the future of music, so entrenched are they in traditional gospel music and creaking studio concepts. . . . I feel like an orphan with a small, isolated voice crying out in a cultural wilderness.[25]

Camp, for his part, was apologetic and seemed to know that he was not quite ready for prime time, writing to Larry that he had just written a batch of songs—"you can imagine how that turned out."[26] But the setback didn't stop Larry from forging ahead with his ambitions.

The dream was enough to keep him going, but the reality was that he still needed to deliver some product to ABC/Word. Realistically, *In Another Land*, the third volume of his trilogy, was still a year away from delivery. On a lark, he sent them *Streams of White Light in Darkened Corners*, a cover record satirizing the spate of "spiritual" songs released by secular rock heroes from the early 1970s. The LP featured "Spirit in the Sky" by Norman Greenbaum, "Presence of the Lord" by Blind Faith (Eric Clapton and Steve Winwood), and "He Gives Us All His Love" by Randy Newman, among others. Word was not amused, and Norman released the record independently years later, in 1977.

Secular artists seemed to understand that spiritual messages could sell records while simultaneously denying the true teaching about Christ. In a blistering late entry in the *Hollywood Free Paper*, Larry reflected upon the phenomenon of cashing in on Jesus in the mainstream record industry. From Paul Simon's "Bridge over Troubled Water," to Tim Rice and Andrew Lloyd Webber's *Jesus Christ Superstar*, there was money to be made from religion. Larry related conversations he had with Leon Russell, who had taken to "preach[ing] during his concerts about 'the need for Jesus, the need for love, I'm talking about the power of love.'" But when Larry talked with Russell about what he meant about Jesus, the soul singer quickly explained that he didn't really have an interest in God. What interested him was "the energy level and communication prowess he had observed in black gospel churches, where the preachers seemed to be able to control the response of their congregations with voice inflections and gesticulations."[27]

Norman persisted in his meditation on the fascination that rock stars had with the power of religion. He recalled being invited with Pam to a Saturday barbecue at Denny Cordell's beach house in Malibu. Cordell, the English record producer who launched not only Leon Russell's career but also those of J. J. Cale and Tom Petty, among others, explained philosophically to Larry (while flipping steaks on the grill) that what most people regarded as "true religion" was really just the power of suggestion. Cordell recounted the story of a time when he saw a girl having a bad LSD trip at a party at his house in Tulsa, whereupon Russell came up to her and said, "I heal you in the name of Leon Russell." The girl revived, Cordell recounted. There you have it, Larry concluded in his "As I See It" column. It was the same message he had preached in "Nightmare #71": "Fadeout. Hollywood be thy name."[28]

For Solid Rock Records to fulfill its true mission, Larry surmised, he and his new cadre of artists would need to avoid the pitfall of, in the words of St. Paul, "having the form of godliness, but denying the power thereof." As a way of proving to himself that he was going to stay on mission, Larry created a logo for Solid Rock. It featured an open mouth, reminiscent of the Rolling Stones' tongue logo, but with a depiction of Golgotha, the place of Jesus's crucifixion, inside.

Larry's conviction about "discipling" his own artists' commune was underscored by his young friend Steve Turner's interview of Eric Clapton in the July 18, 1974, edition of *Rolling Stone*.[29] While the full interview reveals the guitar god's spiritual longing and initial attraction to Jesus, Clapton jettisoned his nascent faith during his romantic pursuit of Patti Harrison (George Harrison's wife).[30] Writing to

Turner days after the interview appeared, Larry said, "Poor Eric—it sounds like he gave up Jesus for a woman he never had," adding that Turner had "done a small service to the Christian habit of speculation." It also gave him an idea: perhaps Turner could help build Team Larry. "I'll pay you a salary, plus hotel and food expenses as you travel on the road with me," he wrote the reporter. "You only need to be on the road for two or three weeks at most out of a possible three months—all of the other work can be done from your home."

As he worked to reestablish his credibility with the Christian public, the fan mail started pouring back in. Typically, Larry didn't directly engage with fan correspondence in the early years, though he made exceptions. During 1974, for example, he replied to at least one fan letter—from one Carl Adkins, writing from the Stanislaus County Jail in Modesto, California. He also responded to accusations that he had no local church affiliation. When a friend/fan from Minnesota wrote saying that Larry's spotty record of church attendance was a barrier to booking future shows, particularly in the mind of one Christian promoter in the Minneapolis area, Larry shot back:

When I asked you to explain my album to people who you happened to hear discussing it, I was just asking you personally, as a friend, to remove the stumbling block of misunderstanding from the feet of troubled brothers and sisters. I didn't know that my request would take on any embellishments. Suddenly, it seems I have to write Dave Klug about the album, and explain where I go to church. . . . I can't understand people's interest in it—I've never thought of asking Billy Graham where he goes to church or even what denomination he is. . . . In fact, I can only think of one reason that anyone would be interested at all, and since my request has suddenly taken on more official tones, instead of personal, I will give an official answer.

I worship regularly at one location and feel that the communion and fellowship is a blessing to me, but I refuse to be inveigled by people who ask questions as the Pharisees asked questions. I am answerable only to God because he is the perfect judge.[31]

Every time he reached out for support, friends and acquaintances requested reassurances that Larry Norman was "safe" for Christian consumption—a concept very foreign, to say the least, to the world of rock 'n' roll. He thought it ironic that people whom he didn't know would demand to know intimate details about his personal life as a Christian. Unfortunately, he would need these people if he was going to make a living again, so he was going to have to figure out a way to make nice. After all, he needed to get out of the house.

With few concerts on the schedule, and no recording session to occupy his attention, he was going stir-crazy staying home with Pam. L.A. itself had started to feel like home—the beautifully painted rock-'n'-roll billboards sprinkled along the Sunset Strip served as re-minders that rock-'n'-roll stardom is the best kind of fame. But the confines of their tiny apartment in "Beverly Hills Adjacent" started to grate on his nerves. He and Pam were almost famous. Rodeo Drive and Century City were mere minutes away. David Bowie lived in the neighborhood, during his period when he was freaking out on coke, and to be certain there were enough B-list celebrities riding the elevator and on the street to make things feel fabulous. Larry and Pam were on the social scene as well, a super-photogenic couple who made quite an impression. In one Hollywood social magazine, a pho-tograph taken from behind the couple ran the caption, "Can you tell which 'twin' is a man under that hair?" Reversing the photo revealed Larry in a tux and Pam in a white chiffon dress. They were attend-ing a celebrity dinner honoring Audrey Hepburn.[32] Larry's growing fame and Pam's budding modeling career made them an attractive ask for parties—gatherings where they rubbed elbows with record producers like Denny Cordell and rock stars like Leon Russell. Living in Beverly Hills Adjacent, however, didn't seem to help Pam's level of contentedness, at least according to Larry.

In a handwritten letter addressed to Pam on *So Long Ago the Garden* stationery, Larry vented about what he perceived as her desire for a more glamorous life—to dine at the best restaurants, and to leave the apartment on South Doheny and "live up in the Hills." All of this he regarded as the selfish demands of a shallow person. His tastes were simpler. He loved strolling down Melrose Avenue to Pink's, the legendary hot-dog stand that had been in operation since 1939.

When they were in public, Larry complained, she wanted to be the center of attention. In a letter, he referenced a fight that he and Pam had one night at the movies. Larry had left his seat before the film started to "wash the butter off [his] hands from the popcorn" and catch up with his friends in the band Oingo Boingo about their new sound. Pam fumed back in the theater, hating being left alone, and took Larry's chat with the boys in Oingo Boingo as evidence he had lost interest in her. In Pam's mind, here she was: a pretty model and aspiring actress with a winning personality whose husband seemed easily distracted from her charms.

In Larry's mind, Pam wanted fame, wealth, and success—an attitude he saw as being unspiritual. He felt smothered and pressured to be someone he was not. "We don't have much of anything in common, and that is the obstacle," he wrote to her. He couldn't understand why "everything is so serious and taken on a literal basis with us . . . it shouldn't be. . . . People are not literal." Their problems could be overcome, he promised, but he said, "If we can't resolve [our problems], then I'd rather be alone. No, I never think about anyone else. The only one you're in competition with is yourself. You don't need to ever fear an outside woman coming between us. You are the only one I want to be with, but if that becomes impossible or unbearable, then I will leave you and live by myself. It might take a lot of pressure off. . . . Let's see if we can become friends again."[33]

It was a reckoning that had been developing for some time. For years, Pam's profligate spending had been a problem. Correspondence between her and Gary Anderson, Larry's former manager from the New Generation Artist Agency days, reveals the extent to which Anderson worried about turning over Larry's paychecks to her. Instead of paying the rent and other fixed expenses while her husband was on tour, she shopped. On January 12, 1974, Anderson wrote her a panicked letter asking what had happened to $1,471.00 that was mysteriously spent before the rent was paid. He told her that he knew she had been having a "grand time" while her husband was out of town, but there's nothing he could do to help her this time when Larry found out.

So imagine Larry's surprise when he read a letter from a sales representative for Rainy Day Advertising, telling Pam how good it was to see her on the cover of *Playgirl*, exclaiming, "You're more beautiful in person!" and going on to say that he looked forward to seeing her the next time he was in Los Angeles.[34] Sure enough, the March 1974 issue featured Pam snuggling up to male model Dennis Newell on the front, with accompanying racy article titles.[35] Pam also posed more than once for the pornographic *True Secrets* magazine, published by Martin Goodman, which ran fantasy rape and sexual-encounter stories with accompanying nude and otherwise titillating photos.[36]

Realistically, how was Larry Norman to fend off rumors that he had backslidden from Christ when his wife was posing for porn magazines? A photo from this period reveals much of the singer's state of mind at the time. Larry is sitting on a leather sofa, facing the camera with a forlorn expression, as though he had just graduated from the fetal position. He is clutching a Snoopy stuffed animal. Over his right shoulder, perched on the back of the couch, was Raggedy Andy, and over his left shoulder hung a picture of Marlene Dietrich, the Golden Age Hollywood star. It was a fitting metaphor for Larry and Pam's marriage: arrested development. On the table next to him in the photo was a copy of *True Secrets* porn magazine with Pam on the cover. A copy of *Harper's Bazaar* was situated next to Pam's cover shoot, with one of the visible headlines being, "The Problems of Sexual Freedom." Problems, indeed.

Meanwhile, letters also started to emerge from various par-amours, pledging their love to Pam, including a string of letters from a Christian suitor who cited references from Oxford University's In-klings one minute, and then breathlessly alluded to a tryst on "Feb-ruary 18th ... an amazing day in our lives" that seemed to "have been too good to be true, but wonderfully I know that this is not so." In another letter, he wrote a poem that promised, "I will come in the morning and wake you with a kiss."[37] Apparently Pamela was also indiscreet, since these letters all eventually wound up in her husband's possession.

Pages written in Pam's hand for a proposed memoir of her life in the 1970s reveal that not only had she posed for the cover of *Playgirl*, she was on a first-name basis with Hugh Hefner, a regular visitor to parties at the Playboy Mansion, and friends with numerous Play-mates, including October 1978 centerfold Marcy Hanson.[38] Writing about her friendship with Marcy, Pam speaks of the tension between Marcy's desire to be a television star, and the lucrative offer from *Playboy* to be their centerfold.[39] When she realized a centerfold might jeopardize her chances at an upcoming television series, Pam recalls Hefner offering a compromise: wait until the series comes out and is established, and then afterward release the photos. When the series failed after just a few episodes, Hugh went forward with Marcy's nude debut. During this time, Marcy called Pam to ask her to help her pray about the decision, and Pam agreed to do so. (Wouldn't the standard Christian response be "Just Say No to Posing for *Playboy*"?)

Hugh Hefner subsequently approached Pamela herself to do a centerfold. But this was to be no ordinary issue of *Playboy*. Rather, as Pam would point out to Larry, the offer was to pose for a special shoot entitled "The Most Beautiful Girl in the World." The gig came with a paycheck worthy of such a distinguished headline: a $50,000 payout, as compared to the normal $12,000 for a centerfold model. Pam immediately went to Larry to tell him the "good news" about the offer and to seek his counsel about what to do. Larry's response was to put his arms around her, give her a hug, and tell her, "Baby,

you're the centerfold of my life and that's all that matters." She recalled asking him for $25 for an upcoming doctor's visit as he tucked
her into bed that night. The subtext was that if she posed for Hefner,
their short-term money problems would be over. As Pam went on to
argue, it's difficult to say no to the prestige of the "Playboy image."
Playboy was, after all, "the Rolls-Royce of men's girlie magazines."[40]
She argued *Playboy*'s legitimacy to Larry; they had interviewed Er-
nest Hemingway, and had run pieces by "distinguished writers" like
Norman Mailer and Gore Vidal.

Larry, on the other hand, was unimpressed, being a devotee of
William F. Buckley Jr., and *National Review*. Larry jotted down the
following notebook entry in response to Pam's request on a page
with the caption "Proverbs": "It is better to live in the corner of the
rooftop than in a house with a contentious woman" (Prov. 25:24).

Meanwhile, back at Solid Rock, Larry nurtured increasingly
grandiose ambitions. In addition to promoting artists, and producing
records for them, what he really wanted was a whole media group
alternative to the Christian mainstream. It would conduct real investigative journalism to help bring the system down. He brought up
the idea to Steve Turner, who immediately caught on. Why stop at an
alternative Christian record label? Turner amplified the idea: "Could
you imagine carrying investigative features into such topics as the
Billy Graham Organization (money, role of statistics, crowd manipu-
lation, computer written letters, follow-up, etc.), Christian publishers
(what are their criteria, what sort of people run them), Christian record companies (same questions) as well as into Christian personalities (Wilkerson, Oral Roberts, etc.)."[41]

Turner also wanted to investigate the practice of evangelists who
asked for money in return for prayer, envisioning the same sort
of "cleansing" pieces that Hunter Thompson had written for *Rolling Stone*. Critiques would originate from a specifically Christian
world view, not from a standpoint of presuppositional hostility to
the claims of religion. But one thing that Larry wanted Turner to do
was a bridge too far: Larry wanted him to write promotional profiles

of him and other forthcoming Solid Rock artists. The *Rolling Stone* writer flatly refused. Why would he jeopardize his blossoming career as a journalist in order to do publicity puff pieces on Larry Norman? It would become a point of tension between the two, but the conversation would eventually result in Turner writing a biography of Norman as an observer on the 1977 World Tour, in exchange for a reasonably generous advance.[42] Still, if he could keep his journalistic integrity intact, sure, Turner had no problem helping Larry build his brand.

The Turner relationship would become an exemplar of a mistake that Larry Norman would make repeatedly: not separating business from friendship. On the one hand, he would speak dreamily of an artists' colony whose output would make the Christian community sit up and take notice. On the other hand, he didn't seem to understand that his setup made him "the boss," with employees who pinned their career hopes on his leadership and organizational execution. It was a role that Larry was particularly ill suited to fulfill. It also put him in the uncomfortable position of being "breadwinner" not only for Pam, whose expensive tastes were a drain on the bank account, but also for the emerging Solid Rock "family."

Despite the fact that Larry's own personal life was increasingly painful and uncertain, he relished the role of big brother, both to his artists and to his actual siblings. Although Larry seemed to drift in and out of contact with members of his immediate family, he checked in on them to see how they were doing. Of special concern was his sister Nancy, with whom he had shared street witnessing experiences in the early, heady days of the Jesus movement in Los Angeles. Larry knew that Nancy and her husband had become associated with one of the more charismatic duos of that period: Tony and Susan Alamo, both of whom had kept their stage names after failing in their respective entertainment careers. Susan was a fiery Pentecostal preacher with bleached blond hair. Tony ran operations. Together they formed a nonprofit organization, the Tony and Susan Alamo Foundation. The couple recruited youngsters to come with them to Hollywood Boulevard, where the group handed out tracts that threatened fire and brimstone to anyone who didn't believe in Jesus.[43] They developed quite a following, which continues to the present day, despite the deaths of Susan (d. 1982), and the more recent passing of Tony Alamo (d. 2017).[44]

Few of the Alamos' followers at the time could have predicted the crazy cult the Alamo family would eventually become, though the Alamos had a habit of claiming to receive special revelations and visions from God. When the sect moved to Alma, Arkansas, in the late 1970s, the environment they fostered got even weirder, and ultimately dangerous. The Alamos hid much of their abusive behavior from the public for years, but Larry had intuited something was "off" for some time. In the early years, the group exhibited typical fundamentalist tendencies and barred members from partaking not only in the usual suspects of dancing and alcohol, but also any pop-culture products of the outside world, including movies, television, and, of course, rock music. In their place, the Alamos provided their own versions of popular music, featured on a cable access television show that Tony and Susan hosted.

Larry sometimes visited the Alamo compound when he was on tour in the South. He relished his role of "interrupting" the cultish bubble. Since he was a famous singer, and most of the members would have remembered him from their days in L.A. during the Jesus movement, the Alamos let Larry in. Larry would appear on the scene in his Chevy Citation rental car, and on more than one occasion mesmerized his bookish and quiet nephew with his rock-star looks and his cool, detached confidence. Larry was a figure exempt from the rule of the Alamos. Tony and Susan, uncharacteristically, bit their tongue when Larry Norman was on the scene. One of his nieces would eventually appear on TV with Oprah Winfrey to talk about her harrowing experiences living in the Alamo compound.

Still, Larry's visits were too few and far between. Although Larry's family members fled the cult before things took an even darker and more abusive turn, things kept getting crazier at the Alamo compound with each passing year. Tony Alamo kept roofs over everyone's head through several businesses: everything from gas stations to a hog farm.[45] Most notably, he gained fame by manufacturing a line of bedazzled denim jackets, and had famous customers such as Porter Wagoner, Dolly Parton, and Michael Jackson.[46] Another source of revenue were his parishioners, and he required church members to surrender their assets to him. In a freakish turn of events, when Susan Alamo died in 1982, Tony and other church leaders mandated that the children in the cult lie down next to Susan's corpse—dressed in a wedding gown, no less—to pray for her to rise from the dead. For months, daily beatings were administered to the children because "the bride of God" didn't revive.[47] Eventually, Tony Alamo was arrested, convicted, and sent to prison for sexual abuse of girls within his congregation, whom he considered to be his wives. A nightmare decades in the making, the Alamo cult was a reminder that unspeakable evil can happen when a couple of con artists convince you God is on their side.

6

JESUS VERSUS THE CRITICS

B ACK IN WACO, WORD RECORDS ANXIOUSLY AWAITED THE RE-
lease of the first installment of Larry's new Solid Rock vision. With expectations and stakes high, Norman set out to
record the final installment of his trilogy, *In Another Land*. What
the record company got was a product that the evangelical community found impossible to resist. *Land* not only sounded every bit as
good as *Only Visiting This Planet* and *So Long Ago the Garden*, but it
was more accessible, from the average Christian layperson's point of
view. It sounded upbeat and happy, not esoteric and cynical like the
previous outings.

Land got off to a roaring start with a power-packed first side that
began with "The Rock That Doesn't Roll," followed up by a bouncy
song that Randy Stonehill claimed to have started but on which he
and Larry collaborated, according to the copyright papers: "I Love
You" (not the same song, for the record, as the hit song recorded by
People!).[1] What gave *Land* its distinctive character, however, were
its anthemic tunes that couldn't have been written by anybody but
Larry Norman. "U.F.O." likened the second coming of Jesus to an
alien invasion, complete with analog spaceship sound effects—a full
year before *Close Encounters of the Third Kind* hit theaters. Ballads
such as "I Am a Servant" captured the mood of the older, but hopefully wiser, Jesus generation. Side Two featured a twist on the paranoid apocalypticism of "I Wish We'd All Been Ready," with a creepy
paean to the Antichrist entitled "Six Sixty Six" that featured a trippy

and eerie banjo solo by John Michael Talbot. "Song for a Small Circle of Friends" was a love letter to Eric Clapton, Paul McCartney, Charlie Watts, Randy Stonehill, and Bob Dylan. The mood of *Land* was pitch-perfect for its audience from start to finish—and lived up to the quality assurances Larry had made to Word Records.

Further, the entire album—and forthcoming promised Solid Rock releases—exuded cool. Dudley Moore guested on a jazzy piano number that started on Side Two. On bass, the album credits list "T Bone"—the musician Tim Ayres.[2] *Land* also featured the innovative and completely original guitar work of Jon Linn, who would be Larry's and many other Christian musicians' guitarist of choice in the 1970s and '80s. Perhaps most important, everything sounded gorgeous with Larry totally in charge of his own production, and having critically acclaimed recording engineer Andy Johns on board. Johns gained notoriety for having been the engineer for the Rolling Stones' all-time greatest record, *Exile on Main Street*, as well as being the engineer for Led Zeppelin's celebrated series of albums. The record was recorded at Mama Jo's and Sunset Sound in Hollywood, and mastered at A&M Studios. Solid Rock spared no expense, and dared to compete with the quality of the best records coming out of Los Angeles at the time.

Land also completed Larry Norman's "trilogy," which detractors would later see as somewhat pretentious—as though he thought his records might be the second coming of Tolkien or Lewis. Larry didn't care. He was building a mythology for his fans and for Solid Rock, and took to his expansive gatefold record sleeve with generous inserts with an extensive biography and interview with photos to lay out the case for faith-infused rock as social commentary. His liner notes were cryptic, but intriguing for young rock fans:

earth is a dying planet, man a dying race. there are strange things in the sky at night. some people say that it is help from other planets, but i fear that it is evil let loose . . .

i've been having dreams at night. i dreamed i was driving

down the boulevard and my car was putting out a black cloud that covered the sky behind me. i saw a young boy hitch-hiking so I pulled over and let him in. "don't you know it's dangerous to hitch-hike?" i asked him. he just smiled and said,

"the garden, the planet, the land of the son . . . the trilogy's done. each life has three parts, when three become one, eternity stretches for aeons to come."

. . . and then he disappeared. i looked all around but i couldn't find him anywhere.[3]

Larry went on in the liner notes to bemoan everything from the corruption of the legal system to the breakdown of distinctions between the genders to the fact that "people are starving to death and we burn and bury food because the economy would fluctuate if we fed them."

Regardless of how history would judge, ABC/Word had to be pleased with the immediate result: *Land* was a real success, selling more than 125,000 records—which made other forthcoming releases from Solid Rock all the more exciting from a distribution and sales standpoint.

Not everyone shared this assessment—Larry's rock-critic friend Steve Turner, for one. For him, *In Another Land* confirmed that Larry had moved away from the edgier, more controversial statements like the ones on *Only Visiting* and *Garden*. He noted that although *Land*'s first mix had included "a choir speaking in tongues" (a Pentecostal church practice) and clips from speeches of the Rev. Martin Luther King Jr., they were left out of the official release to the public. Was this done to make *Land* more commercial? If that was Larry's intention, it had worked. *Land* became the most popular record of Larry's career, in part because it most accommodated its intended audience.

But could Larry demonstrate that he could produce other artists who shared a similar vision and successfully bring such a product to the market? With every new employee hired, and every check written, he kept hoping that by surrounding himself with friends, he could create the environment he had always dreamed of. A few factors worked against him. One was a rolling panoply of indiscretions and poor judgment calls—though not primarily his own, if the record he left behind is to be believed. Another was Larry's penchant for micromanagement. His attention to detail was never exhausted; typewritten letters concerning minor incidents and straightforward misunderstandings went on for pages and pages. Idealism, even perfectionism, would drive him toward fellowship—and just as quickly away from it.

But for the time being, Solid Rock's stock was on the rise. Larry's manager, Philip Mangano, applied his talents as the booking agent for the Street Level Artists Agency. He called promoters, booked the shows, and kept up with all of Larry's business contacts at ABC/Word and international distributors. In hindsight, it was a lot to ask one person to do, but to Larry, Phil was the perfect choice. Mangano knew the business. He had been booking shows for Paul Stookey from Peter, Paul & Mary, as well as members of Buffalo Springfield. But what was more, Phil shared a common vision of Christianity—one that prioritized service to the poor and needy.

For Mangano, who shared Larry's love of Franco Zeffirelli films, the summons to a life of Christian service came after seeing *Brother Son, Sister Moon*, the biopic of Saint Francis of Assisi.[4] When Larry Norman came calling, it seemed like a natural transition from the world of secular rock 'n' roll to Christian ministry. If Larry paired well with Randy as a musician, it was Philip who stood alongside him to build up the reputation and success of Solid Rock artists.

Then there was his relationship with Randy Stonehill, Larry's best bet for the Solid Rock vision. In voluminous, and mostly one-way, correspondence with Randy over the years, as well as in diary entries, Larry expressed concerns about his friend's sex life, substance abuse, and a generally un-Christian lifestyle. Despite any animosity behind the scenes, for the next four years, the pair would project a public image of camaraderie and creative partnership that made them the Christian community's equivalent of Lennon and

McCartney—evangelicalism's dynamic duo. They projected madcap laughs and cool confidence, and they were a team. The image of an upstart record company with a mission from God? It was like catnip to people who claimed the cliché like it was scripture: "be in the world—but not of it." All of a sudden Norman and Stonehill were reunited, and the first order of business was to make records.

Stonehill's first release on Solid Rock delivered magnificently, with the artist turning in ten songs that ranged from tender ballads such as "Song for Sarah" and "First Prayer" to blistering, bluesy numbers like "Keep Me Runnin'." The result was Stonehill's first proper release: *Welcome to Paradise*. With his penchant for mythologizing the art, Larry Norman divided the record into Miltonian halves: Paradise Lost and Paradise Regained. The *In Another Land* team repeated its triumph, with Larry behind the production controls and on backing vocals, Andy Johns as engineer, T-Bone on bass, Jon Linn on lead guitar, Mark Walker on drums, and Stonehill showcasing his formidable acoustic guitar chops. Like *Land*, *Welcome to Paradise* was recorded at Mama Jo's and Sunset Sound.

The art direction and design on the record gave the album a punk feel. Norman was old-school: he put Randy on the front cover standing hands-on-hips with a toothy grin, star-spangled jeans, and wearing a T-shirt of the head of the crucified Christ. Was this for real? The generous double gatefold cover not only offered all of Stonehill's lyrics on the left side, but featured a picture of a homeless man sitting alone on a park bench on the reverse, with an interrogative written in what looked like Sharpie: "Welcome to Paradise?" The message of the record was: there is more to life than what secular thought, art, and music have been offering you.

In bootleg audio from an October 20, 1975, concert recorded in Glasgow, Scotland, one can sense the mystique of the emerging Norman/Stonehill partnership. The pair harmonized beautifully, and there was something sweet about these earlier performances. Stonehill would come out and do his set, introduce Larry, and the two would perform several songs together. Larry would recount Stonehill's conversion story—how Randy professed faith in Jesus sitting in Larry's kitchen—and all of a sudden, it seemed like fans of Christian rock had their own Simon and Garfunkel or maybe Mick and Keith—the Glimmer Twins. Stonehill's humor was goofy, and Norman's acerbic, and the combination paired together well as entertainment. During his act, Larry's humor doubled as social commentary, and he would often improvise during a song like "Reader's Digest." After his dig at NASA's moon program ("They brought back a big bag of rocks!"), he drily muttered, still playing over his guitar riff:

> The latest thing they did was ground up all of the moon rocks into dust and fed them to some white mice. [voice trailing off ... $47 billion] Now I guess if those mice get cancer, they're gonna tell everyone in America not to eat moon rocks.

Larry's stage act in particular hit its stride in 1976, relishing in the lighter touch he took, a contrast to the very intense performances of the Jesus movement era. He commented on how difficult it was for modern audiences to understand who Jesus really was, and found a generous target in Hollywood biblical epics like *Jesus of Nazareth*, *The Ten Commandments*, *King of Kings*, *The Greatest Story Ever Told*, and *The Robe*. Larry's monologue style had turned into a childlike lilt, and he'd deliver bits like the following:

> I guess Hollywood has its own way of doing things ... and they always rewrite the script. I guess the originals aren't good enough for them. I remember seeing this one movie, just filled with a lot of superstars so we'd go to the box office. You know in the Bible it says that when Jesus went into the desert, and he fasted, he came out filled with the Holy Spirit. But in the movie, Jeffrey Hunter played Jesus, and when he went into the desert and came out, he just looked exhausted, wandering around and looking at stones, hungrily [audience laughter].
>
> And then on the Sermon on the Mount, which is so beautiful,

Jesus addressed so many thousands of people, and he didn't have a PA system either . . . and this one here might not have done him too much good [audience titters, laughs, claps, and gasps]. Hey, it's just a joke! [To the soundman] Can you turn this up? And Jesus talked to all of these people. And they must have heard him, because they stuck around for three days. And in the movie, Jeffrey Hunter is walking around the hill, and he's saying stuff like [Larry lowers his voice in a British accent to a feeble notch above a whisper] "Blessed are the meek, for they shall inherit the Earth. Blessed are the poor in spirit . . ."—you know I can hardly hear him [audience laughs]. And he's keeping his hands up into the air like this [Larry raises his hands with the backs to the crowd] like he just had his nails done and he's waiting for 'em to dry [audience roars and guffaws].

If Stonehill's act oscillated wildly between earnest monologues and goofy jokes with funny voices, Larry's steered more toward showing the absurdism of life in a contemporary society that had turned away from God. Solid Rock hit the sweet spot between seriousness and lightness, and neither performer was ashamed to be an entertainer—even if they were singing about Jesus. Together, their banter delighted crowds, and their antics created an air of madcap laughs and brotherly love. Their best bit together was taking requests for Beatles songs and/or songs from the '70s, and Larry complaining that the spotlight literally wasn't big enough for both of them:

> LARRY: I have the feeling that one of these spots isn't the same as the other.
> RANDY: Is this a detergent commercial?

The interchange would become something of a prophecy. Despite Larry's burst of enthusiasm for a renewed collaboration with Randy Stonehill, there was a weird vibe about the pair's relationship. Randy married Larry's ex-girlfriend Sarah Finch in 1975. Larry had met

Sarah in Los Angeles at a church camp, and dated her in 1969.[5] Previously, even before they had met, Stonehill had expressed interest in Larry's sister Nancy. And there was also a weird dynamic developing between Randy and Pam. On February 15, 1975, Pam posted a valentine addressed to Randy at his address in North Hollywood, complete with "I love you" inscribed over a drawing of Raggedy Andy (renamed in pen, of course, "Randy"), complete with a suggestive modeling photo of herself pasted onto the right-hand side. What, exactly, was going on? And yet, here Larry and Randy were, working together again. It was a relationship fraught with potential problems going in, and bitter resentment just waiting to happen. But to the watching world they were Christian music's dynamic duo, and for the meanwhile, they were thick as thieves.

The collaboration with Stonehill seemed to have reenergized Larry. The only other artist he found truly simpatico at the time was Cliff Richard. It was also at this time that Larry and Cliff had become friends with Meg Patterson, the Scottish medical doctor who had developed a "black box" based on neuroelectric therapy for the treatment of drug addiction.[6] Larry kept a file on the work of Dr. Patterson, including a journal article from *Clinical Medicine* in 1974, close at hand.[7] It was the age in which rock 'n' roll became synonymous with heroin and cocaine overdose, and by the mid-'70s, the world's biggest stars sought "Dr. Meg" out to keep their careers— and lives—from nose-diving due to addiction. Over the years, she treated Keith Richards, Keith Moon, Eric Clapton, and Pete Townshend, with varying degrees of success. According to Townshend, "If I hadn't gone to Meg, I'd be dead."[8] With Patterson capturing international headlines, fewer paid attention to the fact that the stars who came to her for care also received the spiritual wisdom of her husband, George Patterson, a Christian missionary who had played an instrumental role during the Tibetan resistance movement during the Chinese invasion of Tibet.[9] Later an honoree of the Dalai Lama in 2011 and given the "Light of Truth" Award for his sacrificial service, George came simply to be known as "Patterson of Tibet."[10] Now the Pattersons found themselves helping save the lives of musicians associated with the counterrevolution. Larry had been introduced to George nearly a decade earlier at a meeting for Christians in the Arts in 1968 in Palm Springs, a group that had been put together by Nigel Goodwin. When Steve Turner and filmmaker Norman Stone befriended the Pattersons in the mid-'70s, Larry reconnected with them.[11]

In April of 1976, Cliff and Larry decided to put on a double-bill charity concert at the Birmingham Odeon to benefit the Pattersons' drug treatment center. Larry found himself in the unusual circumstance of being the opening act in a venue packed with Cliff Richard fans. Richard's music was pure bubblegum, so when Larry took the stage at the beginning of the night, the audience didn't know what to make of him. After playing "Why Should the Devil Have All the Good Music?" he launched into a self-deprecating riff: "I'm from America," he deadpanned. "We're a young country as countries go. Two hundred years is pretty young for a country, but we go around threatening older countries."[12] After playing "The Tune," a mini-melodrama on the decline of the Judeo-Christian world view in Western civilization, the crowd started calling for Larry to exit the stage, and to bring Cliff on. The pairing proved to be an ill-conceived experiment, not unlike the times when Jimi Hendrix opened for the Monkees on tour. When Jimi launched into "Foxy Lady" the throng of teenage girls screamed, "We want Davy!"[13] When Sir Cliff invited Larry to appear on his popular British variety show the following Saturday, however, Larry demurred. Richard assumed that the reason was that Larry wanted to avoid diluting his insistence on gospel music instead of pop.[14] The truth of the matter probably lay somewhere else. Larry's music demanded to be taken seriously; it wasn't teeny bopper–friendly.

Back at Solid Rock, Larry Norman struck artistic gold when, during a visit to a Christian music conference in 1976, a young musician named Mark Heard approached him and Randy Stonehill and asked if he could play a couple of songs for them. "He came up to our cabin

at the retreat center and we all sat out on the porch," Stonehill told
Christianity Today. "I'll never forget listening to him singing 'Appalachian Melody' with the dappled sunlight playing in the trees behind
him. Larry and I looked at each other in wide-eyed delight, and I
thought to myself, This guy is a treasure!"[15]

Everything about Heard was pitch-perfect from Larry's point
of view. Not only had Heard and his wife, Janet, spent time sitting
under the tutelage of Francis Schaeffer in Switzerland after graduat-
ing from the University of Georgia, Heard was a genius songwriter:
literary, gifted as an instrumentalist, and best of all, he had a seemingly inexhaustible supply of subversive and spiritually insightful
songs. Heard turned in a lights-out demo tape of tunes to Larry, and
immediately got a Solid Rock contract. Heard and Larry shared the
same cynical sense of humor, and from Larry's perspective, it was
a completely normal friendship and collaboration. Furthermore,
Heard respected Larry's rules of engagement: (1) a one-year musical
discipleship and proving period so that Larry could ensure the best
Solid Rock release possible, (2) a one-off Solid Rock record deal, and
then the artist is on his own. No clutching at Larry's purse strings or
kitchen apron.

Not only did Mark Heard live up to his end of the bargain without any grousing, the truth was that Larry Norman knew that he
had discovered an artist who was not only his equal, but his superior. Mark Heard would eventually leave the Solid Rock nest, but
with an added bonus: no drama.

With the dual challenges of building a business and the stresses
at home in his marriage, Larry felt the need for more Christian fellowship. In response, he did what every other enterprising Christian does when he thinks his perspective is closer to first-century
Christianity than everyone else's: he planted a church. In all truth,
however, Pam got the ball rolling on the concept. She had friends
and acquaintances in the television and film industry who were interested in learning more about Jesus, but would never darken the
door of a church. The venue alternated between Larry's apartment

in Beverly Hills Adjacent, and (just to keep the Jesus movement vibe about it) the beach. Designed to be a safe place for artists to gather to study the Bible and explore their questions about faith, Larry and his fellow travelers called the gathering "The Vineyard." The Vineyard initially began in 1974 and turned out to be a place for seekers to find refuge away from the prying eyes and judgments of traditional church people. "I decided to start a Bible study for actors and musicians only," Larry recalled.

> No photos. No autographs. No pressure. I hold the meetings in my living room. Two druggies I've been talking to for several years (Randy Stonehill and Keith Green) decide to come. Guitarist and writer T-Bone Burnett comes. By then, "The Vineyard" has grown too big for my living room. We meet on the beach in the Summers and in the colder seasons rent a ballet studio, junior high school, whatever will fit us in.[16]

Eventually, Larry's Bible study merged with another group, led by Christian musician Chuck Girard (of Love Song, the Calvary Chapel band) at the instigation of fellow church planter Kenn Gulliksen. Prior to the Vineyard, Gulliksen had been attending Chuck Smith's Calvary Chapel in Costa Mesa.[17] The Vineyard became a haven for artists, and received kudos from the likes of Martin Sheen.[18] For a brief moment in time it seemed as though Norman's brand of Christianity was not so countercultural after all, but rather right in line with the zeitgeist. One of the trendiest and most exclusive discotheques in Beverly Hills at the time, for instance, was the Daisy Club. This was the establishment where Frank Sinatra was first seen with Mia Farrow, and where the Jackson Five played their first gigs.[19] It had also been the go-to spot for dropping acid in the '60s. In Larry and Pam's view, it was therefore a great place to hold a fund-raiser for the Vineyard.

Martin Sheen and Academy Award winner Julie Harris performed in support of Larry Norman's Bible study in 1977. The event took place on January 5 at the Daisy, and Debby Boone came in tow to sing her number-one *Billboard* single "You Light Up My Life." Larry described the benefit as "a small, intelligent event in support of our artistic, culture-based outreach."

It was a heady time for Christianity in America. *Newsweek* magazine had declared 1976 "The Year of the Evangelical," thanks largely in part to Jimmy Carter being so unabashedly open about the fact that he was a Sunday school teacher in his local Southern Baptist church. A slice of Larry's handwritten personal daily planning calendar reveals his own investment in the new administration. On Thursday, January 20, sandwiched between appointments such as "Meeting with Randy over April Blackwood contract for 'Love Broke Through' at Diamond Jim's" and "Pam started acting class with Gerald O'Loughlin," the following is written in all caps: "JIMMY CARTER IS NOW PRESIDENT."[20]

After the success of the Daisy Club event, the Vineyard Bible study through word of mouth even caught the attention of a Canadian travel agency that sold packages to young Christians: "Fly to California. Go to Disneyland. Attend Larry Norman's Bible Study. See the Hollywood Walk of Fame." But as the Vineyard grew, Larry knew what to do with it less and less. More and more, Kenn Gulliksen took center stage. Larry claimed that the transition to Kenn's leadership of the Bible study took place on the grounds that Larry was touring too frequently to provide adequate leadership from Sunday to Sunday. Before too long, however, Larry groused at his replacement. He complained that Gulliksen would simply plagiarize notes from sermons he had heard Chuck Smith preach, and represent them as his own. More important, Larry expressed concern that the teaching seemed to be unorthodox, bordering on crazy:

> The thing that bothers me the most consistently are somewhat small, but possibly destructive statements he makes. One night he is teaching about Jesus's birth and says that Jesus was God because he had no human blood. He only had God's blood because

God was his father and when a child is born it only inherits the father's blood type. I don't want potential converts to be driven away by erroneous assumptions and misstatements. Christianity is already a laughingstock as caricatured by those who only see the rednecks, churchgoing Klan members, televangelists with strange hairstyles, and overdecorated wives with giant wigs. I think it's extremely important to let it be seen that intelligent people can also believe in a Savior who might also be followed by fools. But it's important to have a true gospel and a logical presentation. I can feel a hedge growing between us because he is embarrassed when I point out these kinds of errors.[21]

Increasingly, Larry felt as though no matter what situation he found himself in, something weird was bound to happen, even in his own "church." Although he had started the Bible study in part to bring some sense of normalcy to his life, it seemed that Pam found herself the object of other men's affections here too. For example, apparently controversy arose at the Vineyard over whether some careers can be profitably pursued and still be done in service of Christ and his Kingdom on Earth. Kenn Gulliksen pointed to the Mafia as an extreme case: your "witness" to the unbelieving world would necessarily be compromised. Being in the mob could not be done to the glory of God. The question arose as to whether Pam's modeling career fit into this category, and it was posed to the congregation by one male admirer of Pam's in the Bible study. Based upon correspondence from Pam to the man in question, he seemed to be insinuating that her suggestive photos were causing him to stumble. Confusingly, he also appeared to be hitting on the wife of the man who had started the Bible study in the first place.

Writing to her fellow "church" member on January 23, 1976, Pam simultaneously flirted with and complained to him: "You're on my case, and I'm not sure exactly why. I believe when you say you love me and that makes me feel really special. But lately, I feel criticized, condemned, and judged by you." Thereupon, she launches into a defense of her chosen profession to a man who just happened to be a television executive and former actor. For her, she explained, modeling was just an outworking of childhood activities like playing dress-up. She certainly did not want to make a fellow Christian stumble. Still, Pam thanked the TV executive for the kiss he had given her during a read-through for his new play for which she was auditioning. She closed the letter by reminding him that her name was Pam and *not* his nickname for her: Bubbles Bathsheba.[22]

Increasingly, the marriage of contemporary Christianity's most visible artist was imperiled by an ever-growing line of Pamela's admirers. Eventually, Larry developed an "I can't take you people anywhere" complex and abandoned the dream of a Christian community like L'Abri through his Bible study. Eventually Gulliksen would get replaced at the Vineyard by John Wimber, whose third wave miracle-oriented theology of "signs and wonders" took hold and grew into a denomination of more than four hundred churches. Despite another failed attempt at fellowship and friendship, Larry walked on. After all, his dreams for Solid Rock were taking off, and his career as a solo performer had reached new heights. But the Vineyard episode kept him looking over his shoulder. Could all of this really last?

7

JESUS LOVES THE LITTLE CHILDREN OF THE WORLD

B Y 1977, LARRY NORMAN WAS ENJOYING A HARD-EARNED reputation as Christian rock's most charismatic performer. With Phil Mangano on board to handle the details, Larry decided to do what all great rock stars do when they reach their prime: embark on a massive world tour. By this point, Larry's carefully honed stage act was a known quantity around the world, and with several acclaimed records under his belt, he felt at the height of his powers. He decided to hire Steve Turner, his longtime friend and *Rolling Stone* writer, to document the trip and write a tour biography. It was a risky venture, not the least because Turner, despite getting paid for his efforts, made it clear he still wasn't interested in writing publicity puff pieces for Larry, ground they had covered numerous times.[1] The "friend-as-hired-gun" routine would put a strain on their relationship when the finished product did not meet the artist's expectations.

Still, at the outset, "World Tour '77" promised something never before seen in Christian rock: several configurations of a crack touring band, fronted by Larry, performing at large venues frequented by major rock acts. Mangano took it upon himself to organize the whole affair. A suitably epic concert poster was printed in black and blue, with a photograph silhouette of Larry with a guitar and his back to the camera as he faced the crowd. Above his head hung the "big blue marble" of Earth with a lightning bolt from above striking through space onto a single point on the globe. Translation: Come see Larry Norman and maybe the Holy Spirit will smite you with a prophetic word from the Lord.

The tour began in South America and took Norman and his entourage through Australia, New Zealand, the mainland United States, Canada, Brazil, Sweden, Finland, Norway, the Netherlands, Switzerland, the British Isles, France, Italy, Greece, Israel, Lebanon, Saudi Arabia, India, Thailand, Hong Kong, Japan, and lastly, Hawaii. For seven months, Larry performed an average of five shows per week. He came out and played an acoustic set first, and sometimes played the second half of each show with a full band, fronted by the guitarist Norman Barrett. Alwyn Wall came on the tour to serve as Larry's opening act.[2] By the time he was through, Larry had traversed more than 40,000 miles aboard forty-five different planes.

Pamela joined Larry for the entire duration, and the couple caused a sensation in each city they visited. Upon arriving in Sydney, the *Daily Telegraph* ran a half-page photo of the two holding hands, and pumped the World Tour with the following notice:

DUET FOR A SOLO SINGER

American rock guitarist, singer and composer Larry Norman arrived in Sydney yesterday at the start of a six-month concert tour of six continents.

With him was his wife Pamela, who will model for an Australian fashion magazine.

The couple will be in Australia for a month.

Norman's first Sydney Concert has been sold out, and his second, at the Hordern Pavilion on September 24, is heavily booked. News of Norman's concerts spread by word of mouth. When he was last here, he built up a cult following, mostly of university students.

Norman is billed as a rock star, although he usually performs alone. America's influential Billboard magazine described him as the "most important songwriter since Paul Simon."[3]

Meanwhile, Larry hired a full-time photographer, not only to chronicle his exploits, but to keep Pam occupied on the road by setting up "shoots." The photographer scouted good locations, and juxtaposed Pam against the exotic backdrop of whatever city the World Tour had found itself in. The strategy didn't always work, as Pam sometimes escaped Larry's not-so-subtle minder. Waking up in their hotel room in Sydney one day, for example, Larry was surprised to find a note from Pam saying that she was already out and about for the day. When she returned late that night, he asked her how her day went, to which she breezily replied that she had been out shopping. The next morning, however, he uncovered the whole truth. There in the *Daily Mirror* was a bikini-clad Pam, posing as the "Page Three" model for Thursday, September 22, 1977.[4] Larry hoped his Australian fans weren't reading the tabloids like he was.

The crowds for the World Tour shows were a curious mix of churchgoers and serious music fans. For some, it was their first major concert experience, given that rock was still verboten at the time for many Christian teenagers. As Steve Turner observed, for many present, "it was possibly the first rock concert, in the electric rock-'n'-roll sense, that they'd been to within the confines of their culture. The first concert to minister to body, mind, and spirit all in their turn. As such it marked a breakthrough."[5] Eager crowds turned out in large numbers and snapped up the merchandise on offer, one of Larry's best sources of revenue. The 1977 World Tour was *the* place for Christian rock fans to be. Photographs of tour posters reveal that the show at the Sydney Opera House sold out two months in advance, but as Phil Mangano would note in a press release, the smaller shows packed more punch. For example, the Larry Norman Band played in Broken Hill, a remote town in Wales, to an enthusiastic crowd.[6] Larry Norman played for his fans in out-of-the-way places other stars didn't go.

The album *Snapshots from the '77 World Tour* captured something of the energy, humor, and emotional appeal of the show. The band was tight, and brought fresh interpretations to Larry's most beloved songs. During "If God Is My Father" Larry improvised in rhymed verse over the main guitar riff. Finishing the verse that appears on the record, "We've got to learn to love, love is the only thing," he freestyled:

> *You've got to learn to love yourself . . . because if you don't love*
> > *yourself*
> *You won't love anyone else . . . the way they should be loved.*
>
> *And sometimes we want to reach out to someone,*
> *but something holds us back inside.*
> *Maybe our father and our mother didn't love us like we wish*
> > *they would*
> *And we'd like to reach out and love our wife or our husband*
> *or our children*
> *. . . if we only could.*

For his most obsessive fans, a Larry Norman show was a psychotherapy session set to music. Because he talked a lot between songs, and allowed for awkward pauses and silence, a fan was encouraged to become more pensive, more introspective about his or her life. At most other Christian music concerts, fans left "encouraged." At a Randy Stonehill concert, there were belly laughs and goofy songs like "American Fast Food," and "Shut De Do', Keep Out De Devil." At a Larry Norman concert, the content was designed to make you uncomfortable, to stir up emotion, and the only outlet was for fans to try to find Larry afterward and open up to him.

In the tons of fan mail he received, person after person poured out their heart and told their life stories to him. Fans (mostly girls) came to expect long post-concert prayer sessions, and extemporaneous one-on-one counseling. Larry took this task very seriously, and even kept a detailed notebook on tour of the different people he talked to after each show, with commentary on the details of their conversations. For instance, regarding one girl he met in Finland, he wrote: "Anne is the girl who said that God never answered her prayers. It turned out that she had never accepted Jesus. And she said she didn't want to, need to, etc. Very argumentative! But something kept me discussing everything. And finally she broke. We went outside when they kicked us out. And she prayed to become a Christian."[7] He copiously wrote down mailing addresses with notes to remind himself: "Send Christmas card and be true friend," "Send her Planet/Garden," and so on.

This approach clearly meant a lot to fans fortunate enough to secure time with Larry, but it also had a downside. Larry Norman expected his fans to be as serious as he was. He refused to simply sign autographs or take pictures with fans. Having chronicled these episodes on the British Isles portion of the tour, Steve Turner turned in a tour diary manuscript that portrayed Larry as one part artist, one part spiritual empath, and one part sadist. In other words, Larry was a control freak who—for reasons obscure even perhaps to himself but certainly to his loved ones—needed to know he could move people emotionally and intellectually. Describing the aftermath of a show in Cardiff, Turner writes:

> Then came the familiar straggle of autograph hunters and people who just wanted to say hello. "I'd like some people to meet you," said one young boy who'd obviously battled his own fears approaching Larry in order to impress his girlfriends. "This is Melanie, and this is Diane." Larry gave the minimum required response, and looked at them, smiling, to see if there was any deeper purpose in their wanting to meet him. There was a sense of embarrassment, the feeling that their teenage adulation had been exposed for what it was. . . . "And I'd like to meet you myself," said the designated leader by way of breaking the silence. "Nice to meet you," said Larry, maintaining the friendly smile.

It was a scene I was to see occur many times on the tour. At first I felt pangs of embarrassment for the fans, knowing that it wouldn't take much for Larry to reach out a hand and make their meeting easy and memorable. . . . The impression he gives onstage is understanding, loving, lighthearted—are they wrong to expect to find the same backstage?[8]

But Larry's tour also gave back to concertgoers in unexpected ways. At the height of "The Troubles," Larry Norman played in Belfast, Ireland, at Wellington Hall. It was during the violent times of the United Unionist Action Council strike, led by Ian Paisley, and 1977 was the year in which the Shankill Butchers, an Ulster Loyalist group, terrorized the city in a gruesome spate of violence.[9] In May of that year, the Butchers, posing as policemen, forced a young man named Gerard McLaverty into their car, where he was transported to an abandoned surgery center, beaten with sticks, slashed across the wrists, and left in an alleyway for dead.[10] It was not safe for Americans, let alone rock-'n'-rollers sporting a quasi-effeminate rock look, to be in Belfast.

Still, Larry was modest enough to know that he was an interloper, and he didn't pretend to have "answers" to their sorrows. As Turner observed, Larry performed in Belfast with a song he had not yet played much in concert, "If I Were a Singer," a song he had co-written with Steve Camp. Although not overtly political, the piece, performed solo on guitar, built with intensity until the following payoff:

If I were a singer, I'd sing my song for you
And my pen would point out all the things you're made of
And the only thing that I could sing would be love.
I would sing till the faithless ones received it,
Until the children of your wayward church believed it.

I would sing it to the governments and leaders
And to the writers who have misled all the readers.

I would sing it though they jailed me and they killed me.
Let them empty me of life, for you have filled me.

These are troubled days, I want to live my life in a special way.
These are troubled days, and
I want to live my life for you and show the way.

Larry Norman was a master at casting a spell upon an audience. He could pivot between comedy and profundity on a dime, and at times, a mystical air of importance hung in the room. It was, for some audience members, the only spiritual moment they had felt in years, even after all their years of church services, sermons, and Bible studies attended. At a Larry Norman concert, you felt an intimacy with the artist, despite his mercurial behavior—sometimes tender, sometimes harsh, and at other moments condescending. But he was always entertaining, even when veering toward being "preachy." Still, for someone like Steve Turner, whose task it was to put all of this into perspective, the antinomies were a little too pronounced. He couldn't quite put his finger on the problem. Norman's music wasn't exactly groundbreaking; it stayed pretty squarely in the rhythm-and-blues vein, time-bound, or so Turner thought, to the 1960s: "Having criticized Christians for being behind the times [Larry] finds that he's very much of another decade trying to communicate in sixties musical forms created back then. He's outspoken in condemning Christians for playing to Christians and yet, there he is, a Christian playing to Christians." Turner had a point. Perhaps by the time of the World Tour, Larry Norman was becoming the very thing he despised: the father of a mediocre Christian music industry.

Larry certainly had a mystique, Turner thought, but most of that inspiration he had borrowed from influences such as the Beatles, Mick Jagger, and Bob Dylan. Where Larry excelled, Turner observed, was in image management and branding, and in a backhanded compliment he compared Larry to another British rock star: "One artist I'd met and enjoyed on the same level as Larry had been David Bowie.

Here was someone else who knew exactly who he was and how he could use what he was to say what he wanted. Not one Bowie strand of hair, photograph, album titling, packaging or poster is without its significance in the scheme of things." Stated differently, Larry's talent lay not in his song craft or even performances. Through marketing, he could trick you into thinking more was going on than actually was, in fact, going on. Embarrassingly for Turner, however, he concluded his comparison of Norman and the Thin White Duke by writing: "I can't see us humming Bowie tunes in twenty years or even five years' time."[11]

Somehow, Turner hinted, there was something sub-Christian about being so concerned about one's image. "At home he doesn't like Pam to display pictures of him and yet at the office he has file after file of photographic material of him." He pointed out how Larry paid for a photographer to accompany him on the World Tour, and that said photographer took 2,675 rolls of film of Larry—"something that might be fitting for an artist on the scale of Bowie but which raises the intention [sic] for someone whose albums, on average, only sell 20,000 copies." And yet, here was Turner himself, following Larry for a portion of a mostly sold-out world tour in which he routinely played to thousands.

Turner also cringed at the Dylan-esque way in which Larry dealt with the press, many of whom were amateurs working on behalf of some local gospel radio program. After a particularly electrifying show in Belfast, Larry found himself seated across from a young, earnest Christian reporter. "I want you to know I don't do religious interviews," Larry explained. "You don't do religious interviews?" the young man inquired. Larry: "No. I don't answer questions like 'What do you think God is doing in the churches these days?' and 'When did you become a Christian?' . . . I don't do propaganda radio." The reporter sat there, mouth, no doubt, agape. No, Larry wouldn't discuss "Jesus music," or the meaning of songs like "Why Should the Devil Have All the Good Music?," stating: "I don't explain my songs . . . I don't think Picasso explained his paintings or Francis Schaeffer explains his books. They should be self-explanatory." Instead, Larry wanted to be asked general questions about the tour, and about his work as an artist. So when the young man asked, "How would you describe your music?" Larry replied:

> It's thoughtful music, you know. There are a lot of questions that aren't easily answered and I try to ask those questions so we can all think about it together. There are big issues in life—God being one of the biggest. Is there a God? Is Jesus really so important that we must go through Jesus to get to God? Things like that really need to be thought about for a long time.[12]

Turner admired Larry's strategy but found his behavior baffling. In Belfast, for example, why did he seem to be so uninterested in the theological differences between Protestant and Catholics? Why did he ask his hosts such basic questions about the violence in Northern Ireland when he had been to the country several times before? Why wasn't he more culturally curious? But when he pressed Larry later about his approach, he began to see a hermeneutic at work in Larry's reply: "I always ask questions right from the beginning again. I like the ritual . . . Everyone I talk to usually gives me a different story so I pretend I'm totally uninitiated and then [they think], 'Here's my chance to give my philosophy to this person.' So I just ask, 'Who's causing the trouble?'"

Still, Turner seemed uncertain why people, both fans and friends, seemed to be enraptured by the "mystery" of Larry Norman: "When his close friends meet together it's inevitable they'll start talking about Larry because so little of his behavior fits conventional patterns or expectations."[13] Turner reveled at drawing attention to the contradictions embodied in Larry: the man who criticized the Church for being too materialistic was the same man who expected fine hotels on tour and complained about substandard service at restaurants.

When Steve Turner contacted Triumvirate—the production team

of Miller, Edwards, and Hand who were behind *Only Visiting This Planet* and *So Long Ago the Garden*—they groused that though they admired Larry, they perceived him as being too controlling in the studio.[14] When Steve Scott, a British poet who was working with Larry for a potential Solid Rock release, was interviewed for his opinion, he concluded, "He's hard to get to know because he does bury himself in his work. . . . Sometimes you really want to love him and be with him; at other times you're wondering what you're doing anywhere near him, how he could be bringing this weird stuff down on your head."[15]

Turner went on to conclude that, in sum, Larry Norman was a control freak. He smothered those around him with an admixture of love, gifts, attention and criticism—as the occasion warranted—as a means of keeping people close: "He encourages his artists to be independent . . . and yet is rarely able to cope with those who learn the lesson. Nearly all of his closest friends are somehow dependent on him for their living, and whether he recognizes this or not, he needs them to stay dependent on him. If his friends gain too much independence, it becomes a threat."[16]

In the end, Turner seemed to have the same problem that other Christians seemed to have with Larry: In evangelical Christianity, there can be no rock stars. No believer should be heralded above any other, an outgrowth of the doctrine of the "priesthood of the believer." There is a flattening effect, a radical egalitarianism, particularly in the Protestant version of the faith. And whenever a pastor or Christian leader becomes prominent, popular, or controversial, a pious litany of detractors will decry that such a thing should not be.

Friedrich Nietzsche saw this feature as being at the very core of Christianity—in which the "sheep" demand conformity and reciprocity from those who desire to be strong, to compete, to lead. In his critique of "slave morality," Nietzsche lamented that the true philosopher is always victimized by Christianity, because the perverse master-slave dynamic upon which the faith relies bars any notion of the "free spirit."[17] Christianity enervates free spirits through an endless string of pronouncements of resentment and regret, by controlling them, editing them, and endlessly critiquing them. After all, the very meaning of the Latin root *religio* means "to bind."

Eventually, Turner concluded that Larry Norman's career sat uncomfortably in-between. Larry never veered from his childhood vision of trying to explain his beliefs to the kids on the playground. The best way he could find to do this was through music. And along the way, he found himself at the vanguard of how Christians thought about culture, and how to deploy art in helping reach those like himself: young people confused about the message and ways of the Church in the modern world. He wanted to show what music "can be and what it must be if it's ever going to reach people like us."

Turner turned the manuscript in and registered a grievance about his contract. He had received $5,000 as an advance, plus all expenses paid for airfare, hotel, meals, and incidentals while on tour with Larry. But he had apparently seen reference to the fact that Word was willing to offer Larry $15,000 for the book, at least at one point. Shouldn't he be cut into that, if that indeed was the number? His contract with Larry didn't specify these terms, but he didn't feel like he was in a good negotiating position to ask for more. All told, however, "I hope the book works," he wrote coolly in his sign-off.[18]

It did not. When Larry received Turner's manuscript, he was gobsmacked. It was not what he was looking for at all. The book failed in Larry's estimation to capture the essence of his ten years as an artist, let alone the World Tour. Most of the manuscript was merely a travelogue of the British leg of the tour, which meant, in Larry's mind, that it would have very limited appeal in America and elsewhere. Furthermore, it seemed as though the second half of the book was an endless series of quotes strung together, mostly from business associates whom Larry hadn't spoken to in years, and most of which had mostly negative things to say about him. As such, the book wasn't marketable to Larry Norman fans who were looking more for a collector's item, not true music journalism. They would want something more commercial, with lots of photographs. But the final straw was this: the book effected a "veiled animosity" toward its subject. "I am not paying you to write an exposé," Larry shot back.[19]

Is it possible that Turner had second thoughts after saying yes to Larry? Whatever the case, it was another episode in friendship gone awry. Co-opting the relationship for the purposes of brand-making turned out to be a bad idea. The two remained cordial, but there had no doubt been a rupture. Unlike other people with whom Larry fell out of fellowship, however, Turner retained a degree of loyalty, even dedicating his book on the Beatles, *A Hard Day's Write*, to Larry, for all of their many conversations about the Fab Four.[20]

Larry had planned for the Turner book to be the summation of an artistic life at its zenith. Instead it proved what he feared: no one understood what he was doing. He wondered if all the work in creating Christian rock had been a fool's errand. The frustration had come out earlier on the tour during a seminar on Christianity and the Arts in Auckland, New Zealand. Speaking before a group of Christian musicians wanting to follow in his footsteps, Larry cast aspersions upon the entire enterprise of Jesus rock. "Here's how it goes," he explained. A bunch of Christians get together and make a record and they sing about salvation, and how to be born again, whereupon said album, made for a Christian record company, is distributed to Christian bookstores. Surely, Larry mocked, "that's where all the non-Christians go to buy their records. Am I getting this right so far?" Pursuing the joke, he continued, "Yes, so all of the non-Christians go and ask, 'Do you have any records by bands I've never heard of? Because I'd like to learn about salvation."[21] No, Larry said. Christian records are not primarily for nonbelievers, but for the already believing community. So their purpose must be to make those people think hard about their faith. To talk about salvation to the already "saved" was a missed opportunity. Echoing the writer to the Hebrews who exhorted his audience to "move beyond the elementary teachings about Christ and be taken forward to maturity," Larry stated: "I believe that clichés are a sin. Maybe not to God, but to the muse of art."[22]

Such thoughts left open the question of precisely what "maturity" looked like for an artist who wanted to follow Jesus. In Larry's mind, the Church once held a place as the prophetic conscience of culture, but no more. Today, he concluded, the world does this for itself, by itself. Christians used to be at the vanguard of environmental reform, for instance, but now their secular peers do a better job of talking like Jesus than the Christians do. Larry feared that evangelical churches were afraid to go deeper, to confront the tough questions being posed by contemporary society.

> So I think we need to dig in. We're not going to catch up to the world now. . . . We've already turned over our birthright to the world, and now the world says striking things. So let's go off in a different direction. Let's not go backwards and talk about the basics of Christianity. But let's tear ourselves from the direction of the world now, and talk about real issues. [For example], is homosexuality a real issue? Well, you can't talk about it on the grounds that the gay [community] wants to discuss it [in today's Church]. They say, "We were born this way." But we "know" that it's not natural, that they're not born that way. But do we know that? Have you thought about it? . . . So you're going to have to struggle with what you're going to write about, won't you?[23]

Larry Norman wanted to restructure the Christian cultural consciousness, moving it away from theologizing and position-taking and into deeper engagement with contemporary daily life. As Larry later remarked to fan biographer Alan Gibson, "God gave me a gift, not to be popular, but to be invasive."[24] He had made it his mission to force his fellow believers to think of life in grittier, more realistic terms. It was an ambitious agenda, and one that never came to be, because everything around him started to collapse.

8

JESUS VERSUS PAMELA

HE SPRING AND SUMMER OF 1979 FOUND AMERICA IN A CRI-
sis. It was the wake of the Iranian revolution in which the
Ayatollah Khomeini rose to power and the American-backed
Shah of Iran fled the country after massive protests. The Iranian hos-
tage crisis was just a few months away, and gas lines had begun to
spread like serpents around neighborhood filling stations. On July 15,
1979, President Jimmy Carter spoke from the Oval Office to deliver a
nationally televised address, now known infamously as "The Malaise
Speech."[1] Carter intoned: "The symptoms of this crisis of the American spirit are all around us. For the first time in the history of our
country a majority of our people believe that the next five years will
be worse than the past five years. . . . As you know, there is a growing disrespect for government and for churches and for schools, the
news media, and other institutions. This is not a message of happiness or reassurance, but it is the truth and it is a warning."[2]

For Larry, personally, his golden era as a successful recording
artist ended not with a creeping sense of malaise but with a bang.
Literally. On April 15, 1978, Larry Norman and manager Phil Mangano were on United Airlines Flight 215 from Denver to Los Angeles.
Norman was seated either next to or near Phil Mangano (their accounts of the event differ), when a ceiling panel came loose and hit
him on the head. Writing to "Passenger Service Supervisor" K. E.
Mason some days after the incident, Larry explained what had happened, how the flight attendant had him fill out an accident report in

quadruplicate, then took the form but never gave him a copy. "I sat on the plane after it landed, waiting for the doctor to come and examine me, but the supervisor, after telling me the paramedics were on the way, later told me that no one had been called after all," he said. He opted to go home after being given the opportunity to wait longer, and was now following up as instructed. In the immediate aftermath his neck was sore, and he had swelling at the top of his head, but now the vision in his left eye had gone blurry as well. "Does this happen very often? Aren't the parts of the airplane bolted down to make them more secure? Why wasn't I given one of the accident forms? All she had me fill out was my name and address and she said that she'd fill out an explanation of what happened. I just put down a description about the panel hitting me in the head. But shouldn't she have let me put down something more?" He concluded by asking if they could recommend a doctor in the Hollywood area; "that would be better than a doctor who works far away. Sincerely, Larry Norman."[3]

United's response was both terse and conciliatory. In a letter dated June 8, the manager of inflight services wrote: "Please accept our sincere apologies for the unusual incident that occurred on your flight. Your report, as well as the report of the supervisor with whom you spoke that evening, is on file." They assured him that the aircraft maintenance department had been notified, and that a representative at their executive offices would be in touch with Larry "in the very near future." "While we regret the need for you to write, we appreciate your taking the time to share your comments with us. We will look forward to offering you a much more pleasant traveling experience in the future."[4]

More than a month passed with no follow-up from United. On July 13, 1978, Larry followed up with another letter. "Considering the unusual nature of the accident I had in your airplane (having a ceiling panel fall directly on top of me and land on my head), I am surprised there has been no real concern on the part of your company." A response from United never came, despite Larry making it clear that he was still in pain.

For someone who seemed elsewhere to be reasonably conversant in legal matters, one wonders why Larry did not retain a personal-injury lawyer. Throughout all of his various disputes with record companies, colleagues, business associates, and the like, he rarely, if ever, resorted to paid legal counsel. One possible explanation is that Larry exhibited some form of elitist narcissism, and it never occurred to him to hire a lawyer to do what he could do himself—even when results indicated otherwise.[5] The second possibility is that the injury was not that serious. That was Mangano's position; when questioned about the incident many years later, he denied that what happened seemed to be that serious to him.[6] The third possibility is that the injury actually did affect Larry physically, enough that his ability to process situations such as this one was skewed.

One thing is undisputed: after the ceiling-panel incident, things changed for Larry Norman's life, career, and fortune. Whether real or psychosomatic, the "plane accident" emerged as a line of demarcation. There was no doubt in the minds of those closest to Larry that something had changed. The creativity, organizational ability, and drive vanished. For the rest of his career, every CD booklet bio that Larry Norman produced would point to the plane accident as the event in light of which everything else could be understood. He described the injury as a "bipolar trauma after brain injury," a condition known to cause psychological disorder.[7] Instead of shying away from the implications of such a diagnosis, he embraced it. He would declare himself, in essence, damaged goods, and force his audience to puzzle through what that meant. As he recalled in one autobiographical entry:

I have brain damage and it immediately reveals itself through an avalanche of unanswered mail and half written letters [that] pile up on my desk, floor, chairs, and couches. And in the studio

I discover that I have forgotten how to produce music. I can't decide if a song needs more guitars, a different bass line, vocal harmonies, or if it's already finished and just needs to be mixed down. But then, should the guitar be louder, placed in the center or on the side in the stereo spread? Is there enough reverb on the voice? Is the voice loud enough?[8]

While the glow of the World Tour still shone, Larry was in negotiations for a new record deal with Mike Curb, who had recently moved to Warner Bros. Records. Larry had written and already begun to record the material for his next album, *Something New Under the Son*, a raw, electric blues offering.[9] But things were starting to drift badly off course at Solid Rock.

Larry's particular obsession in 1978 was Eldridge Cleaver, the black radical intellectual who had recently made a profession of born-again Christianity after surrendering to police upon his return from France as a fugitive from justice. It was one of the greatest biographical turnarounds in American history. Cleaver gained notoriety during his incarceration at Folsom State Prison on a rape conviction, where he wrote *Soul on Ice*, published in 1968. The memoir was a bracing tour de force of black liberation philosophy that prompted the *New York Times* to name it one of the best ten books of the year.[10] A disciple of Malcolm X's teaching, Cleaver became the information minister for the Black Panthers, and emerged as one of the most recognized activists of the era. "We shall have our manhood," Mr. Cleaver announced, speaking on behalf of the Panthers. "We shall have it or the earth will be leveled by our attempts to gain it."[11]

After the 1968 shootout with police officers in Oakland that left seventeen-year-old Bobby Hutton dead, Cleaver fled the United States, first for Cuba, then Algeria, and then finally France, where, on the verge of committing suicide, he had a vision of a blinding light that caused his Marxist heroes to fade and Jesus to emerge.[12] By the time he returned to the States, Cleaver let it be known that he was a born-again Christian.[13] Upon hearing the news, Larry wrote a song about Eldridge with a title that anticipated the subject's next memoir: "Soul on Fire." He fired it off to Word Records. Buddy Huey, Word's A&R man, immediately replied that the record company had no interest whatsoever in releasing this particular track: "We are returning 'Soul on Fire' to Solid Rock."[14] Big surprise: Christian record company in Waco, Texas, wants nothing to do with song about black radical activist, even if he does claim to be a believer.

Unbowed, Larry replied to Huey in September of 1978 and tried to persuade him that Cleaver held the potential of being for this generation of Christians what G. K. Chesterton had been to his: a broadside against "shallow Christian thinking." In his mind, a radical black intellectual who had come to Jesus could be the best possible answer to American evangelicalism's intellectual stupor. Cleaver could lead all of the white evangelicals into the "beloved community." He urged Huey to obtain a copy of Cleaver's new memoir. But "even better," he urged, "read *Soul on Ice* before [listening to] 'Soul on Fire.' Eldridge Cleaver was, and possibly still is, one of the brightest and best subculture-politicos. He was brilliant. When I read *Soul on Ice* for the first time, my mind reeled. I thought, if this man could only become a Christian, and still have the pervasive insight to say such things . . . then Christianity shall have some books well worth writing and some words well worth heeding."[15]

In Larry's mind, the Cleaver phenomenon bore a striking resemblance to Solid Rock: both men were radicals hoping to subvert "feckless" traditional institutions by making a direct appeal to the mass market. And Larry believed this could translate into big record sales—bigger than anything Word Records had experienced before, including *In Another Land* and Stonehill's *Welcome to Paradise*.

Alas, Larry sometimes promised more than he could deliver. For instance, he expressed his desire for a "true friendship" with Word executive Buddy Huey, and conveyed his hope that "this next Larry Norman album is all that it needs to be. I have tried to make it the best album I have ever recorded."[16] But *Something New Under the Son* did not arrive in a finished state until 1981, long after the

relationship with Word was on the skids. Perhaps there was something to the brain injury after all.

Back at Solid Rock, Larry needed to catch a break, and he found
one in the talents of Mark Heard, his "favorite son" at the label. Larry
had worked diligently with Heard to give his career in the music
business the shot it deserved. The initial result of this mutual fan
club was *Larry Norman Presents: Appalachian Melody*, released in
1979. From track one, you can hear the promise of Solid Rock, as
Larry Norman intended it: Norman, Stonehill, and Heard singing
like happy schoolboys. The musicianship is impeccable, and there's
not a cheesy Christian track on the record. It made a case for being
one of the great albums of the late 1970s—of any kind—unheralded
or not. "Once Again (Here I Am)" is likely the greatest track Larry
Norman ever produced.

Mark Heard turned out to be the ideal Solid Rock alumnus. After
the release of *Appalachian Melody,* he opened his own recording
studio (Fingerprint), and began producing records for other artists,
including Randy Stonehill, Pat Terry, Tonio K, Phil Keaggy, The Rev.
Dan Smith, Steve Taylor, and others. He amplified and built upon the
foundation that his friend Larry had given to him. Secondarily, there
was no "awkward parting of the ways" after he went on to pursue
his own career. The correspondence between Heard and Norman
remained intelligent, warm, and funny. In a letter from the early
'80s, Larry wrote Mark after one magazine called Heard a genius
who unfortunately had not completely found his own "voice" yet,
since he sounded "like everybody else." "Hey, I used to sound like
Peter Noone until people forgot who Herman's Hermits were," Larry
wrote in solidarity, "and then I sounded like Nilsson until he started
charting singles, and then I sounded like Paul Williams, or maybe I
just looked like him and that made me sound like him."[17]

But not all of Norman's protégés fared well critically or commercially. Tom Howard was a gifted musical arranger and pianist who
played on many Solid Rock releases. Larry repeatedly said he signed
Tom to make a record on Solid Rock as a favor to Pam, as she and

Tom had been friends since their days in Minnesota. Larry wanted to show Pam a willingness to listen to her ideas.[18] But Howard's record on Solid Rock, 1977's *View from the Bridge*, failed to be a critical success in Larry's mind, even if it was not an abject commercial disaster. Likewise, Pantano & Salisbury's *Hit the Switch* (1977) was something just short of a major disappointment. One of the singles, "I'm Just a Record," seemed to pretty much sum things up for the group's overall appeal. These recordings weren't charting new territory for Christian music.

Part of the lack of impact, however, was Word's fault. Larry wrote to executives at Word—Stan Moser and Buddy Huey—expressing his dismay that the record didn't have an insert like other Solid Rock records did. These extras explained who the band was, and what they were trying to accomplish with their music. "If you examine my own career I think you'll see that the big obstacle in my path for years was Who is Larry Norman and What in the World Is He Talking About? It was only when I started doing extensive interviews in magazines and putting insert-like material in my concert programs and albums that people finally 'understood' Larry Norman."[19] He continued, "Without an insert, I have no hope for [the Pantano & Salisbury record] surviving this mortal wound . . . The death of this album represents . . . the death of this group as a unit. I saw not even a sticker on the album proclaiming "New from Solid Rock and Larry Norman," which we had earlier agreed would give any 'unknown' group a needed point-of-purchase push."

And then there were the actual misfires. In 1978, Larry Norman helped produce two records, for artists Dave Mattson and a bluesy group named Salvation Air Force. When he concluded that the results were not up to Solid Rock standards, he gave them to Myrrh Records, another label operated by Word, for distribution. But his heart sank when he got the records in the mail: not only were the records not shrink-wrapped, there was no insert, and nothing to guide radio DJs as to what to play. Was this indifference or incompetence on Myrrh's part? In either case, Larry believed it made him look bad.[20] Additionally, he produced a record for the British poet and spoken-word artist Steve Scott entitled *Moving Pictures*. The album never came out. According to Larry, there wasn't much interest from Word in the release; Scott's low profile in America was not something they felt could be overcome. Scott was understandably upset: he had signed a record contract for three albums to be released on Solid Rock, and nothing happened.

By 1983, Scott had moved on and recorded a new wave album— *Love in the Western World*—on Exit Records/A&M that sounded reminiscent of the Thompson Twins. The highly regarded Steven Soles was behind the production controls. Michael Roe, the brilliant guitarist and front man for the '77s, and Charlie Peacock, another phenomenal new Christian talent, were involved in the making of the album. All of a sudden, it seemed like the best Christian alternative musical talent was developing naturally elsewhere—outside of the Christian-music industry altogether. It occurred to Larry—in November 1983, nearly five years after the recording of *Moving Pictures*—that maybe it was time for Scott's album to come out, and called to find out if Scott had any interest in releasing it.[21] Answer: no. Scott had moved on. Moreover, why was Larry picking up on this now? The answer was simple: now that Scott had some cachet with a critically well-received album on Exit/A&M, *Moving Pictures* might get a hearing. Scott, clearly annoyed, wrote a five-page manifesto to Larry dousing cold water on the notion, and asking for the copyright for his songs to be returned to him.[22] There is no record that Scott received a reply.

The flow of new product from Solid Rock began to dry up. Larry renegotiated his contract with Word. There was a renewed promise for monthly promotional dollars to promote Solid Rock releases, this one from Word Records CEO Stan Moser in an addendum to the contract. Despite the attempt to "make things work," between 1978 and 1982 Larry's attitude was to punish Word by withholding finished product until they indicated a seriousness about living up to their commitments about getting behind Solid Rock releases with real marketing dollars. At the time, he thought it was good strategy. After all, he claimed that not only were Solid Rock records artistically superior to run-of-the-mill, poorly produced Christian albums, they routinely outsold their peers on Word by 10 or 15 percent. As Larry would later explain in a postmortem to Moser:

> The reason "Something New Under the Son" and other product which was ready in 1977 was not given to Word on time was because I had agreed with a certain artist on Solid Rock that our albums should be withheld until we could get publicity/promotion support GUARANTEED in writing, since we hadn't been getting it otherwise. When the '78 contract guaranteed it I went back to finishing the previous albums but when it was suddenly rescinded I stopped work on them and I "sat" on them until I finally gave up and [delivered them] to you in 1980. I think I foolishly decided it was a "matter of principle" because it was from that moment on that our relationship unraveled. . . . I can guarantee you that if these earlier abrogations and rescissions hadn't occurred, there would have been no break in the product flow from Solid Rock.[23]

What Larry hadn't counted on was that Word was content with mediocrity. In effect, the Christian record industry counted on a certain religious economic socialism: God's people will purchase your tapes and records just because they are Christian, regardless of whether they are good or bad. Remember, a not-so-small number of youth ministers in the 1970s and 1980s would routinely stage burnings of records, tapes, and CDs. *Teens! Bring your secular records to be destroyed*, they inveighed. *We'll give you Christian music to replace it.* When it came to art, evangelicals weren't very discriminating.

Back on the home front, the tension with Pamela was mounting as well. The two had agreed to a trial separation. Questions about Pam's drug use, as well as about her supposed relationship with Larry's former manager Gary Anderson, hadn't cleared the air. Her appearances on porn magazine covers, her series of paramours (which, according to Larry, included an All-Pro NFL defensive end), and profligate spending all added to the strain. Pam also intercepted Larry's royalty checks while he was on the road, forged his name, and then cashed them at the bank. Larry never saw the money, and only discovered the deception when the canceled checks—to the sum of nearly $7,000—were returned in the mail. Larry confronted Pam about the incident, and, with her approval, recorded a conversation with her to ascertain what was going through her mind at the time.

> PAM: I praise the Lord that we've been able to have this separation because I know I've grown in Him ... and He has been a husband to me ... and He's ... He's taken care of me ... and I've grown in Him.
>
> LARRY: Well, to grow in Him you also have to count on Him. ...
>
> PAM: I do.
>
> LARRY: You rely on Him?
>
> PAM: I totally rely on Him for everything.
>
> LARRY: When those checks came did you feel that He was providing those checks for you?
>
> PAM: Yep, I did [laughing].
>
> LARRY: You did? That He would want you to do something illegal?
>
> PAM: Well, I felt that, I felt that it was okay at the time to do it. ...
>
> LARRY: It would have *blown my mind* if you would have brought me those checks!
>
> PAM: I know.
>
> LARRY: I would have just been amazed ... I would have been very impressed ... Instead I knew about it and you brought me over a few checks, you know, that you couldn't have cashed. You would have cashed those if you could have, but they just weren't made out to Larry Norman. How did you endorse them on the back? Mrs. Larry Norman?

PAM: Uh-huh.
LARRY: Ugghh [sighs].[24]

Later, Pam's lawyer forced her to surrender half of her 1979 tax return refunds to Larry out of fear he would report the matter to the police. In a letter dated July 2, 1980, she sent in approximately half of the amount she had misappropriated through the forgeries.[25] Money would continue to be a sticking point in their relationship. In countless correspondences Pam complained of "having no money," and expressed her yearning for high-end designer clothes, new furniture, and a bigger house.

Larry occasionally received external confirmation of his view of Pam as self-absorbed, dying to be the center of attention, and clueless. One example came in a letter from the head of a modeling agency in Florida. Pam had complained about both her treatment on assignment, as well as the pay scale. James A. Long, president of JLA Modeling Agency, replied: "Dear Mrs. Norman: I have no apologies to make . . . You seem to have the misapprehension that you were the focal point of the assignment. I must remind you that the main attraction was the Space Shuttle Columbia, and that your work with it was just a small fraction of what my company was doing that day." He then took her to task for inviting other photographers to the shoot at Edwards Air Force Base, and conducting her own photo shoot alongside the one for which she had been hired.

To be fair, Pam wrote dozens of love notes, ardently professing her love for and devotion to Larry, even amid claims she felt abandoned by him. But mostly these letters came in 1979–1980, when the marriage was already in deep trouble. To Pam, Larry Norman remained an alien. He felt "distant" and sometimes inaccessible. When he was "on," Pam loved it, and responded. When he showered her with gifts and attention, she rallied. But she resented his need for privacy, his late nights at the studio, and his weeks away on tour without taking her along. She took it as a personal affront, even though her own diary reveals how regularly Larry called and checked in with her, even while touring far-flung places like Australia.[26]

She wrote to one boyfriend, this one named B.J., that while she "hated games" and wanted to "share special times," she would never leave Larry. She wanted a relationship of "loving but not possessing," but warned that if she was placed in a cage, she would "die." "Dear, dear B.J.," she wrote, "I don't want to hurt you. I love you too much. It's in a category all its own. How shall I love you?"[27] Still, Pam couldn't understand why she couldn't continue to do "ministry" with Larry.

Two events, however, prompted Larry finally to move out altogether of the apartment on Doheny Drive and take up residence on a roll-away cot in his offices at Solid Rock. The first was that Larry had discovered that Pam was having an affair with a youth minister from a local United Methodist Church. When he confronted her, she blamed Larry for making her feel lonely. Some unhappy people drank, did drugs, got sick, spent money, she protested—"anything to escape the loneliness." But in this instance, she had encountered a young man who befriended her and, according to Pam, really communicated with her. She explained that while her intentions were pure, "I fell into sin."[28] According to this particular paramour, and as he detailed in a break-up letter, Pam had come to him because Larry was not "covering," "protecting," and "listening" as a Christian husband ought to do.[29] He went on to apply an analogy of a time he raced a thoroughbred horse, and he lost control of the beast, who raced them both into a ditch. This was how he viewed his relationship with Pam. Still, he wrote ardently, "Everything I think or feel or plan, or see just isn't complete unless I can share it . . . with you."[30] In the final analysis, however, the young pastor felt it time to call it a day with Pam.

The second event stands in the foreground of Larry Norman mythology. The string of personal invitations to the Playboy Mansion infuriated him. When he found out that Pam had attended a cocaine party with a group of men from the Middle East, he implored her to stop. In response, Pam stared him in the eye, wiped her hand in front of her face, and simply said, "Erase." She didn't want to talk about it. But the final straw was his discovery of Pam's purported tryst with another woman on the grounds of the Playboy Mansion, and a diary entry detailing this sexual encounter. He moved out, hoping that a separation might convince her to change her ways. But he wasn't optimistic.

To Larry, Pamela's fundamental problem was that she possessed no center of self. Her life was reflected through the glory of others, derivative of the famous people with whom she sought to surround herself. Writing to Mark Heard in the year that his impending divorce became certain, he explained a moment of illumination in his own understanding of Pam. "Pamela is a terrible actress," he explained, "but one night in acting class she played the Marilyn Monroe character from *After the Fall* (an Arthur Miller play written after Marilyn's death). Pamela had never seen the role portrayed onstage or in a movie, so she just played it the way she understood it. [Her acting teacher] said that the reaction was a mixture of tears and silence. It was such a transformation. People were moved by the performance and thought that perhaps Pamela had finally learned how to act. Even Pamela had come home and said that she had made everybody cry in class."[31] Pam intuitively got Marilyn, her neediness and disappointment, but never got to play that sort of role again.

Despite the friction between them, and to keep up appearances, Larry decided to take Pam along with him to Washington, DC, in September of 1979, when President Carter invited him to play at the "Old-Fashioned Gospel Singing" musicale on the White House South Lawn. President Carter had been an admirer, and included Larry despite the fact that the rest of the invited artists, such as the Archers, the Mighty Clouds of Joy, and the Howard University Gospel Ensemble, mostly came from Southern or black gospel backgrounds. The invitation included a reflection from President Carter on the music that he held dear to his heart: "The beginnings of Gospel Music were as humble and direct as the human need to express our deepest feelings of a divine presence in the world. Today this music may have almost as many forms as worship itself. It can be heard around the world. Still it brings the same simple good news to all people in our only universal language. For the true message of Gospel music is peace. Its instruments are goodwill and understanding. Its mission is hope."[32]

Larry and Pam arrived at the White House on a beautiful day; for one last moment, they turned heads and appeared once again as the gorgeous duo that American Christianity and the Jesus movement had hoped they would be. Larry wore a sculpted inverted A-line leather jacket and a black polka-dot silk scarf. Pam looked stunning in a gold-pleated chiffon dress, and her gold locks were adorned with a flower crown. Larry tapped the White House photographer to take some of the most iconic photos of his career: Larry wandering around on the South Lawn. Larry talking to the Secret Service. Pam and Larry sitting on a lawn blanket next to the president of the United States. Larry, Pam, POTUS, and FLOTUS posing together like old friends. Video footage of the event from the National Archives reveals a cameraman quite taken with Pamela.

As far as the event itself went, Gretchen Poston, the White House social secretary, gave just one set of instructions to Larry: don't say or sing anything political.[33] After the gospel group Mighty Clouds of Joy finished their numbers, Larry was introduced as the pioneer of "so-called" Jesus rock. Taking the stage before the leader of the free world and several hundred other guests, Larry greeted the crowd and expressed his surprise at the invitation, given the fact that the other artists sang traditional gospel music. Still, he wondered why "Bobby Dylan wasn't invited," since his new record, *Slow Train Coming*, was, in Larry's opinion, the greatest artistic statement ever produced in Christian music. And then, despite Ms. Poston's warning, Larry sang something political, and said something political. He played his incendiary song "The Great American Novel," and followed up with "If God Is My Father," which contains the memorable lyric:

What's happened to the message, given by our Lord
To take his gospel to the streets, and share our money with the
> *poor?*

At which point, Larry started free-associating and riffing over the A major 7 chord:

And those in power know, it's a wicked time we live in,
and wicked men know best . . .

The next time you see Kissinger, tell him
What we need are men of God
Not some Chase Manhattan messenger.[34]

Carter didn't seem to mind. The call to care for the poor, root out racism, and defend the weak were right up the president's alley. When Larry finished playing, Carter took to the stage to make some closing remarks about the power of gospel music. "Earlier this spring," he told the crowd:

Rosalynn, Amy, and I went down to Calhoun, Georgia, to see our first granddaughter christened. And at the First Baptist Church, they had a college choir, who was doing a nationwide tour—highly professional. And then following that, they had a local group of mentally afflicted children, and they sang a gospel song . . . that stole the show. It really impressed me, and I think that performance was a demonstration of just how deep within a person Gospel music originates. Because when a group of mentally retarded children can move a sophisticated audience with a simple Gospel song, it shows that there is something special about that music.[35]

During the president's remarks, Larry flanked Carter—the ultimate photo op. And as the whole assembly joined in singing "I'll Fly

Away," led by North Carolina congressman Bill Hefner, Larry smiled and shook his hair and, uncharacteristically, clapped along. Stepping offstage, Larry spoke to the president for about a minute or two while others waited in line. Apparently Larry enthusiastically told Carter about Dylan's conversion, because days later he followed up by sending the POTUS *Slow Train Coming*, explaining, "As I promised, here is the new Bob Dylan album. Bob goes to the church which started in my living room and we have all been very glad for his conversion. I am happy for his sake. I realize that others might be excited because he is a celebrity. We live in such a media-centered era that even Christianity has become a pop art form in the lives of some."[36] Both Poston and the president sent back enthusiastic thank-yous for Larry's performance, one with a personal handwritten note from Carter.[37]

Meanwhile, Larry was still sleeping at the offices of Solid Rock, with Pam keeping residence at the apartment on Doheny Drive. By Christmas of 1979, Larry wrote a ten-page letter that addressed all the relevant "wrapping up" details, as well as his grievances about their marriage and her modeling career:

> You have saddened me terribly. I can't believe eight years is really coming to an end. I just can't live with you anymore. You are not only self-destructive but you are destroying me and deeply affecting my ministry. The gossip that is spreading about you is beginning to have a very negative effect on my reputation as a Christian and as a lay minister of the gospel. . . .

He expressed dismay at passages in her diary in which she breathlessly described a chance to go on an all-expenses-paid trip to the Bahamas for *OUI* magazine to do a semi-nude couples shoot with her *Playgirl* cover partner, Dennis Newell. He was further incredulous that she "prayed about it" and thought that if she got the job, she would turn the escapade into a "mission project for the Lord." "Fortunately," Larry concluded, "you did not get the job." He wearied of dealing with this sort of spiritualizing of bad choices. Perhaps an outside observer would say that he had held her back—that posing for *OUI* and *Playboy* would have advanced her career. "That would be a matter of opinion. Ultimately, of course, I am concerned with your spiritual life and the disposition of your soul for eternity."[38]

And then he really let it all come out:

> You have not needed me for years. Oh, you say you need me as your husband. But your definition of "husband" (and "wife") is completely different from mine. The truth is that you have not been a PARTNER to me. You haven't even attempted to follow in the direction I was going. . . . You have been completely self-reliant . . . willful to the extent that if I ask you not to do something then that almost assures me that you WILL do it.

He addressed one of the most central complaints Pamela had expressed about Larry not letting her into his career:

> I do not want to "dress up my stage act." Your idea of having you sing with me so that girls would be more attracted to us as a "Sonny and Cher" team of happily married people and the boys would be attracted to my concerts because of your looks is exactly the ANTITHESIS of what I am saying to the world, if not the antithesis of Christianity. . . .[39]

Larry concluded his missive by recommending some books on divorce law, and reviewed the different kinds of lawyers she could retain. He reassured her that he did not want to rehearse the infidelities in a trial, but simply that he wanted an equitable division of their assets. He did not care to embark upon an expensive legal fight. His tone was dry, analytical, and cold. Then, after his traditional sign-off, "Love in Jesus, Larry," he added the following postscript:

> P.S. Don't forget to look for an apartment out in the valley that is affordable (not more than $250 a month) and be packed and

ready to move by the time the condominium owners ask us to leave. It's around January 28th or 29th isn't it? If you know where you want to move I will organize the movers for you, and pay for the van, etc. If you don't have a place, the owners will make us move just the same. Remember, you don't need to organize the moving of the furniture. I'll do it for you. It's beautiful out in the valley. Maybe some of your friends don't think that the valley is "where it's happening," but it's sure close enough to drive to wherever it's happening. Give your friends my love at Christmas if you remember.

In the remaining correspondence, Larry offered his advice on which one of the boyfriends that Pam had been seeing would be good for her and which ones would not. Stay away from musician B.J., he warned; he would be no good for her because he would cheat on her, and he'd had run-ins with "Mafia loan sharks" in the past.[40] He also chided her for doing "relationship evangelism"—dating men who promised to become Christians if they could be with her. The only thing that Larry confessed he would miss about the marriage was contact with Pamela's family, whom he adored. Larry admired her father greatly, and corresponded with her brother Dale over their shared admiration for the writer G. K. Chesterton.[41] Pam wrote back without directly replying to Larry's bits of advice. She repeatedly expressed her regrets that the marriage didn't work out. She wondered why they couldn't at least be friends. She fondly recalled their travels together on the World Tour, and reminisced about the good times in their marriage. Despite her repeated overtures, Larry did not reciprocate in kind.

Once news of the split began to spread among Pam and Larry's social circles, there were expressions of concern and a desire that the pair stay together. Even noted Christian author Os Guinness, and his wife, Jenny—herself a former *Vogue* model—sought to offer counsel to the couple. After meeting with them, Guinness penned a letter to the embattled couple on August 8, 1980, in which he urged them to

The typical Larry Norman concert setup, solo onstage with a nylon string guitar, taken during the 1977 World Tour.

Larry at age five
with his parents,
Joe and Margaret.

Larry with the author William Golding
(*Lord of the Flies*) in 1963

People! perform in 1968 on KPHO Phoenix's variety/comedy
show *Wallace and Company,* the show that launched the career
of a young Jerry Springer.

The March for Jesus on the state capitol in Sacramento, 1971.

Larry and Pam's wedding, December 1971. Charles Norman, the ring bearer, is also pictured, age 6.

An insatiable consumer of
tabloids, Larry takes a break
during the recording of
Only Visiting This Planet.

Larry leans over the then state-of-the-art
56 channel Neve mixing console at
George Martin's AIR Studios in 1972.

The album cover photo for *Only Visiting This Planet,* taken in Times Square.

Larry and Randy Stonehill in the studio during recording sessions for *Welcome to Paradise.*

The scandalous cover photo for Larry's 1973 LP *So Long Ago the Garden* on MGM Records.

Larry Norman in concert in the late 1970s.

Larry and Pam send up the album cover from Bob Dylan's *Bringing It All Back Home* LP. Note the Cliff Richard memorabilia and Pam's *New West* magazine cover photo on Larry's lap.

Larry performs for President Carter on the White House South Lawn in 1979.

Larry flanks President Carter
in the aftermath of the
"Old Fashioned Gospel Singin'"
at the White House, 1979.

The Solid Rock Records artists' stable, circa 1980 (*left to right*): John Pantano, Ron Salisbury, Larry Norman, Mark Heard, Tom Howard, Randy Stonehill, Terry Taylor, and members of Daniel Amos.

A frail, post–heart attack Larry, performing sitting down in Oregon in 2003 with his brother, Charles, and sister-in-law, Kristin Blix.

work it out. Still, he admitted that a marriage proposal from another new suitor—a musician named Joey Newman—placed the marriage on "dubious grounds, biblically speaking."[42] Writing back to Guinness and Jenny, Larry lamented: "Marriage is supposed to be more than living together in the same house. I think what God wants is a whole and healed relationship between two people, not just legal marital status."[43] It was simply too late in the game, he lamented, for recovery. When a friend in New Zealand wrote a concerned letter to Larry about the perils of divorce, he replied: "She's had quite the variety of admirers. About ten that I know of. And every once and a while I find out about someone else."[44]

Someone else. Elusive happiness. The life one wants but never knows. It all got folded into Larry Norman's mythology. On *In Another Land*, Larry made a cryptic dedication in his liner notes: "To Fehrion . . . wherever you are." He repeated the same phrase on subsequent albums, leaving fans to scratch their heads for years, trying to decipher the meaning of the reference. When asked what the dedication meant, Larry gave multiple, conflicting answers to the question. This was on purpose. "Fehrion" was an ambiguous concept to which the listener could ascribe his or her own meaning; "wherever you are" is a signal that the quest to find one's true love, the source of one's desire, never ends. It encouraged listeners to make up their own mind about what Fehrion meant to them. Larry never found Fehrion himself. And he would die never having found it.

9

JESUS VERSUS FRENEMIES

EANWHILE, BACK AT SOLID ROCK HEADQUARTERS, THINGS weren't exactly happy good times. Randy Stonehill's second record on Solid Rock, *The Sky Is Falling*, sounded great. But aside from *Something New Under the Son*, which Larry Norman was not delivering until 1981, the only other album in the hopper was Steve Scott's *Moving Pictures*, which was a question mark at best for release. Although Larry had discovered Mark Heard and launched him into an independent career, the subsequent records Larry produced failed to make waves. Larry needed a new act, and a good one—someone with artistic merit, commercial viability, and a real chance of communicating truth to a non-Christian audience. If he could not fulfill the mission of Solid Rock, he would find himself facing mounting acrimony and accusations that he did not want others to succeed where he had. And behind that lurked another question: Was it even Christian to want to make it big?

Having been aware of the music scene at Pastor Chuck Smith's Calvary Chapel for years, Larry decided to rescue an existing act, Daniel Amos, from a rival Christian music label in Southern California, Maranatha! Music. Daniel Amos (aka DA) was an outlet for creative front man Terry Taylor. Their initial shtick was as a country rock act. A mid-'70s video clip shows the group, all wearing cowboy hats, playing under the Maranatha! Holy Spirit "dove" logo before a packed room of docile white kids.

DA was almost comically mismatched with the Maranatha! label, although their presence on the roster was understandable given the group's near cult status with the Calvary Chapel Youth Group. Their self-titled first album failed to sell enough units to recoup Maranatha!'s initial investment, but DA's second release, *Shotgun Angel*, gained considerably more interest, and their shows started drawing larger crowds. Their gig alongside Pastor Chuck Smith and the Sweet Comfort Band at the Anaheim Convention Center on September 7, 1977, attracted 18,000 people, with hundreds of would-be ticket seekers turned away at the door.[1]

Around this time, the band came to Larry's attention. DA claims to have entered into conversations with Mike Curb at Warner Records about taking the band there, but the negotiations never went through, with one band member saying that it was not the sort of deal they were looking for.[2] Sensing an opening, Word Records stepped in to try to get DA out of Maranatha!'s contract by paying the debt still owed on their first album. Meanwhile, Phil Mangano came to Larry, explaining that DA had approached Street Level to be their booking agents, but since Street Level didn't represent anyone not on Solid Rock, such a deal would require that the band join the Solid Rock family of artists. Larry was initially reluctant and implored Word A&R man Buddy Huey to place the band on the Myrrh label instead. But Phil persuaded Larry it would be good for DA to be a Solid Rock/Street Level hybrid.[3]

DA knew from experience that a band's real path to sustainability was money made from playing on the road, so they were amenable to the Street Level/Solid Rock package. Larry ultimately agreed to purchase the forthcoming DA album *Horrendous Disc*, their third effort, which was almost finished. Larry realized they held significant commercial potential. What was more, he thought the guys were full of madcap laughs and good fun. He attended an all-night-long "pajama party" with the band, along with Randy Stonehill and Tom Howard, and according to Terry Taylor, the evening kept Larry in stitches.[4] Could this be the rebirth of the artists' colony he had long dreamed of?

On August 24, 1978, the six members of Daniel Amos signed and executed a five-year contract with Larry Norman to be their sole manager and "attorney in fact," with 15 percent of their gross income due to Larry in exchange for the "development, promotion, and exploitation of [our] name, talent, career, and engagements in all entertainment fields."[5] So with the recording contract with Word via Solid Rock in place, a management contract, and the booking arrangements via Street Level, the conditions were set for a new phase in DA's career.

To help them jumpstart their touring schedule, Larry secured for the boys a 1979 beige Dodge Custom touring van through a lease, on which they were expected to make payments, but for which Larry was ultimately liable. According to the leasing paperwork from Beverly Hills Lincoln-Mercury, the van came with a $15,189.48 price tag, a $1,054 down payment (paid by Larry), and a $410.00 monthly payment.[6]

Based upon the band's touring itinerary for the remainder of 1978 and into 1979, the van got a lot of use, and alliance with Street Level proved to be a winner. The quality of the venues they played increased, with fewer churches and more colleges and festivals on the itinerary. They toured often with Randy Stonehill, and even played a Disneyland gig (with Larry and Randy).[7] Larry and Phil covered DA's expenses both while on the road and as the band kept working on *Horrendous Disc* in and around L.A.

DA was a conscientious outfit as far as their tastes went. Their expense report from September 5, 1979, reveals that the entire band ate at El Taco #12 at 1701 North Western Avenue for a grand total of $11.73.[8] The whole band was able to stay at the Friendship Inn on Hollywood Boulevard that night for $80.64.[9] Hitting the road that October in their brand-new van for a tour with Stonehill, they grossed nearly $25,000, of which DA's net share was $14,081.50, and Randy's was $7,040.79—not a bad intake for artists touring in the midst of a national economic malaise.[10] Larry and Phil were pleased with how the arrangement was working out. By August 1979, the band had largely finished mixing their record with someone that Norman had recommended.

Word made a test pressing of *Horrendous Disc*, but the band claimed that the company got the track order wrong. Solid Rock placed an ad in the November 1979 *CCM* magazine announcing the forthcoming release. Larry took album photos of the band and worked on the art direction for the record. Mostly he'd been hands-off regarding *Horrendous Disc*, save for one critical insight: he felt that the song "Hound of Heaven" (a nod to the poem by the nineteenth-century English poet Francis Thompson) should be included, as well as a track titled "I Love You #19," a number that lay in the balance. Larry's reasoning was that these two songs had a stronger Christian "message" and were thus more consistent with what he felt a Solid Rock record should be about.

As spring of 1980 dawned, Larry learned via Phil Mangano that DA was revisiting their conversations with a Warner Bros. A&R representative for a true secular record deal. Larry proposed that he release DA from their management contract with him. He saw very little for him to do in DA's forthcoming pursuits:

> I hope you will never abandon your plans to take your conceptual ideas and your Christian message with you [as you go]. Otherwise you will appear to, and for all purposes be, just an ordinary everyday rock-'n'-roll band. And this is something you certainly are not. . . .
>
> But now, I would prefer that Daniel Amos would retain more autonomy, and more of their contract, especially if I am not really needed to provide creative direction in the studio. I don't see the need for Solid Rock Productions to receive 15% of anything simply for being intelligent enough to sign you to a production contract.[11]

His obvious replacement as band manager, he explained, would have been Mangano, given his experience in the industry, and the fact that "Philip is the best agent I've ever personally known." But California state law prohibited a scenario wherein a booking agent was the same individual under contract to provide a band's management. Since they would need a new manager for their secular career, Larry volunteered his counsel for any forthcoming Christian projects they might have, but gratis, as an act of friendship. It could all be done with a handshake, he hoped, and that went for Stonehill too. He wanted to give everybody their management contracts back. "Secular management is what you're really going to need if you intend to enter the secular music scene," he concluded.

It was almost as though Larry was telling DA, "Knock yourselves out." He'd been on Capitol and MGM himself, but that in and of itself hadn't earned him a following—only his own wits, self-mythologizing, and hustle did. Now he seemed to be challenging DA and Stonehill to do the same. Still, there was one "gotcha" at the end of the tale of Larry's letter: he was contractually bound "with Word, to maintain recording contracts with Solid Rock artists." Solid Rock's agreement with Word included the right to release, publish, distribute, and control songs from artists under the terms of the contract. Translation: *Horrendous Disc* was going to come out on Solid Rock, as per Word's prerogative, and as stated in the band's contract with Word.

When DA returned from their tour, they were surprised but a bit relieved to get Norman's letter. They happily agreed to take Norman up on his offer to be released from the management contract, but they also wanted everything back: their recordings and the publishing rights too. Writing on behalf of the whole band, Alex MacDougall, the percussionist/drummer, pleaded for all contracts to be declared null and void, and that doing so was "tantamount to the survival of the group."[12]

Larry's reaction was predictable: he couldn't give back what wasn't his to give. Word had a right to release *Horrendous Disc* through their Solid Rock label, as the contract stipulated, and to publish and distribute the songs as they saw fit. Daniel Amos was free to leave

Solid Rock and Street Level. But as a partner with Word Records, he was running a business, not a charity.

Word via record executives Stan Moser and Buddy Huey concurred, but not all was well in the relationship between Larry Norman and the parent company. The slow flow of product, Larry's mercurial correspondence, and his charges regarding Word's inadequate promotion of Solid Rock contributed to increasingly choppy waters in that relationship. Wondering where things stood, Larry called Huey. Was all well with the home office? Huey said no, that Word was planning on dropping Larry's label.

According to Larry, Huey expressed dissatisfaction with the business relationship between the two entities. When pressed why, Huey hedged. "Is it me?" Larry asked. Huey demurred. "Is it Philip [Mangano]?" According to Larry, Huey's answer was yes, and that he would not work again with Solid Rock if Philip remained in charge of day-to-day business there. Huey subsequently denied ever saying such a thing, but only after Larry had already reported his recollection of the conversation to Phil. In any event, the damage was done. Phil felt personally hurt by the accusation that he had anything to do with Solid Rock's denouement with Word. As for Larry, he had reached the point where he really didn't care.

Once close friends, the relationship between Phil Mangano and Larry Norman began to disintegrate. Lack of clarity regarding business roles and responsibilities had been part of the brewing misunderstanding from the beginning. When things were good, those blurred lines worked beautifully; but in bad times, they made the whole operation look shoddily run. For example, correspondence from Norman Miller and Ian Hamilton to Mangano shows that in the mind of Chapel Lane Productions and Word/Scope Records in the UK, Mangano was the business manager both for Street Level and Solid Rock. In this particular instance, the issue seemed to be that a cash advance sent to Mangano to purchase airfare to England and Sweden was insufficient to cover the cost of the flights. Miller maintained that had the tickets been purchased when the check had been requested two months previously, the amount would have been adequate, and so on. The exchange turned acrimonious. Other correspondence to Mangano seemed as feisty as that between Larry and record companies and promoters, which obviously made them quite the pair.

Adding to the difficulties was that Mangano saw Solid Rock disintegrating as a meaningful entity—and it was. Tom Howard was released from his contract. Daniel Amos sought to extricate themselves from theirs. Mark Heard, although not agitating for release, showed signs of moving on, and Randy Stonehill was quietly planning his escape too. In the coming vacuum, Mangano saw himself as the answer to everyone's need for both management and booking. This would provide much-needed revenue (that is, 15 percent from all earnings in management fees) for Mangano's expanded vision for Street Level, in addition to the 15 percent Street Level took from concert bookings.

Larry made it clear to Mangano that he did not need management, only the assistance of the booking agency.[13] What was more, he increasingly saw little purchase in having management contracts with artists at all, adding that Mangano's new proposal would mean a whopping 30 percent of the artists' income siphoned off to one source.

Previously, Larry had split the management fee with Mangano down the middle, but now he felt it was of little benefit to artists who in reality would never sell that many records, regardless of the "conflict of interest" California state law. "Dear Philip," Larry wrote on April 15, 1980, "I've considered your proposal and I am not interested in pursuing that direction although I would be willing to discuss it with you on a low-key level." He did not wish to be represented by Mangano in any formal capacity. "I'm afraid that I disagree with your philosophy of what artists need. And I disagree with your impression of what Solid Rock needs." He added that he should not have signed Tom Howard up for management. "Any advice he needed could be given freely to him. He simply doesn't have a career that needs the dynamic of management at this point. Not 15% worth."

To this Larry added a series of accusations: Mangano's attitude toward certain promoters and contacts was "very destructive"; he had a chip on his shoulder; "you strain to swallow the gnats of their errors and crucify them for their failures."[14]

Mangano expressed anger and frustration at these charges. Couldn't Larry see that the common denominator in all of the confusion and acrimony was not him, but Larry Norman?

On May 1, 1980, Larry wrote a nearly forty-page letter to Mangano airing all of the various matters in dispute between the two and the relationship between Street Level and Solid Rock Productions. The gist: "Solid Rock shall have absolutely nothing to do with Street Level. Both companies are completely separate and independent from each other. I shall not be involved in any partnership with you on any level."[15] He thought the management fees were harmful to the artists. No more. Then there was the matter of some $10,000 from Word Records earmarked for Solid Rock Records' pursuit of radio and publicity for its artists' albums. "Somehow that check was never deposited into Solid Rock's general fund or its promotional or publicity fund. And none of that money was dispensed from Solid Rock accounts for any of the expenses invoiced on Solid Rock's 'behalf' nor has Solid Rock even received a single invoice or duplicate of an invoice." Where had the money gone? "Somehow Word was convinced to make the check payable to either Street Level or Phil Mangano. I'm not sure which," Larry wrote. "Or did you convince them to make it out to a third name? You controlled the disposition of the entire fund. And I know NOTHING of how that money was spent because I never received a memo or invoice. So would you please send me an invoice of all expenditures immediately?"[16]

Mangano denied any wrongdoing whatsoever, but Larry couldn't shake the feeling that he had let people draft off his name and reputation for far too long. He had been subsidizing the purchase of records for the artists to sell while out on tour. Larry sold them for

$1.00 to Street Level, who then charged artists $2.00 to purchase them. Now everyone would have to pay the wholesale price. Larry also didn't like what he believed was Phil's practice of charging promoters for round-trip tickets when only one-way-trip tickets were needed. He expressed that he never felt properly thanked for selling Street Level to Mangano for nothing, or for buying the office furniture, filing cabinets, equipment, free film and film processing, or for access to his entire Rolodex of booking contacts that he developed over the past decade.[17] Consequently, Larry fired Phil Mangano as his personal manager.

All of a sudden, the founder of Jesus rock and Solid Rock found himself asking himself some probing "what ifs." What if he simply walked away and let Solid Rock collapse? What if the Street Level booking agency didn't survive the split? He theorized about the lives of the employees, not to mention his own, and wondered to Mangano whether they might all be better off just walking away from it all. Maybe people would actually lead more peaceful, productive lives without feeling the daily pressure of doing something worthy of the kingdom of Jesus. Maybe losing the dream of success might actually make them better Christians. Maybe not mattering was an option.

"Daniel Amos and Randy seem to be very convinced that they NEED to make it, don't you think?" he queried Phil. "Well, none of us 'need' anything, anything, really. You don't NEED Street Level and they don't NEED to be secular rock successes, do they? And I don't NEED to ever write or record again, do I? What we really need is to become more true in our Christian walk. We NEED to walk where God leads us, not where we choose to go in service of him."[18]

Phil called for an agency-wide arbitration meeting. After a preliminary get-together, the date was set for June 17. The purpose of the meeting was to clear up the relationship between Solid Rock and Street Level Artists Agency, and to deal with Daniel Amos's request to have all of their contracts back from Solid Rock—management, recording, tapes, publishing, and so on. Larry had the foresight to bring a tape recorder, and the whole conversation has been preserved for posterity. Minutes for the meeting, taken by Sarah Stonehill, indicate that those present included Phil Mangano, Larry Norman, the members of Daniel Amos (with the exception of percussionist Alex MacDougall), Randy Stonehill, Tom Howard, Bobby Emmons, and Ray Ware (Randy's best friend and Street Level executive), along with a handful of lower-level Street Level employees. Hitting the Record button on his device, we hear a dispirited Norman say: "The day today is the seventeenth of June, 1980, and I am on my way upstairs to have a meeting with Philip and his staff and my staff, and the artists are going to be there. I don't know what Philip is going to say, but this is likely to be his big, dramatic staged tabula rasa exit, or announcement. And the drama rolls on and on."[19] He announced to everyone at the table that he was recording the meeting.

The nearly two-hour conversation is painful to listen to; Mangano's and Larry's voices are both exasperated and angry. Mangano, chairing the meeting, opened by expressing his hope that once both business matters and personal grievances had been aired, God might bring some sort of "reconciliation" to the situation.

He then announced that Solid Rock management was dissolved. This led to the next question: the recording contracts that Solid Rock issued to the artists in conjunction with Word. Some movement had already taken place along these lines: Tom Howard had been released from all aspects of his contract, principally because Word had no interest in releasing another record with him. Daniel Amos, on the other hand, was a rising star. Larry had released them from their management deal but felt like he couldn't let them out of their recording contract. After all, Word had both paid to extract them from their Maranatha! contract and fronted the money along with Solid Rock to have them complete *Horrendous Disc*. Word clearly thought the album had potential to earn back its advance and even make money, so for Larry, it was a matter of ethics: he didn't feel at liberty to free DA from all their obligations unless Stan Moser and Buddy Huey gave the green light for them to walk away from Word and take their record with them. Why in the world would any business do that?

DA, however, couldn't comprehend why a commitment from Larry to release them wouldn't also mean a release of their record and songs they had written on Solid Rock. They wanted to take the new material to Warner Bros., and perhaps another Christian record label for the material appropriate for a Christian release.

Horrendous Disc was slated to come out in July. It wouldn't make sense, Larry explained, for Word to release them until the album had lived out its initial life cycle. Why, he deadpanned, would Word put promotional money into a group that was no longer associated with them? "You have my permission to leave," Larry reassured them. They would be freed from their obligation to release another record through Solid Rock. They might, however, have to sign a separate contract amendment with Word because the company had a vested interest in at least making *Horrendous Disc* work. Mangano pressed Larry: if Solid Rock released them, weren't they clear of any responsibilities to Word too? Growing testy, Larry replied, "Look, if they want to buy their contract back from Word, and return all the money that Word gave in their behalf, I'm sure Word will give them a release in their sleep."

Larry explained that if he and Mangano called up Buddy and Stan and they were okay with releasing DA, then things could be resolved more quickly. But Philip pressed the point that there was no legal contract between Word and the band, only with Solid Rock. Technically speaking, Philip added, Buddy was not involved in the contract. At this point Sarah Stonehill chimed in. How, she queried, could Philip say Word was not involved? There was a lot of money involved. Word's money. Wasn't Larry bound to honor his arrangement with Word? Don't you "have to clear the entire road here," Sarah asked, to make the separation complete? Was not DA, because of their financial investment in their record, indirectly bound to Word? Randy piped up, uncharacteristically, and underscored that there was indeed an ethical obligation to Word, even if there was some way legally to skirt the issue.

Neither Philip nor DA seemed able to concede this line of thought, so Larry made a fateful move in the conversation. He dug in his heels. He brought up other matters about the separation with DA. What about the masters of the recordings that had been made, in terms of the physical tapes? What about the demos of the songs that had been recorded? What about the songs written while DA was under the Solid Rock contract? Contractually speaking, those were owned and controlled by Larry too. What would happen to them? Well, obviously, DA replied, they would want those back too. And then Larry fired the shot that upped the ante of the conversation: "Well, that's what you want. But maybe there's a few things that I want too."

Larry was on a roll, so he kept going. Was there a reason DA never paid a dime in management money to Larry? Who decided it was okay to default on the payments? How long after the first payment was missed was it decided not to give remuneration for Larry's work in finalizing the record deal with Word, for art direction, for the opportunity to be booked through Street Level, and so forth? Terry Taylor's defense was that they weren't making enough to pay the management fee on top of living expenses—and since all the money they made passed through the Solid Rock/Street Level office, Larry and Phil knew it. Then what about that beige Dodge van? DA had been making the lease payments, but Larry wanted to know what his financial responsibilities were, since the debt was his. Another member of DA asked if Larry felt entitled to keep their songs because they owed him money. (The invoice sent to them when Larry terminated their management contract came to $14,000.) No, Larry said, he was entitled to keep them because there was a contract stating that what was his, was his.

Ray Ware, Randy's longtime best friend and a Street Level employee, pressed the issue of why Larry simply couldn't let DA walk away with all of their possessions, simply in the spirit of Christian charity. Larry's response: "Why can't you simply give to me what is owed to me" under provisions of the contract during the time that it was in full effect? "So you see," said Larry, "it's not simple, is it?"

Sarah interrupted to point out that the matter of Christian charity was a two-way street. It needn't only apply to Larry. Mangano, incredulous by now, repeated the assertion that Larry had said that if an artist wanted out, he would graciously give back to them anything that was theirs. That simply was all that was being asked for in this case.

Larry responded, "Well, then, I suppose that anything that's mine should be given back to me, is that correct?" He denied that he universally promised that anything an artist wanted back they could have back. "Yes, you have," insisted Philip. Anything DA defined as "belonging to them, belonged to them." Randy, again, spoke up in defense of Larry, saying that when he signed his contract he never imagined that absolutely anything he wanted he could have back "just 'cause," but that there would be negotiation and compromise. The whole conversation had reached an impasse. It was tense and awkward.

By the time everyone had moved on to the discussion of the breakdown between Word and Solid Rock, nerves were frayed. The matter of whether A&R man Buddy Huey had complained to Larry about Philip created an uncomfortable environment. Since both Huey and Moser had denied that Huey had ever said such a thing, both to Larry and Philip, the question arose: who was lying, Larry or Huey? Larry's position was that Buddy said it, then denied it. The whole affair ended in a shouting match between Larry and Mangano, the latter of whom expressed utter confidence that mendacity had been involved, on Larry's part.

But then the tape recording captures something else: Larry Norman snapped, even as he continued to defend himself. His voice broke in anger and despair as his soon-to-be-former friends looked on. The dream was over. He was broken. In some ways, he would never recover from the events of June 17, 1980.

After the meeting concluded, it was official. The relationship between Solid Rock and Street Level was over. So was Larry's friendship with Philip. What wasn't over, however, was the animosity. On
one afternoon during the summer of 1980, Larry showed up to the
offices of Street Level/Solid Rock on Hollywood Boulevard after a
trip, and was met with a shock. Everything was gone: the furniture,
phones, typewriters, and the filing cabinets with industry contacts.
Later, he asked a friend to walk with him to a telephone booth, where
they called the Street Level Agency booking number. Apparently,
Street Level had quickly and mysteriously moved to Pasadena. Larry
asked his friend to pose as a promoter wanting to book Larry Norman for a concert. Expressing both regret and concern, the Street
Level representative who took the call replied that Larry wasn't doing
concerts anymore, and would they please pray for Larry because he
was going through a divorce, and having a lot of personal problems.
They hastened to add, however, that Randy Stonehill was available
for bookings. Without access to his contacts, business files, and other
paraphernalia, Larry was effectively checkmated. To him, it seemed
like a coup d'état, with the company he had built taken away from
him under cover of darkness.

Philip suggested an arbitration between the two of them. Larry
was having none of it, and engaged in a few business maneuvers
of his own. For starters, after Daniel Amos retained Schlesinger &
Guggenheim in Hollywood and threatened legal action against him,
he composed a letter to Daniel Amos, dated July 7, 1980, informing
them that all legal contracts between Daniel Amos and Solid Rock
Productions, Inc., were still in effect, though "Daniel Amos' recording contract is under suspension until further notice." He concluded
to DA: "I love you all, but what is right is right and I can't allow the
kind of universal sovereignty you presumed at the last verbal meeting to be given any more latitude in my life. I'm sure that Philip
is wholesaling you a lot of impudence, but what is right is right.
And I'm not going to give a good-natured response to any further
suggestions along the lines proposed at the last meeting."[20] Larry

pledged to forgive DA the thousands of dollars they owed him, but that he wouldn't let them, as he put it repeatedly, "leave and take the furniture." Having shed his image as Solid Rock's spiritual community leader, Norman added and signed the peroration, "Love in Jesus, Larry."

Looking back on these proceedings, one sees how torturous it was for all parties to keep up the linguistic game of Christian discourse and catchphrases while trying to extract from each other commitments of a very secular nature.

AT PAINS TO introduce some serenity into his life, Larry rented a small house with some fruit trees and a flower garden in the backyard. He adopted a pet, which he repeatedly enthused about to both friends and colleagues. Writing to Alex MacDougall, Larry beamed:

> I rescued a crow from being killed by animals and took him to a vet to see if his wing could be fixed. It was broken clear through and the doctor said that it would never mend, and that he'd never be able to fly again. So, now I've got a pet crow. I didn't realize crows were so friendly. He's not at all violent like the crows in Alfred Hitchcock's *The Birds*. The throaty CAW voice they have makes them sound unfriendly but he sat on my hand the second day. I have him in a big Aviary type room and he didn't want to go anywhere near the cage I bought for him so now he's living in a dog house inside the room.[21]

Larry named his new pet Horace (think: Horus), and the bird became his constant companion. One wonders whether Larry's description of Horace was really a description of himself, metaphorically speaking: supposedly scary but actually a beast who was broken and could no longer fly. Horace stayed with Larry through the rest of his bird life, and when he died, Larry took him to a taxidermist to preserve him. He sat perched atop Larry's grand piano until the day Larry died too.

In spite of the hard feelings, Larry helped DA out in a pinch at the Kamperland Music Festival in Holland that August. Terry Taylor fell ill, and the band wouldn't have gotten paid if they failed to perform that afternoon. Larry volunteered to step in and played front man for the band. Despite that fleeting moment of solidarity, however, DA submitted their grievances with Larry and Solid Rock to a lawyer. They engaged first the services of Schlesinger & Guggenheim in Hollywood, who promptly fired off a directive to Larry demanding that he release the band from all aspects of their contract, citing "below industry standard" provisions of the agreement, and the fact that DA trusted Larry as a friend and did not seek proper counsel before signing.

Upon receipt of the letter, Larry not only responded, but developed a strategy in dealing with DA's lawyers. This included:

1. Concede nothing and reassert full rights of the original contract.
2. Assume neither the firm nor DA wanted actually to file a suit, or take the matter to trial. That would commit DA to money they did not have, and Larry knew it.
3. Hold the ball, and wait out the clock. Larry surmised that the law firm would bill DA for every lengthy exchange with Solid Rock. If they wanted to pay expensive lawyer's fees when things could have been resolved more amicably, so be it. Larry never engaged legal counsel or paid a dime to respond to DA's lawyers. Like Muhammad Ali's "rope-a-dope" strategy, he just let the other side throw punches until they exhausted themselves.

Larry politely explained to Schlesinger & Guggenheim that if DA wished to pursue this matter, he was prepared for a lengthy litigation that would place the band and Mangano in financial jeopardy, if not bankruptcy.

Meanwhile, the divorce with Pam was finalized on September 2, 1980. Larry carefully boxed up her diary and all of the love letters her boyfriends had sent to her over the years, and which she had left behind. He read through, once again, the ardent professions of love from Pam's boyfriends, including "Brucey" from 1975, a Christian praise and worship songwriter, who included dashing photos of himself shirtless on a sailboat. Larry got one last chuckle out of one entry in which Pam recounted being offered a role in a David Carradine (of TV's *Kung Fu* fame) vehicle: *Death Race 2000*. But when they informed her that she would have to film nude scenes, she prayed to God as to what to do. Maybe change her name? Wear a wig?[22]

And then there were all the letters Larry himself and Pam had exchanged over the years, many of them the tender offerings of young love. In one, dated March 6, 1973, Larry proposed that he and Pam pose nude for *So Long Ago the Garden* in the double gatefold inside cover. Larry would be Adam, and Pam would be Eve, pulling the apple down from the tree. "What do you think, Eve?" he wrote, illustrating a self-penned drawing of his idea that never saw the light of day.[23]

It wasn't the only marriage to dissolve that fall. Randy Stonehill divorced his wife, Sarah, in September 1980. Although Sarah, who also worked as Larry's secretary at the time, had pleaded with Randy to stay together, Stonehill confessed that he felt the marriage had been over for some time, and nothing could be done about it. Communication between the two was chilly, and the separation included a tangle of charges that Randy had emotionally abandoned Sarah. Randy seemed in a hurry to finalize things, and only three weeks after the marriage was legally declared over he married Sandi Warner, a young woman he had been seeing in the last days of his marriage to Sarah.

Randy did not wish to alienate Sarah entirely, however. He posted her a "whatever happened to our friendship?" letter, but seemed far from repentant. Why, he queried, had their relationship become so very volatile? Her reply was angry and resentful. Why, she wondered, did Randy get to ride off into the sunset with his perky new wife and life while she was left wearing a scarlet "D" for divorce around her neck? In her opinion, her marriage to Randy was stillborn; in fact, it had been dead for six years. Little wonder it was so easy for him to move on.[24]

The fall of 1980 also brought a conclusion to Philip Mangano's relationship with the Street Level Artists Agency, which he sold to the remaining parties involved in the business, including Holly Benyousky, an employee, and Ray Ware, Randy Stonehill's longtime childhood friend. Philip moved back to Boston to start a ministry to the homeless, fulfilling his desire to be a modern-day Saint Francis of Assisi. His efforts did not go unnoticed, as later President George W. Bush and then President Barack Obama tapped him to be the nation's first "homelessness czar."[25]

Meanwhile, Daniel Amos dug in their heels. Upon receiving Norman's response, they switched to the law offices of Schulenberg & Warren in Los Angeles. Schulenberg, a man whom, incidentally, Larry had once taken a course in contract law from at UCLA, wrote Larry a cheery, new restatement of Daniel Amos's desired terms: Larry could release *Horrendous Disc*, and release an EP of DA's new songs with his voice on vocals, but no mention could be made whatsoever of Daniel Amos as a group on the release other than songwriting credits. Further, the five new songs in dispute—as well as the song "Happily Married Man," which DA hoped to shop to a secular label— would revert back to DA's control for publishing. Ergo, if Larry wanted to record them, he would have to pay DA to release the songs on Solid Rock.

Miffed, Larry wrote back that, although Schulenberg's proposal seemed "very civilized and cosmopolitan," it didn't cover any of Norman's concerns about what he was owed. Again, stalemate.

It was now 1981, four years since the band's last album. Understandably, Daniel Amos was very concerned. The January 1980 edition of *CCM* magazine featured the boys on the cover with the headline: "Christian Music's Angry Young Men?"[26] In the interview, Taylor boasted that a major secular record deal was forthcoming, and that once that happened, "our dependence won't be on the church for a living." The article talked in depth about *Horrendous Disc*, but nearly a year had passed and still, nothing had happened. They hadn't released a record since 1977's *Shotgun Angel*, and although they toured extensively, it was hard to win over new fans without a recent LP to market. Four years between records was not unheard-of in the secular music industry—two to three years is standard, and five years is common with more established artists.[27] Still, DA was a band whose time was running out. Attempts to secure the Warner Bros. deal had stalled. They had been playing legitimate clubs like the Whiskey a Go-Go in Hollywood and Madame Wong's, but then again, this was hardly difficult; these clubs moved acts through in rapid succession.

By spring of 1981, the rumors were swirling. Why was Larry Norman trying to end DA's career? *CCM* published an article that March entitled "Whatever Happened to *Horrendous Disc*?"[28] The writer Karen Platt had contacted Larry as her final interview, and found him openly wondering how she could be unbiased when she knew DA so well, and him not so much. After all of the controversies he had withstood within the Christian subculture in the early to mid-1970s, he explained, he had finally come to enjoy some respect in the broader evangelical community—and now this tempest in a teapot with DA threatened to upend this new stasis. Yes, he admitted to Platt, it was true that *Horrendous Disc* had been delayed by Word, but that was because the record company wanted not to get drawn into any pending legal action between Solid Rock and the band. Once that was resolved, the album would see the light of day, almost immediately.

For Larry, the brouhaha with *Horrendous Disc* cast him in the minds of a lot of fans and colleagues as a bad penny, a troublemaker who couldn't keep his artists. As Mark Allender would claim in DA's biography for allmusic.com, the delay of *Horrendous Disc* was largely Larry Norman's fault.[29] Knowing the rumors to this effect, Larry placed Phil Mangano and DA on notice. Writing to Schulenberg, he averred, "I'm very serious about all of this, Richard. I'm in no hurry, whatsoever, and I am prepared to wait until the terms of this settlement are ripened to a season of fullness.... And if Daniel Amos and Philip Mangano continue to disparage my professional and personal reputation within the Christian community I will actively pursue legal avenues in response to their slander and libel. To try to steal a man's property is robbery, but to steal his reputation is murder."[30]

At this point, Robert Schulenberg seemed to have exhausted every avenue of pursuit in dialogue. If the money didn't matter to Larry, as he repeatedly stated in correspondence, then the only possible motive that he could see would be revenge.[31] A volley of more correspondence ensued, with Larry exhibiting renewed resolve to take the matter to its bitter conclusion. Larry included an audiotape of the exchange he previously had at a Mexican restaurant with Terry Taylor and Alex MacDougall about these matters, in order to refresh their memory so that Schulenberg would "be surprised to find out how much more I was willing to give them than you ever believed of me."[32]

The eventual settlement, arrived at on April 15, 1981, basically conceded to Larry Norman's demands in broad outline. Copyrights would stay with DA, but Solid Rock could release any of the material that was legally "theirs"—including ownership of the five songs on the masters recorded by DA for their prospective secular record deal. DA would have to earn back the full production costs of the record before realizing a penny of royalties, which would be paid by Word, not Solid Rock. Additionally, Solid Rock could release the songs with DA's voices erased, replaced by Larry's, and DA's management fees would be waived. Also, DA was free to seek their fortune and fame on another record label. The final agreement looked remarkably like

Larry's original proposal more than a year earlier.[33] All that had changed was that more than a year had expired, and a lot of legal fees were incurred.

The full-page *CCM* ad (also part of the settlement) for *Horrendous Disc* repeated the ad run in the November 1979 edition of the magazine, with the addition of the following tease and taunt: "after 744 days held captive . . . it was released on April 1st. Vanishing now at your corner Bible store." Only six weeks later DA released their grittier, leaner new wave offering, *Alarma!* This left them with two very different-sounding records to support at the same time. *Horrendous Disc* was a gorgeous, lush-sounding rock record, and contained some of the most melodic songs of the band's career. *Alarma!* further demonstrated Taylor's brilliance for brainy, funny lyrics, but was far too avant-garde for the Christian public at the time. The secular album deal never came through.

DA continued to release records throughout the '80s and '90s, to great critical acclaim, if not commercial breakthroughs. But for fans of Christian music, the debacle with *Horrendous Disc* amounted to the end of the innocence. Christian rock was quickly becoming big business. Events such as the Cornerstone Music Festival and the Creation Festival were drawing tens of thousands of fans by the close of the 1980s, and record sales soared into the millions of dollars.

At the time, however, fans of Christian rock looked upon the breakup of Solid Rock as a dream dissolved. This wasn't ministry. This wasn't even rock 'n' roll. It was just a shame.

10

JESUS VERSUS THE SOVIETS

NOW THAT SOLID ROCK HAD GONE THE WAY OF THE DINO-saurs, Larry's performances became less concerts and more like teaching sessions from a grumpy uncle. His mono-logues between sets lengthened. At moments one had to wonder whether he was actually addressing his audience, or engaging in self-therapy. During his historic appearance at the Greenbelt Festival in the summer of 1980, he intoned:

What are we doing with our lives? Some of you right now are planning what you're going to do. And you have to plan a lot, like, you gotta remember to take your cigarettes out of your back pocket before you sit down. Some of you are planning which sins you're going to get back into when you get home. Or maybe you've got some sins planned for tonight. Why? What are we doing? Don't we know what we should do, what our conscience tells us to do? Why are we sneaking around so much?

[...]

What are we doing with our lives? This isn't a rehearsal. All these holes you put in your body, all of these slices taken out? A lot of that is your fault. That's not the world coming up from behind you. The devil doesn't need to sit around, making us sin. We've figured it out pretty good by ourselves. He can go away on vacation.

You can't blame your sins on other people. You can't blame

them on your parents, your heritage, your karma, peer pressure. It's our life. We lead it. Nobody can force you to do what you don't want to do. We've become immune to sin, because, you know, we can do them and they won't really hurt anybody else. They're mostly private sins that nobody sees. Nobody knows! Nobody gets hurt except for God, and hey, he'll understand. He'll help us out.

And so we get older, and harder, and then we get colder. And we just don't care as much. Our attitude changes. We're comfortable with our own hang-ups. Let somebody else who's younger, who's more optimistic, who's less realistic, let them resist sin, and worry about every little piece of it.

Be careful with your life. You only have one. Don't screw it up.[1]

Larry Norman entered the 1980s like a fugitive on the run from the Christian image police. In the minds of the Christian record-buying public, he would always be a mythic figure, the icon of the Jesus movement, a wild boar in Christ's vineyard. But for the rest of his career, he would be cast in the literary role of the "gothic double"—an angel to friends and fans, a monster to his enemies and the castaways of Solid Rock.

The year 1981 signaled a different era in American history too. No longer was Jesus cast as a rebel, the friend of freaks and misfits who inspired his acolytes to protest war, racism, and the space race as much as they did promiscuity and the drug culture. With the arrival of Ronald Reagan, Jerry Falwell, and the Moral Majority on the national scene, a seemingly very different strain of Christianity was now suddenly in the mainstream of power politics. "Evangelical" now increasingly meant "the churchgoing Republican Party." Larry's mission to bring traditional Christianity and rock 'n' roll together now seemed—strangely—both quixotic and redundant. Imagine learning your team won, but through a process that rendered them unrecognizable. The new Religious Right was not Larry Norman's tribe.

Larry himself reached new heights of defensiveness. A burst of correspondence between him and Chuck Smith, founder of Calvary Chapel and another leading figure in the Jesus movement, saw him facing more accusations that he was failing to be wholly above reproach, in every meaningful way. "Pastor Chuck" wrote Larry with concerns over allegations that: (a) Larry had financially mistreated Daniel Amos, (b) he had "appeared" nude on a record cover, and that such "art" was not a way to "reach the world" for Christ, and (c) Larry had chosen to focus his ministry outside the Church and as such had nothing to say to people inside the Church, namely in this instance, Calvary Chapel. Larry shot back to Pastor Chuck, irritated. No, he replied, he had "NEVER NEVER EVER EVER EVER EVER" taken a penny from the Daniel Amos band. On the contrary, Word Records had put in $35,000, and Larry had personally sunk more than $10,000 into their project. What's more, he added, DA had left with an unpaid $15,000 bill to Solid Rock. Further, he piled on, did Pastor Chuck know what he was defending?

> However, there came a time when I went out on the road to see the "Amos and Randy" tour they did with Randy Stonehill and witnessed a most desolate secular presentation on stage and then rode with them out to a restaurant afterward and further witnessed them smoking, drinking, and making vernacular street jokes using unusual vernacular adjectives. I returned to Los Angeles and it was at this time I drafted a letter to them pledging continuing friendship and free advice, but disassociating myself from them professionally. Certainly, I was not trying to judge them myself. I'm certain that most people have let a curse word slip now and then . . . and certainly more and more Christians are drinking and smoking . . . the whole issue was not to "compare" sins and lifestyles, but I did not feel I could represent them anymore and I also didn't want to manage Randy anymore after that, although I also desired to maintain a friendship with him.
>
> I suppose you're not really interested in any of this, are you?[2]

As for Pastor Chuck's charge that Larry disparaged the kind of Christian contemporary music played in his church in favor of "ministry" to non-Christians, Larry replied:

> The REASON I perform outside church walls is merely to provide a more neutral setting for the non-Christians who attend my concerts. I've never backed [out] of my message and have never tried to popularize or commercialize my Christian witness or my preaching from the stage. I've never changed my lyrics or made my concerts less Christian to try to appeal to any audience or promoter.[3]

By the dawn of the '80s, Larry was also getting more combative with the Christian press. In an interview with Don Gillespie from *New Music Magazine*, Larry was grilled regarding his statement that he didn't sing gospel music. Larry's response was, well, of course not. He didn't sing about mansions in the sky, or "I'm a gonna walk dem golden stairs." When Gillespie asked where exactly Larry's songs did "fit in," Larry replied: "I don't know if they fit in at all. Do they?" And when questioned again about whether or not he was anti-Church, he drily reversed the question:

> Are we including the apostate Church in this? Commitment to any church for the sake of commitment to a religious structure? We must first be committed to God. If the church that we attend is a church that is Christ-centered, one of the true churches of God and not one of the social Western-world religious look-alike cults, then we should be part of that church.[4]

In the same interview, Larry recounted a recent experience in which a woman came up to him in a restaurant and asked him if it was true that he had been appearing in porn films. "Where did you hear that?" Larry asked. In all occasions, the rumors were sourced from someone who purportedly possessed "inside information." The truth is that, at this point, after all these years, maybe many people in the Christian subculture secretly hoped the rumors were true. They expressed somehow a repressed hope that someone like Larry Norman, someone so free of typical religious conventions, was a fraud. Because if people like Larry were frauds, then the black-and-white distinctions did hold true, and being old-fashioned was synonymous with the faith. Larry Norman as onetime hero turned villainous porn star was a fantasy that far too many people couldn't resist. The alternative, to them, was unacceptable. There couldn't be any way a person could fly in the face of religious convention and Church authority and still have something to teach them.

Meanwhile, musically speaking, Larry seemed happy to be a one-man band again. He got over his squabbles with Word's marketing department and finally released *Something New Under the Son* in 1981. The record fit both his mood and the times. The album cover featured Larry in his trademark leather jacket, wearing white shoes, emerging from a city record store and flanked by black brothers on the street—a clear protest against the lily-white image of much Christian pop music at the time. *Something New* was a blues record so raw and gritty that it greeted Christian listeners as a veritable slap in the face. It featured the inventive lead guitar work of Jon Linn and the loose, confident drumming of former Daniel Amos percussionist Alex MacDougall. Linn's virtuosity is so striking, it's hard to think of a better guitar album from the era. Meanwhile, the harmonicas, horns, and bass on the album "stank" with the best of funk. Larry's subject matter alternated between the suffering of being human, and feeling lost in the face of warnings from an elder brother to get one's act together.

Track one was the searing "Hard Luck, Bad News," and was followed by the positively creepy stalker song "Feeling So Bad," about a man perplexed by why his ex-girlfriend has found religion and is attending church. The latter was inspired by Larry's reading of Graham Greene's *The End of the Affair.* Larry's voice throughout the album is soaring, ragged, and confident. For many fans, the highlight of the LP was "Watch What You're Doing," which featured a very odd guitar riff and began with the quirky lyrics:

> *Mama killed a chicken, she thought it was a duck*
> *She put it on the table with its legs sticking up*
> *Papa broke his glasses when he fell down drunk*
> *He tried to drown the kitty cat, turned out to be a skunk.*
> *You gotta watch what you're doing.*

The song ended with the catchy entreaty: "Come On Pilgrim. You know He loves you. He loves you more than you'll ever know. He'll make your life glad, unless you start acting like an idgit!" It's the kind of weird, arresting lyric that got the attention of Charles Thompson, lead singer of the Pixies, who in 1987 would title the band's first EP *Come On Pilgrim*.

Something New was so far "out there" that Word Records didn't know what to do with it. It certainly wasn't an uplifting, dreamy, gold record like *In Another Land*. From a Larry Norman fan perspective, however, it was their hero's crowning achievement. It said something to the punks, lone-wolf kids, and freaks who didn't fit in church or the Christian subculture. *Something New* would be a record that Larry could re-release over the years with bonus material to the delight of diehard fans.

Fed up with the tensions of life in Hollywood following his divorce, as well as the Solid Rock wars, Larry entered into a self-imposed British exile for much of 1981. He rented a room near the Bunch of Carrots pub in Hereforshire, which was a reasonable commute to Chapel Lane studios in Hampton Bishop, where he struck a distribution deal with promoter Norman Miller of Chapel Lane Productions for the next phase of his career. For a musician, it was a magical time to be in London. New bands were making new sounds, and punk was ascendant. The Stray Cats, the Clash, and the Jam were happening, and Larry met the charge in the air with a burst of productivity. Miller gave Larry free studio time in exchange for his lack of royalty payments for records sold in the UK, upon which Larry recorded thirty new songs in a fortnight, and eventually seventy songs altogether.[5]

He played the Royal Albert Hall again that February, in support of new artists including Sheila Walsh (Norman Miller's wife) and others.[6] He also began playing live with the Norman Barratt Band as part of an outing called Friends on Tour. Larry's performance at London's Dominion Theatre in May captured him at the height of his powers as a live performer. His press appearances, however, seemed born of a determination to double down on his reputation for acting combative, and maybe even a bit crazy. To wit, speaking to *Buzz* magazine:

Buzz: What is the main aim of your ministry?

Larry Norman: I don't think music is a ministry. Music is just a bunch of notes.

Buzz: Are people expecting more from your music than you want to give?

Larry Norman: I've started to get the impression that they are expecting less from me.

Buzz: Are you sure?

Larry Norman: I'm not sure about anything. Do you expect my music to be more evangelistic?

Buzz: No, but a lot of people simply ask the question "What are you trying to achieve through it all?"

Larry Norman: But I never achieve evangelism through my music. If I'm going to say anything evangelistic I say it with words and not music. Music is art, not propaganda.

Buzz: That sounds a bit like "Larry Norman—Anti-Hero" strolling out onto the stage, hands in pocket, standing like a statue in front of the microphone.

Larry Norman: Well, it's a particular mannerism, isn't it?

Buzz: A friend turned to me and said, "That man is so conceited it's unbelievable."

LARRY NORMAN: If he had me over for dinner he'd probably say you were wrong. The guy's not conceited he's just boring.

BUZZ: He didn't think you were boring. He thought it was a non-verbal statement of arrogance.

LARRY NORMAN: I must make a note of that. Do not go out with your hands in your pockets—it looks conceited.[7]

Back in Hollywood, Randy Stonehill had left Solid Rock, opting for Myrrh, Word's pop/rock label. He sided with Terry Taylor and the other exiles from Larry's former stable of artists, and was vocal about it when asked. Having freed himself from Solid Rock and the shadow of Larry Norman, Randy was "feeling it," and getting ready to release his first non-Norman album.

In June of 1981, it was also Stonehill's turn to stand in the spotlight at the increasingly important British faith and music festival, Greenbelt. It was to be his coming-of-age. At his previous 1979 outing at Greenbelt, Stonehill had announced to the audience, "My brother just flew in from America," to a roaring "Johnny B. Goode"–style guitar riff, then: "Will you please welcome Larry Norman?" The crowd had gone wild. A professional film crew happened to be on hand to capture Larry singing "Let That Tape Keep Rolling," and it wound up making it onto the television documentary *Greenbelt Live*, which included an interview with Cliff Richard, also playing Greenbelt that year, gushing about what a talent Norman was.[8] By 1981, however, it was time for Stonehill to own the spotlight alone.

Although Larry had not planned on attending 1981's Greenbelt festival due to a cash-flow crisis, an unexpected windfall of promoter advances led him to pack his bags, along with his kid brother, Charles, eighteen years younger, who was staying with him for the summer. They arrived at the venue and went to the ticket booth to purchase passes for him and Charles. The Greenbelt representative stammered out: "You don't have to pay, you're . . . uh . . . Larry Norman." His arrival proved a shock to the fans—he wasn't on the schedule! He wasn't even supposed to be there! Charles later recalled the crowd parting down the middle, as though Larry were a rock-'n'-roll Moses. It was the first time he understood that his brother was famous.

Not that everyone at the festival was enthused by Larry's presence. When the brothers made their way backstage to see Randy before his set, one of Stonehill's posse stood in Larry's way and told him, "We'd like you to leave."[9] Apparently, Randy and his new wife, Sandi, were angry that Larry refused to attend their wedding due to his reservations about how quickly Stonehill had ended his marriage to Sarah and immediately wedded someone he barely knew. Larry retreated and made his way to the press pool in front of the stage and pulled out his camera to snap photos of his erstwhile colleague and "best friend." Writing to Randy a few weeks later, Larry damned Stonehill's Greenbelt set with faint praise, telling him that while his band was hot, Randy sounded "tired." Anyway, he had bailed after four or five songs. "I like your new songs," he wrote. "I had to leave . . . because the crowd was weird. . . . They seemed unreceptive. How did they seem from the stage?"[10]

Meanwhile, Randy was settling scores of his own. Sitting down with Devlin Donaldson of *CCM* during Greenbelt, Stonehill gave an expansive and vulnerable interview in which he distanced himself from his association with Larry Norman. Yes, he admitted, Larry was "there" when he accepted Christ, but reports of Larry being an unrelenting evangelist who would not give up until Randy knew the state of his own soul were perhaps exaggerated. Despite the version related in the song "Norman's Kitchen," Stonehill demurred: "I just don't think that it is totally accurate to say that Larry Norman came to me in a blaze of light and led me to the Lord."[11] When Donaldson asked the looming "What ever happened to Solid Rock?" question, Randy played it smoothly. It was just time to move on. He had outgrown both Larry and Solid Rock. When pressed about his divorce, as well as Larry's, Stonehill danced around the subject.

By the time Randy returned from his tour, Larry and Sarah Finch (who had reclaimed her maiden name) had begun dating—years after their first romance back in the late 1960s. Misery, as they say, loves company, and sensing a common foil in Randy helped turn their longtime friendship into something more. And thus the rumor began to spread throughout the CCM community that Norman had "stolen" Stonehill's wife—and Larry's own secretary, to boot—while poor Randy was out on tour. It was a rumor that would circulate even after Larry's death.[12]

The supposed "inappropriateness" of Larry's deepening friendship with Sarah had caught the attention of a youthful staff worker at Street Level named Brad Durham, even before the breakup of Solid Rock. Durham thought it untoward that Larry and Sarah would work late into the evening together before the Stonehills' marriage was officially dissolved, and got the impression that something funny was going on.[13] To a young man like Brad, even the appearance of shenanigans was bad enough. Larry denied the insinuations of wrongdoing, but the allegations spread nevertheless. It turned out to be a boon and quite lucky timing for Randy, who could dodge questions about his own divorce and remarriage while stories about the more controversial and polarizing Larry Norman swirled.

The clouds did part, however so briefly, for Larry when he and Sarah wed in April 1982, in Santa Barbara. And if there was ever a time in Larry's life when he was really happy, this was it. Sarah came from a family of relative wealth and privilege. When Sarah and Larry honeymooned in Hawaii, several months later in December 1982, they brought other family members in tow.

Still, they couldn't get away from the Solid Rock meltdown. As Randy's new wife, Sandi, wrote in a letter to Sarah in October of 1982, the Stonehills weren't to blame for the rumors spread about the newly coupled Normans, but hey, people talk, and we don't live in a very understanding culture for that sort of thing, she wrote. People were free to draw their own conclusions, aren't they, even if those conclusions are unfair to the truth.[14] Randy added a personal footnote and told Sarah that the "lies and smoke" of the gossip about her and Larry, while regrettable, did not originate with him.[15]

But Larry was not in a mood for understanding. He penned a screed to Randy that may not have been sent, as it was found in his papers upon his death. Still, it proves Larry's fury at Stonehill during the time. At issue was that he felt it was slander about his marriage to Sarah.

> Old Rand:
>
> I think your life is a filthy tragedy. How dare you accuse me of breaking up your marriage. You dumped your wife when you were bored and Liza was a hot blonde you wanted to marry. When she dropped you Sandi bounced into the picture . . . Now that I've married Sarah you're telling people that you walked in on us making love and that's why you got a divorce. You're pathetic. Can't you take responsibility for your own failings and lusts?

The letter goes on to list a number of accusations about Randy's failings as a husband and a Christian role model, before ending with a note of dismissal: "Hey, I could care less. You poseurs don't exist as far as I'm concerned. . . ."[16]

The war between Larry Norman and Randy Stonehill would continue for more than a decade, mostly on vinyl, in the form of passive-aggressive, sometimes veiled lyrical digs leveled at each other. Randy fired the opening shot with a song entitled "Even the Best of Friends," which lamented friends who fall away into sin and go to the dark side. Stonehill was singing about Larry, and everyone knew it. By far the subtlest warning to Randy came in a song Larry released toward the end of the 1980s, "He Really Loves You," which contained a clear reference to Stonehill's conversion in Norman's kitchen, followed by a lyric that pinpointed Randy's former street address in North Hollywood. It further cryptically referenced Larry's charges of an affair Randy had with his ex-girlfriend: "I had a vision near Otsego Gate," Larry intones. And then he says something unintelligible. Look up any lyrics website, and it will say that the next line is, "I saw you in

Su San Dupheay"—which, of course, is nonsense.[17] A number of listeners think Larry was singing a woman's name in that faux French accent. Then: "unborn children weep and wait for the resurrection day. The Savior sits in heaven and he's calling out your name. He really loves you." Was Larry intimating that Randy and his girlfriend had an abortion? It seemed so.

In the midst of this relational Sturm und Drang, there was one silver lining: affirmation from Larry's father. Joe Norman was recently retired and recovered from a heart attack. Somehow, the man who once forbade his son to go into rock music and tried to persuade him to settle down, get married, have kids, and live a "normal" life, turned into Larry's biggest supporter. First by becoming the business manager of Phydeaux, a label Larry had formed in 1979 to disseminate his bootlegs and new recordings but had not yet seen the light of day. Joe ran interference at the office, worked with promoters, and kept overenthusiastic fans at bay. He got product out on time, and took the burden that had fallen on his son's shoulders for so long.

The name Phydeaux was a Cajun gloss on the pet name Fido. As Larry explained, if Christian music was going to the dogs, he wanted to be on the cutting edge. And the business model was innovative: having used major record labels and tours to build up his name and mythology, Larry decided to cut out the middle man of a record company and distributor altogether, selling directly through the mail to fans. This approach accomplished two things. It allowed Larry to compete with bootleggers obsessed with chronicling his every appearance. He could release what he previously considered inferior live recordings like *Roll Away the Stone* and *The Israel Tapes* (a quasi-reunion of sorts with members of People!) that captured the raw, "in-the-room" appeal of his concerts. He also released a cleaner, more traditional live album from his recent performance with the Barratt Band at the Dominion Theatre in London that was entitled *Larry Norman and His Friends on Tour.* The subtext was not so sub: Larry Norman still had friends.

Phydeaux also gave Larry the chance to double down on his sto-

ried "battles" with Pam, DA, and Stonehill. On the promotional release *Barking at the Ants*, Larry featured UK artists such as Sheila
Walsh and Alwyn Wall, but he didn't put them on the cover. Instead,
he splashed on an old Solid Rock photo of Stonehill and Terry Taylor
with a white banner obscuring their faces and big block lettering
announcing "The British Invasion." Black Sharpie scratched out the
old Solid Rock artists' names, and the flip side announced the roster
of new British artists. As the album artwork was being sent off to
be photographed, Charles, who was staying with his brother at the
time, grabbed a pen and drew long black fingernails on Terry Taylor's guitar-strumming hand. For the younger Norman, a skater kid
developing an interest in punk, there could be no bigger compliment
to a guy playing guitar than fingernails befitting a punk.

Larry adored Charles, who had shown signs of solidarity with his
older brother from the start. In a photo at Pam and Larry's wedding,
then six-year-old Charles is seated in front of the beautiful bride, with
his chin resting on his hand, looking annoyed. Larry looks similarly
exasperated, as if intoning *"serenity now"* under his breath. Larry
introduced Charles to the Sex Pistols during his early teens, and his
little brother ran with it. Now as he was entering early adulthood,
Charles had gone from being a skateboarder, whose good friend was
the legendary skater Steve Caballero, to becoming the lead guitarist
in the San Jose cult-favorite hardcore band Executioner.[18]

In 1982 Larry took Executioner into the studio and helped them
record an EP, *Hellbound*, which is still regarded as a classic of the
early San Jose hardcore scene. Larry offered to pay for the entire
session on one condition: the band needed to record one of Larry's
songs, a lost gem entitled "Take a Look at the Book, It'll Show You the
Way." For the boys in Executioner it was, needless to say, quite the
departure from their own lyrics. Larry enjoyed the contrast, preferring to hang around honest albeit crass-talking punks than to hear
pious spiritual mumbo-jumbo from his fellow CCM artists. Years
later, in something of a role reversal, the youngest Norman started
to introduce Larry to leading figures in the L.A. scene, including

Steve Jones, the guitarist for the Sex Pistols. Larry was pleasantly surprised when Charles brought Steve around to the studio, where the trio made some off-the-cuff recordings together.

With Joe in the office at home, Charles ventured out on tour with his brother in a new backing band dubbed the Young Lions that was originally intended to bring the old Solid Rock artists together in one band. (Think: the Traveling Wilburys.) But now that there were no Solid Rock artists, Larry had to start from scratch. For the first time on tour, Larry brought backup singers, including Beki Hemingway, a distant relative of the famous novelist.[19] The group played Cornerstone in 1985, a large outdoor alternative Christian music festival in Illinois. The band then flew to play the Sydney Entertainment Theatre in Australia, to a capacity crowd in the 13,000-seat arena. Charles brought along his friends the Hoodoo Gurus—a group that, at the time, was the top pop act in Australia.[20]

Unable to finish a proper record in the studio due, according to Larry, to ongoing effects of his plane injury, he happened upon what he felt was a novel idea: a record of new songs, recorded live in Australia. Entitled *Stop This Flight*, the actual recording had been made previously at the Dallas Brooks Hall in Melbourne, on June 15, 1984. And the new Larry Norman songs weren't very, well, rock-'n'-roll. Some songs, such as "Woman of God" and "Messiah" (which made its way as a single onto the Christian charts), appealed to fans who liked more explicitly straightforward Christian messages, but struck others as being disappointingly middle-of-the-road. Photos on the album cover underscored the new "all in the family" Norman narrative—candids of Sarah and Charles, Sarah laughing in the back of a jeep in the Australian Outback, and so on.

Back in Hollywood, Sarah gave birth to Larry's son Michael in August of 1985. Larry told fans that in Sarah he had finally found his "Woman of God," and now he had a "baby of God." Born ten weeks prematurely, Michael spent the first two months of his life in an incubator—a detail that made it into the George Formby–inspired "We Three Twogether":

Held our breath for a baby boy
Big fat bundle of joy
And now we three are happy twogether

Our dearest friend, old faithful Phydeaux
He could not come along to the baby ward
But he tried, though

Love abides, life makes sense
Great big house with a little white picket fence
And now we three are happy twogether

Sarah underwent a period of postpartum depression, which set in motion a range of new and difficult family dynamics that Larry later immortalized in his song "Baby's Got the Blues." A need for a steadier financial footing was one of the Normans' main concerns. The 1985 Back in America Tour put together by New Jersey promoter Bud Pirollo promised to be a needed windfall; it was slated to be a 250-date, year-plus itinerary, at $2,000 a show. But Back to America began to crumble when the money promised for gigs mysteriously vanished or was never paid. Promoter advances and merchandise sales netted enough cash for gas, hotels, and food while the band was on the road, but it wasn't the lucrative tour the family had hoped for.

Then Jon Linn, the virtuoso guitar player and musical linchpin, abruptly left the tour, battling with alcohol addiction. Sarah was understandably concerned. At a low point, Larry found himself in the awkward position of pressuring a local concert promoter in Fort Lauderdale for the contracted fees when he didn't have them at the time. He decided to bring the tour to a close, but when he announced this to the band, he was met with howls of protest; they were supposed to be on the road for a full year and a half. But after the Solid Rock breakup, Larry couldn't handle head-to-head conflict anymore. He called up Joe, who flew to Florida, and under the cover of darkness, the three Normans packed up for home, ditching the two remaining

band members in Florida without saying goodbye. Pirollo booked
the remaining duo on a series of dates back up the East Coast. The
drummer, Kenny "Bam Boom" DeRouchie, wound up living in Pirollo's garage upon return. Needless to say, none of this helped Norman's already sour reputation in America. Neither did it help project
the image that this was a new season of wedded bliss, friendship,
and life making sense.

  A new record deal was inked in 1986, but it caught many people
in the industry by surprise: it seemed like, all of a sudden, Larry Norman was going to make nice with the CCM industry. Like the func-
tional sadist he was, Larry chose Benson Records in Nashville—an
odd choice, given that their roster included mostly light adult contemporary Christian musical artists. Benson was excited to receive what
was being billed as Larry Norman's "comeback album." But Larry's
real reason for choosing Benson was karma. Since 1970, their subsidiary NewPax Records had been pressing and selling *Upon This Rock*,
Larry's first solo record. The album was, anecdotally at least, ubiquitous, and international sub-distributors had made the album popular worldwide. But Larry never received a penny in royalties from
Benson/NewPax. Part of the negotiations for the new record deal, at
least verbally, was for Benson to make good on being in arrears—in
addition to having the honor of distributing Larry Norman's return
to form. Benson inked the deal, and sent Larry $50,000, ostensibly
to commence work on the record. Time passed. When Benson demanded the record, Larry asked where the back royalties were, since
that should come first. When they didn't make good on his request,
he lost interest in giving Benson what they wanted—an irresistible
Larry Norman record. In public, Larry continued to assert in interviews and liner notes of re-releases that the United Airlines ceiling-
panel incident had left him unable to finish a "proper" record.

  On the home front, Larry and Sarah tried to make things normal. Initially, they lived in the historic Calabasas Colony in a home
designed by Austro-American architect Rudolph Schindler.[21] They
subsequently moved into 11800 Kling Street in North Hollywood, a

Cape Cod house with a white picket fence. After years of controversy, Larry was trying to develop a "home and hearth" image. It didn't suit him well.

Meanwhile, the late 1980s saw the fall of numerous charismatic television evangelists. There was of course the sordid story of Jim and Tammy Faye Bakker, who took millions from people watching their *PTL Club* television ministry for memberships in a theme park called Heritage USA, while simultaneously paying off a woman named Jessica Hahn, who claimed that Jim Bakker had raped her. Robert Tilton made millions off followers sending in their "seed of tithe money" in exchange for a prayer hankie that had been "blessed" by the TV evangelist. Tilton was eventually exposed for his fund-raising practices by Diane Sawyer of ABC News, and was sued for fraud.

And then there was Larry's old archnemesis Jimmy Swaggart, who'd joined the parade of televangelists who endured both sex and money scandals in the 1980s. Before being caught with a hooker (actually, multiple hookers), Swaggart had doubled down on his criticism of Larry in his 1987 book, *Religious Rock 'N' Roll: A Wolf in Sheep's Clothing.*[22] When Swaggart finally had to admit to the charges against him, he delivered his now infamous "I Have Sinned" speech to his congregation in February 1988, in which he tearfully pleaded to God, his family, and his followers: "I beg you . . . forgive me." Oh the irony, Larry must have thought to himself. Larry wrote a song to be included on his forthcoming record, which included the line "My songs are spiritual fornication—that's what this television preacher said. I guess he knows a lot about it. I heard he wrote some sermons in a prostitute's bed." Benson, perhaps wisely, faded out the song before that lyric was uttered on the record, but Larry would perform the whole version live in concert anyway.

Perhaps the larger point was that the broader American public was forming the impression that evangelical Christians were a bunch of fakes and hypocrites. This was certainly a far cry from the postwar mainstream evangelicalism of figures like Billy Graham, Boston pastor Harold John Ockenga, Francis Schaeffer, and *Christianity*

Today's founding editor Carl F. H. Henry. Now, in the minds of the public, the whole movement was lumped into one big group of blustery dirtbags, and Larry Norman had little interest in it. Increasingly, he would spend as much time as he could outside of the United States.

Conveniently, he simultaneously began to realize that his brand was much bigger in Britain, Australia, and Scandinavia than it was at home. Larry fell in love with Norway while on tour there, drawing large and devoted crowds wherever he went. Evangelicals in the Scandinavian countries were not as fussy as the American evangelicals. His show at Rockegalla '85 in Norway, filmed by the cinematographer Odd Hynnekleiv and broadcast on Norwegian television, showed what a happy, confident performer Larry Norman could be.

It seemed like little good happened while Larry was at home. One morning in 1988, Larry was at home with Sarah, and was roused from sleep by the doorbell. Standing there was an officer of the court, serving him divorce papers. He took the documents up to Sarah, who confessed that yes, it was true, that she needed time to process her feelings about their marriage. The end would not officially come until 1995, and it ended slowly and rather quietly. Sarah moved to Salem, Oregon, and eventually, Larry would follow her there. They partnered in raising their son Michael together, and stayed close friends, even traveling together. Larry tried his best to convince Sarah to stay in the marriage. He even cut his hair at one point—as he had for Joe many years earlier—and applied for a real estate license in Salem in the hopes that taking up a regular job might persuade her to stick around. When master stampers for *Home at Last*—the "comeback record"—came to him on vinyl, he etched on them, "I Love You, Sarah." On the cover he would put a picture of their house on Kling Street, white picket fence and all.

The situation looked particularly bleak for him in Los Angeles in the fall of 1988. And what did Larry do when he needed to feel appreciated and understood? He returned to Europe. He teamed up with a Finnish band named Q-Stone, and planned to set out from

Helsinki for a gig in Tallinn, Estonia, then part of the USSR. The fall of 1988 found the Eastern Bloc countries tiring of the illusion of Mikhail Gorbachev's doctrine of glasnost. In June of 1987, David Bowie had returned to West Berlin, where he once lived and recorded some of his best work, and with his back to the Berlin Wall, belted out "Heroes" with his band, crying out for liberty to the crowd in German. Thousands of East Berliners pressed up against the other side of the wall to hear him. Subsequent protests against the Communist regime got the attention of the West, and one week later Ronald Reagan stood near that same place and uttered the unforgettable words: "Mr. Gorbachev, tear down this wall." As he commented on the event some years later, it was clear the event moved Bowie, who remembered that "when we [played] 'Heroes,' it was really anthemic, almost like a prayer."

Larry Norman would get his own chance to stick a thumb in the eye of the creaking Communist regime. Driving south around the Baltic Sea and the Gulf of Finland, Larry, Charles, and the boys from Q-Stone stopped initially in Leningrad (St. Petersburg), where the locals offered them ten times the government-sanctioned exchange rate for rubles to dollars, and pleaded with them to sell their Levi's and Western-style clothing. The band trod on, making their way to Tallinn. Unlike most Westerners at the time, Larry and company did not stay at the typical tourist hotel. Instead, they were booked into the Viru Hotel, which was used more frequently by government officials. Unbeknownst to them, the twenty-third floor of the Viru was local headquarters for the KGB.[23] Antennae atop what was then the tallest skyscraper in the city could pick up signals from some fifty miles away.

Although they hadn't planned it that way, Larry and Q-Stone had arrived at the zenith of what is now referred to as "The Singing Revolution"—a massive series of protests in which the people of Estonia gathered in public places to sing their national folk songs and remember what life was like before Communist rule. On September 11, 1988, 300,000 people jammed into the Tallinn Arena to declare to the Soviet Union that they intended to regain their independence once again in an event called "The Song of Estonia," a moment immortalized in the documentary film *The Singing Revolution*.[24] Apparently, the Christian promoter in Tallinn wanted to see the good news of Jesus represented during this political revolution. Who better to be the torchbearer than Larry Norman?

The band checked into the Viru late on the evening of November 14. The next morning, they walked around Tallinn. Returning to the hotel, they settled in for lunch, and a hotel employee announced to the group that, in addition to welcoming his Finnish brothers (Q-Stone), with whom Estonians shared a fraternal bond, they wanted to know who the Americans in the group were, because they had prepared a special meal of local cuisine for them. Plates were brought out, and everyone ate their fill, but shortly after the meal, Charles went to his room complaining of a raging headache. He was sweating profusely. Larry confessed to feeling strange too. He held on to the table, as it seemed the room was spinning. Asking at the front desk for aspirin, the clerk instructed Charles to return to his room and they would send someone up. Larry had already returned to his room, and that's where Charles found him.

Within minutes, an ambulance backed up onto the front steps of the hotel. Out of the vehicle scrambled three "nurses," who entered the hotel, and next the room, pointing at Larry and identifying him as "[the] sick one." One nurse demanded that Larry lie down for an examination. She proceeded to fumble with a blood-pressure monitor, uncertain, apparently, of how to use it. Prodding and tapping hard around the solar plexus, the nurse declared that Larry had a swollen appendix that was about to burst. He had to go immediately to the hospital, the nurse barked. Another nurse produced a vial and syringe and prepared to administer an injection. Larry waved off the syringe and protested vociferously that he didn't want to go to the hospital unless he had to. In the midst of this chaos, the front-desk clerk appeared in the doorway. Larry asked whether or not he had to go to the hospital, and the employee hesitated, telling Larry that it was his decision, that he could not say anything or give him any advice. Larry paused to pray to God for his situation and Charles's condition. He bowed his head and asked for the sort of moment when God confused the Moabite and Ammonite armies when they came up against King Jehoshaphat of Judah. According to Charles, an argument broke out among the nurses at that moment. During the verbal melee, the duo made their way out of the room and down to their van to drive to the show. Crisis averted.

Soviet soldiers approached them outside the venue and told them to cease and desist from proceeding indoors—that the show wasn't happening. When the show's promoter realized what the soldiers were up to, he came out and berated them for attempting to preempt the show. This was precisely what the Estonian people were sick of, he bellowed, the Soviets always telling them what to do. The band was instructed to set up and play after all.

The show had been under way for more than an hour when Soviet soldiers returned and ordered that the concert cease. Pulling the plug on the PA as well as on the video recording device (the concert was being filmed up until this point), the Normans and Q-Stone made their way backstage, where they were told to leave the country immediately. When Charles asked whether they'd be able to return to the hotel to recover their luggage, the promoter recommended that they simply get out while they still could. They drove back to Leningrad, stopping at various checkpoints where the van was searched for stowaways or contraband. By the time they returned to Helsinki the next day, the leading newspaper, *Sanomat*, filled them in on the details they seemed to have missed. They had played Tallinn, Estonia, on November 15, 1988, on the same day and at the same town hall in which the Estonian government had officially declared national sovereignty from the Soviet Union.[25] Although Estonia wouldn't fully realize independence until 1991, Larry Norman could say he had been an eyewitness to a key instance of the demise of the USSR. He too had been a part of the "Singing Revolution."[26]

Safe back in Helsinki, Larry and Charles were still feeling the after-effects of the "special meal" prepared for them in Tallinn, which they now suspected was an attempted poisoning by the KGB. The "nurses" who had attempted to administer a liquid injection to Larry and then take him to an undisclosed hospital—that scene seemed too strange to be mere happenstance. Their story bears similarities to other KGB "nurse" sightings and activities. Historian Robert Royal has chronicled the fate of Roman Catholic priests and nuns under Soviet rule, noting the role of "nurses" in poisoning religious dissenters.[27] Other reports abound of KGB nurses stabbing, for example, a family member of a sailor on the Russian submarine *Kursk* with a liquid injection in order to silence them. In this case, the cover story was that it was "medicine" for a "heart condition."[28]

According to Larry and Charles, the poison lingered in their system for a while. Charles awoke back in Finland with his head swimming, and began hyperventilating. Making his way down to the lobby, he found Larry with several other people, including Larry's friend Jennifer Robinson, who had been running the merch table at the concert in Tallinn. He complained of shortness of breath. After lying down on the couch, Charles went into convulsions and started seizing. Jennifer, a registered nurse, later told Charles on an audiotape, "You could have died." Someone called an ambulance and Charles was hurried to a hospital, where he was given oxazepam, a heavy tranquilizer, and had lab work and X-rays done.[29] Larry was also examined and treated for his symptoms (shaking, headaches), according to the hospital receipts in Larry's archive.

Originally scheduled to leave Helsinki for Sweden the following day, Charles and Larry instead stayed at Q-Stone band member Mikko Kuustonen's apartment for several days to recuperate. They spent five days doing little more than watching VHS tapes from a local video rental store. From there, they transferred to Stockholm for one night in a Gothenburg hotel, and then spent seven more days at Royal Music Studio's artist bunk rooms in Mölndal, Sweden. Then Larry began experiencing convulsions as well. When the brothers returned to America, blood tests revealed certain unidentifiable toxins in their systems. Their symptoms continued for months until gradually subsiding. This near miss with the KGB would become a legendary piece of Norman lore for years to come.

When Benson Records wrote Larry to inquire how close he was to finishing *Home at Last*, he demurred, saying he had assumed that the $50,000 was a first installment for unpaid royalties from *Upon This Rock*. More time passed. Benson eventually dispatched a processor to Larry's home to demand delivery of the record or face legal action. Larry cobbled together existing studio recordings and demos, and turned it in as the finished record. It was a pretty cheeky, if self-destructive, move, but Larry had finally had it with the Christian record label industry.

11

JESUS VERSUS LARRY NORMAN?

B Y THE DAWN OF THE 1990s, LARRY NORMAN WAS FACING THE prospect of being relegated to the Oldies category. *Home at Last* was greeted eagerly by fans and panned by critics. For both, it prompted a question: Why did the record sound so contented? Why were there so few political statements—long a staple of Larry Norman records? In a press interview, one reporter asked why Larry Norman seemed to be stuck in the '60s. Rather than take the bait, he feigned umbrage: "Stuck in the '60s? That's not true! I'm stuck in the '50s!"

By this point, Larry had moved out of the white-picket-fence house with Sarah, and was living with Charles on Riverside Drive in L.A. Living with Charles was an altogether new experience for Larry. Charles inhabited the world of punk rock and glam-metal bands, which sometimes gave the Father of Jesus Rock the chance to show up at parties where he did not quite know how to behave. The two befriended Martha Quinn, one of the original MTV VJs, with whom they had dinners and played Scrabble.[1] But if Larry felt somewhat disconnected culturally, it was nothing compared to his overall scattered approach to life since the plane accident. Phydeaux record label associates like Bill Ayers noted Larry's inability to complete everyday tasks, and family members testified to his literal inability to bring back milk from the grocery store. Although he seemed able to perform songs in concert well enough, he complained that he couldn't remember how to produce a record or hear the right mix. Every LP since the accident—including *Something New Under the Son*, which sounded decidedly "unslick"—seemed to confirm his testimony.

For the first time in a long time, Larry Norman was largely at loose ends. "What did it matter anymore? I feel that my life is over," Larry recounted in his diary. "I am alone, and I will have brain damage for the rest of my life, and I have little to offer anyone, except to give them the gospel of Christ."[2]

Other than hanging out with his five-year-old son, Mike, there was not much to do. Charles was busy with Jetboy, a new band he'd joined. Mostly, Larry hung out in Los Angeles, going to the movies, and hitting the magazine stand to get the latest copy of *Vanity Fair* or *The Atlantic* and bringing home matzo-ball soup from Jerry's Famous Deli in Studio City. Then in February 1991, on the heels of a British tour, something unexpected happened. Larry went to Croydon, in south London, for a meeting of fellow believers in the home of his friend Dave Markee. A fellow musician, Markee had played bass in Eric Clapton's band, in addition to performing the signature bass line for Henry Mancini's "Pink Panther Theme." During the evening, a pastor, John Barr, singled out Larry to give him a "word of knowledge." Barr uttered a cryptic prophecy about a plane being unable to take off due to too much baggage. He laid hands on Larry, and Larry claimed to have felt a crackling in his head. Whatever actually happened, the result was that Larry claimed to be healed, and ready to reengage the creative process.

He felt clear-headed once again, even "back from the dead."[3] Larry teamed up with Charles to begin work on a new record. Charles had acquired an Apple computer with a digital sequencer and a new mixing board. He would write chord progressions and guitar hooks, and pass them along via cassette to Larry, who would write the lyrics and come up with melodies. An invitation from a charismatic preacher, Aril Edvardsen at Sarons Dal, Kvinesdal, Norway, for Larry to have free rein at their recording facilities in exchange for a concert at the church was too good to pass up. The brothers Norman bought one-way tickets, and Charles sequestered himself at the church's spartan studio for months at a time, while Larry shuttled back and forth to the United States and Europe for concerts.

The result was a creative triumph. *Stranded in Babylon* was filled with quirky sampling, synth loops, and innovative guitar work. The finished product possessed an early electronica feel (there were no live drums), and was universally regarded as Larry Norman's return to form. Although Charles played all of the instruments on the record, Larry brought the goods as far as lyrics and melodies went. The writing reclaimed the social and political commentary that had gone missing on the last few records. A standout was "Step into the Madness," which featured the following critique of both the nation and the Church:

> *Where the local church is closed except a couple times a week*
> *And turns its face from all the homeless in the street*
>
> *This is America*
> *Land of the free*
> *Everyone gets justice*
> *And liberty*
> *If you got the money*
>
> *Bankers and controllers make deals on foreign shores*
> *And the CIA ships heroin to finance their secret wars*
>
> *They sell the madmen weapons then send soldiers to their*
>   *land*
> *And in the name of God we battle for all the oil under the*
>   *sand*

Larry Norman was back. *Babylon* demonstrated that he could rock 'n' roll again. Throughout the album, Larry portrayed himself as a protagonist engaging in dangerous behavior that still seemed curiously righteous, as evidenced in the song "Come Away," which spoke of Larry's experience street witnessing in 1973 to prostitute Hope Valentine in London's Shepherd's Bush neighborhood. Valentine later became a Christian.[4] All of this rekindled the Larry Norman mystique, and confirmed in the minds of admirers that no one could balance on the knife's edge quite like he could. Riding high on the renewed sense of success, Larry mounted an extensive tour, traversing ground in Sweden, Finland, the UK, Germany, Holland, Norway, the USSR, Poland, and Belgium. By this point, Larry Norman was a much bigger act in Europe than in the States. In the Scandinavian countries especially, he was a household name, as his appearances on television and frequency at festivals attested. In the United States, he embodied the "prophet unknown in his own town," but who cared at this point? He had survived.

Then, just at the peak of his renaissance, disaster struck once again. On February 27, 1992, Larry called his brother from a Kinko's in Studio City, California, complaining of chest pains. Could they go to the hospital? Charles drove him to North Hollywood Hospital, where they hooked him up to an EKG, concluded nothing was going on, and sent him home. The next day Larry visited his general practitioner, Gerald Labiner, and was told he probably just had esophagitis, and not to worry. The next morning, Larry and Charles grabbed breakfast at the Four 'n' 20 Restaurant in Laurel Canyon. Charles was gearing up to travel with Guns N' Roses on their *Use Your Illusion* tour, and the brothers had a lot to celebrate after the success of *Babylon*. During breakfast, Larry began to experience chest pains again. As the discomfort transitioned to explicit pain, he phoned Dr. Labiner, who reiterated his diagnosis of esophagitis. When Larry called back a few minutes later, he was screaming to the office receptionist about being in pain, but the doctor demurred again, and told Larry that he was overreacting to his symptoms. After several hours, a phoned-in prescription for antacid pills that Larry promptly vomited up, twice, and a referral to a chiropractor who referred Larry to another chiropractor, who finally insisted they make haste to the nearest hospital, Charles rushed Larry to

Cedars Sinai Hospital, where, after waiting on a gurney in a supply closet for hours with no attention, an EKG confirmed that, in fact, Larry had suffered a major heart attack. Doctors performed an angioplasty, at which point he became unconscious. Larry later commented on his disappointment that, while he was near death during the procedure, he did not see a bright light above him, or any recently departed relatives beckoning him on. What he experienced was, well, just nothing. Darkness.[5]

The physicians' order sheets and cath lab reports from Cedars Sinai read like a horror show. The list of medications and labs ordered was pages long, and included Dilaudid, a high-powered opiate, in addition to various blood thinners, such as heparin, to address Larry's "sinus tachycardia" heart attack, an "acute septal infarction."[6] Keeping a low profile, Larry nonetheless had family and other well-wishers coming to pay him visits, among them his old friend Andraé Crouch. When he emerged from the hospital, his medical bills were astronomical. Larry's health insurance had lapsed after he separated from Sarah, since she took care of such details when they were still together.

Meanwhile the city of Los Angeles itself was descending into chaos. On April 29, 1992, the four LAPD officers on trial for the beating of Rodney King—a cataclysmic event captured on amateur videotape—were acquitted of all charges of police brutality. As angry protesters gathered outside police headquarters, riots broke out on the corners of Florence and Normandie Avenues. By 6:45 that evening, news choppers captured truck driver Reginald Denny being pulled out of his vehicle and assaulted. Meanwhile up in the Hollywood Hills, a convalescing Larry Norman had brought his son, Michael, to Andraé Crouch's home to be baptized in the swimming pool. Videotape of the event shows Crouch pronouncing the Trinitarian formula in the water standing over the six-year-old while Los Angeles was in flames in the background.

Larry eventually sued Cedars Sinai for malpractice, and won. His court case took place, incidentally, at the Los Angeles Superior Court, down the hall from where the O. J. Simpson trial was simultaneously occurring. Charles remembers passing Johnnie Cochran and Marcia Clark in the corridors during lunch breaks. In another strange celebrity crossover, Dr. Labiner would eventually be investigated for treating Michael Jackson before the singer's untimely death.

Facing mounting deadlines on medical bills, Larry took a gig in Dallas, Texas, for some much-needed cash. The intimate show, later released under the title *Totally Unplugged: (a)Live and Kicking*, featured the new Larry Norman: relaxed, weak, and genuinely grateful for his fans, who now to him seemed indistinguishable from friends. The recording documents the appeal of later Larry Norman shows. It was less a concert, and more a meditation on the perverse core of a society that had forgotten God. As always, Larry's voice was drenched in reverb, but gone was his itchy response to fans clapping during the songs. With all of the blood thinners he was on, Larry had grown a big, bushy beard, and looked something like Gregg Allman meets Grizzly Adams.

Two days after the show, he collapsed on the sidewalk and was rushed to Parkland Memorial Hospital, where doctors diagnosed him with congestive heart failure. This time, the culprit appeared to be medicine that slowed his heart down.[7] When he returned to Los Angeles, his medical team strictly instructed him to cease and desist performing until a new regimen of medicine and treatment placed him in a stronger position physically.

The year 1992 continued its string of terrible events when Mark Heard suffered a heart attack onstage at the Cornerstone Music Festival, while performing with Pierce Pettis and Kate Miner. He was rushed to the hospital, but died two weeks later after going into cardiac arrest. The news hit Larry hard. Mark had not survived, but he had. Why? Mark Heard was the one friend Larry felt understood the dark absurdities of the world of human affairs—but never succumbed to cynicism. "He was perhaps the gentlest and kindest of any musician I have ever known," Larry would later reminisce. "He rarely said anything negative about anyone, at least not to me."[8] By the time of his death, Heard had become one of the most critically acclaimed songwriters and producers of his generation, and had long since left the idiosyncrasies of the Christian music industry behind him. In 2012, twenty years after his death, *Christianity Today* feted Heard with remembrances from such artists as Buddy Miller, Bruce Cockburn, Victoria Williams, and others. Among those contacted for comment was Randy Stonehill. His entry read: "Stonehill says though he spent a lot of time with Heard, they never become close friends: 'Mark was a complex, deep man who valued his privacy and, more often than not, held his cards pretty close to his chest.'" But Larry had a different perspective. In one of the final interviews he gave before his own death in 2008, Larry remarked:

> I've never gotten over Mark Heard passing away. He was really my best friend, and the one who was the most similar to me in Christian music. And I still miss him so much. And I don't know if I'll ever get over that.... I think Mark Heard was very funny. I don't think most people sitting in the room would say he was funny, but to me it was hilarious because it was the truth.[9]

Diminished by his most recent cardiac event, Larry nonetheless trod on. He took opportunities to play when, and if, he could. Meanwhile skepticism mounted from the emerging Internet community, and holdover grudges within the CCM community wondered aloud whether Larry Norman was really that sick. If his plane accident wasn't as serious as he had made out, couldn't he be capable of faking a heart attack? Old animosities continued to simmer. At one of the large outdoor Christian music festivals in 1993, Randy Stonehill took on duties as emcee. Although Stonehill took great pleasure in introducing the various acts at the concert, when it was Larry's turn to perform, Randy allowed someone else to do the honors. Taking the stage, Larry ignored the snub, and told the thousands of fans gathered that, given his health situation, he didn't know if and when he would be able to perform again. Still, his old friend's refusal to introduce him did not go unnoticed. Onstage the Christian rock stars spoke of love and forgiveness, but the real message came through loud and clear: old wounds die hard and pettiness is forever.

FROM THAT POINT on until 2007, the announcement of a Larry Norman concert took on a macabre, voyeuristic appeal. On a tour in Holland in 1993, scheduled performances were abruptly canceled when Larry spent ten days in a hospital in Drachten, suffering from a ventricular arrhythmia.[10] The incident became national news in the Netherlands, and a TV host was dispatched to Larry's bedside to ask him what it felt like to come back from the dead. Larry corrected the reporter. He had died once, at Cedars Sinai in L.A., but his recent two episodes were something like aftershocks. The Dutch interviewer then asked how his perspective on life had changed. What did the "real world" look like on the other side?

> It looks pretty silly—that I would have worried about small things so much that didn't matter. When you realize how much control God has over your death and your life, then why should you worry about what happens in five years. [Will] I lose my job? [Will] I ever find someone to love me? We shouldn't worry about that, we should just think about today, and give each day to God. "I trust you to take care of me today, and I will also try to take care of myself, to live in a right way." And don't worry about tomorrow, worry about right now.[11]

After being discharged from the hospital, Larry convalesced at a bucolic goat farm in Oudebroek—which translates into English as "old pants." And that's what Larry, in a manner of speaking, had become. The father of Jesus rock now felt like a grandfather. Charles peeled away from the Guns N' Roses European tour (where he had been a special guest to the band) to rejoin Larry on the farm, as nurse and friend. For weeks on end, the brothers did little but amble around the pastures, and bottle feed the baby goats. Two of the kids were albino goats, which their owner appropriately named Charlie and Larry.

The time had come, however, for a different kind of divorce for Larry Norman. Since 1968, he and L.A. had been entwined—both the glamour and the horror inseparable from one another. But when the Northridge Earthquake, which measured 6.7 on the Richter scale, shook the San Fernando Valley in January of 1994, Charles returned home to find their apartment building rendered uninhabitable. It was the last straw for the "Albino Brothers," as they dubbed themselves, where L.A. was concerned. Preferring to be near both Larry's son and their parents, who had also moved to Salem, Oregon, the brothers loaded two semi-trucks filled with personal effects, master tapes, and equipment, and struck out for the Pacific Northwest.

The ensuing decade of Larry Norman's life was a tale of both rapprochement and remonstrance. In 1995, a group of prominent CCM artists recorded a cover album called *One Way: The Songs of Larry Norman* on Forefront Records, but some of the artists had to get permission from their pastors before paying tribute to the controversial star. *CCM* had run an article saying that Larry Norman was a "black cloud" whose friends had all abandoned him.[12] As a joke, Larry took Charles out behind a restaurant, and asked him to photograph him on the ground, looking dazed, next to a Dumpster: "Larry Norman on the skids." At least he wasn't taking himself so seriously anymore. He began bringing Mike onstage with him to sing. He appealed to his fans to contribute to his medical fund. The biggest expense was an implanted defibrillator to prevent dysrhythmia, which could lead to a fatal cardiac event.

The medical fund was seen as tasteless at best and a scam at worst by his many detractors in the Christian media. One night in Anaheim in the early 2000s, Charles's band Softcore was playing a showcase for NAMM. The group had been working with actor Kiefer Sutherland on a new album, and were on the cusp of signing a major label deal. Unexpectedly, Charles and his wife, Kristin, ran into Michael Roe, the front man from the Christian alternative group the Seventy Sevens, and Terry Taylor, from Daniel Amos. Roe launched into a litany of rumors that had been swirling around his social circles, not least that Larry's health problems were being exaggerated for personal financial gain. Roe was caught off-guard when Charles began weeping openly. Charles explained how sick his brother really was. A couple of years later, Roe wrote Larry personally to apologize. In truth, he confessed, Larry had never been anything but kind to him at festivals such as Cornerstone, and even to the point of appearing with Roe in concert when the musician was passing through Oregon.[13] Another Christian journalist admitted his own skepticism of Larry's condition until he met with the artist in person. When Larry unbuttoned his shirt and displayed the defibrillator, he was shamefaced.

By the year 2000, a new season of openness seemed to characterize Larry's relationship with Randy Stonehill. While lingering questions still hung in the air, the pair teamed up for the CD re-release of *Welcome to Paradise* in commemoration of Solid Rock's twenty-fifth anniversary. Then, having escaped the threat of Y2K, Randy greeted 2001 by sending Larry the news that their mutual friend, Jon Linn, the guitarist extraordinaire of numerous Solid Rock records and tours, had been struck fatally by a car while walking near his home in Palmdale, California. Randy noted the irony that, just as he and Larry were starting to work together again, a member of the gang had been taken away from them.[14]

By April of that year, Stonehill also felt emboldened enough to ask Larry for financial assistance. He had been asked to "pay up" or face the consequences for medical bills that had recently surprised him. Could he receive $3,000 in advances against the royalties for the *Paradise* re-release? Given their "colorful and unique history" together, Randy felt slightly sheepish about asking, but Larry immediately responded that while he didn't think the forthcoming record would ever recoup that much money in mechanical royalties, he'd like to give the money to Randy as an outright gift.[15] Within days, however, Randy managed to come up with the cash via alternative means, and wished Larry a happy birthday on April 8.

The spirit of reconciliation continued later that summer. On Wednesday, July 4, Randy was slated to play the side stage in the "Legends" tent at the Cornerstone Music Festival. Having run through his acoustic set, Stonehill launched into his popular gospel song "Good News." His backing band was Daniel Amos, of all people. Just like at Greenbelt 1980, Larry bounded out onstage to a delighted roar of the crowd, and Randy cried, "Will you all please welcome Larry Norman!" At that announcement, Stonehill remembered, "the whole place lit up with flash bulbs. It reminded me of a pop show at the fabulous Forum. We spent the next couple of hours hanging out backstage and then watching Daniel Amos play."[16] The moment came, and then passed. In a subsequent interview after Larry had died, Randy indicated that he allowed the joint appearance because he was trying to help Larry out during a difficult time.[17] That explanation seems somewhat implausible, given the fact while Stonehill was playing one of the side-stage tents, Larry would headline the main stage with a full band the following Saturday.[18]

Larry's main-stage performance at Cornerstone 2001 stood out as perhaps the last time he could perform with a band and still sound like Larry Norman. The festival organizers apparently requested that he stick to hits from his 1970s golden period, so he launched into classics like "Why Don't You Look into Jesus?," "Shot Down," "I've Searched All Around the World," and of course, "Why Should the Devil Have All the Good Music?" Speaking to the crowd, Larry reflected on the huge commercial industry that had grown in the wake of his pioneering work in light of the fact that, physically speaking, he felt like every day could be his last:

> It's nice to be here. It's nice to be anywhere. There's a lot of different kind of music here. Christian reggae, like Christ-afarian. Christian rap. [mock tone] "Whatever the world's got? We've got it too! Hey, we're imitators of Christ!" But hey, there's a lot of

different kinds of Christian music now. I kind of liked it better
when I was the only one.[19]

The year 2001 also marked the last year that Larry was able to release a proper record. With the help of Charles and his bandmates in
Guards of Metropolis (which included Charles' wife, vocalist Kristin
Blix; bassist Silver Sorensen; and drummer Jason Carter), he was
able to finish *Tourniquet*. The record featured the environmentalist
screed "Turn," and also "Feed the Poor," whose lyrics seemed to suggest that the final evidence of Christian conversion was how much
money one gave to the poor during one's lifetime. Although *Tourniquet* lacked the epic scope of his earlier work, it made up for it in its
sheer cool factor, with the Guards providing the sonic template. Not
unlike Bob Dylan, he realized in his later career that he could not
recapture the muse of his earliest writing.

After his triumph both with Randy and on the main stage at
Cornerstone, Larry flew to the UK to play a few dates. When he
landed back in the States, he was taken straight from baggage claim
to the hospital. With a few exceptions, his career as an active touring
and recording artist was effectively over. When the Gospel Music
Association invited Larry to Nashville to receive their Hall of Fame
introduction that November, he was not well enough to be there
in person. Appropriately enough, he was inducted alongside Elvis
Presley—both artists whom the Church had difficulty recognizing
as their own throughout their careers, and yet could not ignore.

Elvis had received his award posthumously, and Larry seemingly
barely pre-posthumously. His son, Mike, traveled to the ceremony to
accept the award on his father's behalf, and the Christian hip-hop
group DC Talk performed their rendition of Larry's song "I Wish
We'd All Been Ready," which they had included on their bestsell-
ing 1995 record *Jesus Freak*. The printed program for the evening
included the following assessment of Larry's contribution: his music
"exemplified the goals, ideals, and standards of everything the original architects of contemporary Christian music intended it to be."[20]

Oh, the irony! The Christian music industry was honoring Larry Norman for helping to give them standards? He must have felt like a failure.

LARRY'S REMAINING YEARS in Salem were a revolving door of hospital stays, doctor visits, and ambulance rides. When he felt well enough, he could get out with family and local friends. His mother was still alive, and the two remained close. When Jason Carter, who also worked with Larry on graphic design for his steady stream of album rarities and re-releases, invited him to join his bowling league, Larry was game. His bowling team featured another musical legend, finger-style guitarist John Fahey. In 2003, Larry told Christian music journalist John J. Thompson:

> As for my current health, I still have congestive heart failure problems and was even in the hospital this last week. . . . It happens often enough that it's more of a cliché than an exception to my current problems.
>
> I can rarely go to the computer and get on the internet because the electricity in the room makes me so sick that my heart starts to speed up and the electricity affects the defibrillator/pacemaker. So, for instance, I am typing this on a laptop. I have to stop when the battery goes down and re-charge it. I can't type on it if it's plugged in.
>
> Two or three nights a week I feel on the verge of throwing up and my pulse starts going up toward 180 beats a minute—which would set off my defibrillator which means I'll end back up at the hospital. So my sister often sits up with me and I have to take medicines to slow my pulse down and then when I'm asleep she can go to bed. Or my son has to sit with me because my sister is gone, that is very hard on his health since he has to get up at 7:00 a.m. [to go to school]. . . . [and] despite what's happening to me on and off all the time, I try not to concentrate on that. I read the

Bible, I call my mother, I pray until I fall asleep. I wake up every morning being so glad that I get to see the sun shine in the windows again. I'm really in love with life. And in love with God.[21]

Thanks to his family's efforts, Larry was able to record occasionally and keep re-releasing albums and rarities from his extensive archives. Although he invited friends like former People! drummer Denny Fridkin to live with him to help take care of his medical needs, at the end of the day, he leaned most heavily on those nearest and dearest to him: his relatives. As long as Larry kept it "all in the family," everything went just fine. Although he had fine working relationships with Bill Ayers (Phydeaux) and Kerry Hopkins (the later Solid Rock Records, based in Oregon), Larry loved working with his sister-in-law, Kristin Blix, most of all. A painter of extraordinary ability and a gifted vocalist, Kristin was intellectually and artistically Larry Norman's match. She kept the Solid Rock business office humming, would book concerts for Larry when he felt well enough to play, and was gloriously free of the Christian subculture. While she was interested in Jesus and spiritual things, her independence and intelligence came as a welcome, late-in-life gift to Larry, who had, by his own admission, never understood the opposite sex. She challenged him when he was wrong, but would stay up into the wee small hours with him talking about the Bible. Later, in his last few months of life, Kristin asked him if there was anything left that he wanted to do before he died. He thought about it, and said yes. Larry owned a Porsche that had been given to him by a friend: "I wanna take that car out and drive it really fast." Blix remembers a harrowing tour of Oregon backroads, playfully regretting climbing into the car with a cardiac patient whose motor skills were not exactly top-notch.

Although he definitely was descending into old codgerdom, Larry enjoyed, at least to some extent, not mattering anymore. Mark Rodgers, Wedgwood Circle founder and former aide to Sen. Rick Santorum, had introduced Larry to Bono, who was delighted to meet

Larry, and take him backstage at a U2 concert. Rodgers also arranged for Larry to meet President George W. Bush at the White House and perform, but storms on the East Coast caused him to miss the opportunity. Additionally, Larry found out that Daniel Smith of the alternative rock band Danielson was an admirer, and sent the young artist a kooky, ALL CAPS email of introduction. In Oregon, Charles introduced his brother to Mark Lemhouse, an American blues and roots musician. Black Francis of the band the Pixies, who lived an hour south in Eugene, also came around frequently to spend time with Larry. On Friday, June 24, 2005, Larry's friends and family staged a show at the Elsinore Theatre in Salem, Oregon, for another concert that could very likely be his swan song. *Christianity Today* covered the show as the end of the road for a polarizing and consequential figure in modern Christianity.[22] The end of the concert featured the venerable Guards of Metropolis as the band, Mark Lemhouse on guitar, and Black Francis trading vocals with Larry on "Watch What You're Doing." What other Christian rock act was performing with the front man of the Pixies?

But it was Larry's intimate, solo performance at the piano during the show that resonated most. With his voice weak and cracking on the high end, he sang songs that he remembered his mother and father liked, such as "The Moon's a Harsh Mistress" and "Few Days with You." Walking out onstage, he was dressed, uncharacteristically, in a tux and tails. He sat down at the piano and, Victor Borge–style, made a comedic production of getting ready to play, and launched into a children's song he'd written, sung in the voice of a five-year-old, with the *r*'s and *l*'s replaced by *w*'s:

> *Oh the Wabbit Woved the Twain,*
> *and the Twain Woved the Wabbit*
> *They would play and play all day.*
> *Then a man told the Wabbit that the Twain*
> *Would move to Baltimore*
> *And that's when they decided they would both wun away!*

And so the Wabbit started Wunning for the Twain
The Twain caught the Wabbit and they never looked back.
And the last they were seen
They were disapeawing
Down the twacks

It is hard to know what Larry meant by this performance, but one cannot help but see it as a metaphor for the singer's life. Larry and Jesus are the rabbit and the train. He wanted to be Elvis, and yet tell people about Jesus. He rode on the Jesus train for four decades. Despite the narcissism of his youth, the grandiose ambitions of an artists' colony and Solid Rock, and two failed marriages, in the end it was just Larry Norman and Jesus, disappearing down the tracks. He simply left behind anyone who didn't fit into that narrative.

With his health continuing to fade, Larry still managed to make one or two more performances. In 2007, he reunited with his fellow bandmates from People! for an induction into the San Jose Rock and Roll Hall of Fame. Larry was twice inducted—once for the band, and additionally as a solo artist.[23] His last official concert would be on August 4, 2007, in New York City, at Calvary Baptist Church, the same venue he had played thirty-five years earlier at the height of the Jesus movement. Former People! bandmate Denny Fridkin joined Larry to play bongos and sing along, for old times' sake. The trademark humor was still intact, however: "In China, if you become a Christian, you may be imprisoned. In India, your parents may disown you. In the Middle East, they might execute you. But in America, if you become a Christian, you just have a broader selection of Christian CDs to choose from."[24]

The concerts at Elsinore and in New York would have been a fitting farewell, but as fate would have it—and perhaps appropriately, given the controversy he generated all his life—Larry Norman would die amidst a brewing and very public scandal. For years, Larry was dogged by allegations that he had fathered the child of his former associate Jennifer Wallace (née Robinson), who had distributed his records and merchandise and worked as a sometimes promoter for him in Australia. A blog post written after Norman's death in 2008 laid out the details.[25] Her story was as follows: She was with Larry during the fall 1988 tour, which included the infamous swing into Tallinn, Estonia. She claimed that this is when she got pregnant. Jennifer further alleged that Larry was aware of the pregnancy before Daniel was born, and promised to marry her. She claimed that Larry repeated this promise over the years, as well as his intention to bring her and Daniel to live with him in the United States. Jennifer and Daniel had visited Larry when he was still living in Los Angeles in 1994. But Larry broke his promises, she claimed, and acknowledged his son Michael as his only child. For Jennifer, the story was as old as Isaac and Ishmael.

The charges were picked up by an enterprising documentary filmmaker named David Di Sabatino, who had begun to investigate the story after getting in touch with Robinson years earlier. He found her story credible, and decided to take it upon himself to expose Larry Norman as a fraud and a predator. Di Sabatino had corresponded with Larry over the years about his interest in the Jesus movement, and he had done a bit of scholarly work documenting the movement as a cultural phenomenon. That research initially resulted in a film on Lonnie Frisbee, a rising star preacher and wunderkind in Chuck Smith's Calvary Chapel Church in Costa Mesa, California. Frisbee died of AIDS in 1993, and the film chronicled his rejection by the Christian community in general, and by Calvary Chapel in particular, for being gay. Larry's attendance at the film's premiere wound up engendering a "scene" when he made his presence known to the audience during the Q&A following the screening. The kerfuffle bizarrely ended up attracting the attention of Mark Driscoll, then the star pastor of Mars Hill Church in Seattle. Driscoll was curious as to why two long-haired hippie Jesus Freaks had warranted so much attention.[26]

Di Sabatino's *Fallen Angel: The Outlaw Larry Norman* was released a little more than a year after Larry died. The film was possessed of a split personality: on the one hand, it assailed its subject's life and character with glee. On the other hand, the movie almost functioned as a group therapy session for everyone who had ever felt wronged by Larry Norman. Fans thought some of the material in the film hard to swallow, including a charge that Charles was actually Larry's son, not his baby brother, and that he was conceived when a witch wandered out of the forest at a Christian music festival in 1969 and made love to Larry in the center of a pentagram. Despite producing his certified birth certificate from 1965, with Joe and Margaret Norman listed as his parents, Charles still couldn't convince the doubters. Even Pam repeated the rumor on Facebook. Charles couldn't believe it; he had photos from Larry and Pam's wedding in 1971, in which he was a ring bearer, and very clearly more than two years old. When interviewed about this, Charles repeatedly expressed his exasperation at his attempts to settle the matter once and for all.

From a media perspective, and most important, *Fallen Angel* dropped the bombshell about Larry's "love child." It is important not to bury the lede. Di Sabatino was telling a tragic story: there was a young man living in Australia who wanted to know his father, and both he and his mother were convinced Larry Norman was that man.

"Larry Norman's tragic post-mortem," as a story in Christian news-magazine *World* put it, painted the portrait of a late-in-life, narcissistic rock star who couldn't admit he had fathered a son out of wedlock.[27] Emails they had obtained from Norman to Daniel Robinson were, in fact, at one point signed "Dad." Larry purportedly admitted to the affair with Jennifer in these emails, and blamed the rumors surrounding it for the decline of his popularity and concert bookings. In one email, he blamed his 1994 heart attack on stress caused by the allegations—a cruel thing to write to any adolescent young man, for certain.

If the allegations were true that Larry indeed had a son with a woman he never married, and never acknowledged the child, a different lens is needed to understand and assess the central figure of this story. For years, he rather righteously judged the sins of his erstwhile friends and colleagues. Was he just as guilty as the rest? Is this story true? Did Larry Norman ever privately admit that this young man was really his son?

Some anecdotal evidence suggests he did. When Larry was preparing his will, his response to his attorney when asked how many children he had was the following: there was Michael, and there was a young man in Australia who claimed to be his son. Larry conceded that it might be possible that such was the case but would not acknowledge it as a certainty. Daniel was not included in Larry's will. And yet, on the other hand, there was Daniel's birth announcement, which was sent to all of Jennifer's friends and family. It listed Jennifer as the mother, and under the name of the father, it read: "David Rose." Who is/was David Rose?

If the allegations were true, Jennifer and her family had the patience of Job. They waited some nineteen years to reveal the truth to the media, and only after Larry was dead. Digging through the archives Larry left behind reveals the events that unfolded behind the scenes. Emails sent from Larry to Jennifer in March 2006 confirm his invitation to fly Daniel to the United States to begin the process of determining if the boy was his son. Larry suggested that the two take a DNA test, and if the results showed that Daniel was his, Larry would host an event, invite him onstage, and make an announcement to the effect that he was the boy's father. Kristin and Larry arranged for a bank transfer for Daniel's airfare. Then things seemed to hit a snag. Jennifer Wallace proposed that Daniel might not want to fly to the USA to see Larry unless that could be combined with a trip to Europe too. Larry wanted Jennifer and Daniel's social security and/or "person" number, Jennifer's home address, and the name of another relative to call in case of emergency. "There is too much liability in hosting a young man to visit without comprehensive information and a written form. Signed by you and witnessed by a notary public," he wrote coolly. But then Kristin Blix insisted on a change of plans. Instead of wiring money to Jennifer's bank account, she suggested Jennifer should pick a date for Daniel to travel and that Larry would buy a ticket for him.

At this point, communications between the parties ceased. Larry and Kristin did not hear back regarding these requests. For whatever reason, Jennifer and her family stalled for nearly two years . . . until Larry died. There would be legal correspondence about Larry's will in the year following his death, but the window for bringing a definitive conclusion to the case had passed.[28]

For many believers, Christianity contains two essential elements: certain doctrines about who God is and how he acted in the world through Jesus; and a series of rules as to when, and with whom, a person may have sex. For Larry, there was irony in all of this. His sister-in-law, Kristin Blix, once remarked that her assessment of Larry's life was that he never had enough sex. The double irony is that Larry was quite possibly the only honest-to-goodness rock star who was expected not to act like one. His strange marriages to Pamela and Sarah both fizzled, although he remained faithful to them as long as they were together. When Sarah left him, he felt lost, and when finally confronted by a woman who genuinely seemed to be in love with him—Jennifer Robinson—he froze. Yes, in biblical terms, he appeared to have committed fornication somewhere on tour in the fall of 1988. But it also seems almost certain that he never truly found love, let alone found it combined with sex. Some of his most beloved songs contain references to abstinence, or present sexual relations as something with deeply frightening results. This theme popped up throughout Larry Norman's career, as evidenced by an article he wrote at the height of the Jesus movement entitled, generically, "Love and Sex." He wanted to send it to *Time* and *Newsweek* for publication, but never finished it. But the words he wrote would turn out to be prescient in terms of his own biography:

I remember a time when I thought sex was an act of inter-urination, and earlier thought it was a bumping of behinds, and finally came closer to the truth when I later thought it to be a strange *labor* of trying to melt together to get inside each other. For what purpose I didn't know.

Somehow, I have come to long for those days of innocence. Not that they were realistic or practical or even desirable, but because I am so over-burdened with the knowledge of precise intercourse, I am repulsed by it. Not by sex. But repulsed by the diagrams, charts, and descriptions that are printed on my mind.

Sounds, words, and images [are thrust at us] like sitting through a film festival and then [being] asked to discern between the real and the unreal—only in life we must deal with the real and the imposed real. . . .

Sex is not everyone's media, and that is nothing to feel guilty about. There are a whole array of other interests to excel in. . . .

And so here we are.

Just as it is more regrettable to die if life has not really been lived, so it is more lamentable to have had a life of sex without love.[29]

Larry found out the hard way: waiting for true love meant waiting for a lifetime. In the meantime, he mostly missed out on sex too. Whatever had happened in the fall of 1988 with Jennifer, it was a grim reminder to him that both sex and true love are all too rare and vexing to find in the world of the real.

IN THE LAST few weeks of his life, as Larry declined further and further in his hospital bed in Oregon, he couldn't see any of this coming. Gone were his long, flowing locks of blond hair, the clicks of cameras, and the furious correspondence. A hospital nurse had shorn him of his hair, like he was Samson. What he could see all around him were his family and friends. Charles Thompson, aka Black Francis, came to say his goodbyes, as did longtime fans turned friends such as Derek Robertson, a Scot who volunteered vacation days to help Solid Rock with day-to-day business. Family gathered around. They whispered their final I-love-yous.

When Larry passed away, on February 24, 2008, Christian journalists went in search of Randy Stonehill for comment. Randy released a statement to the effect that while he probably knew the late Larry Norman better than anyone, he was a cipher whom no one could really get to know, and who never even really understood himself. He signed off by both acknowledging Larry's contributions to his *Edge of the World* CD, and to the kingdom of God, but left one zinger for the end. In conclusion, Randy mused, Larry Norman had finally laid his "struggles with his demons" to rest. For Stonehill, the only exorcism that could cure Larry was death. The Christian media seemingly nodded along with this sentiment.

The secular media was far more kind. NPR feted the late father of Christian rock, and interviewed his brother, Charles, on *Morning Edition*.[30] *Rolling Stone*, NPR, and other leading music journals gave glowing reviews to the two-CD retrospective, *Rebel Poet, Jukebox Balladeer*, that appeared in the wake of Larry's passing.[31] The *Times* of London wrote: "Many of the younger generation of Christian musicians have spoken of their debt to Norman, and hundreds of cover versions of his songs have been recorded. Modern Christian rock has moved away from its hippyish beginnings, but Norman welcomed the vitality of the many Goth and metal-influenced acts who play to packed festivals of young people across the US. 'Christian music isn't supposed to be polite.' [Norman said] 'It's supposed to be relevant.'"[32] The *New York Times* took special note that while Larry preached "conventional spiritual messages," he was willing to take on the Church's real problems, like rooting out bigotry, confronting poverty, and talking about real life.[33] *Entertainment Weekly* remembered Christian rock's seemingly only "maverick."[34] The Grammy Awards honored him in the tribute segment of the year's departed artists. For their part, *Spin* magazine honored Norman's memory with a full-page back inside cover tribute, complete with custom artwork. The author, Andrew Beaujon, enthused over Larry's antiestablishment stance, and his confession that "the church never felt like home." Beaujon interviewed Black Francis, and enjoyed what he heard:

> Black Francis met Norman at an early Pixies show at the Roxy, in L.A., and the two stayed in touch. He was struck by the company Norman kept—"the studded nose-ring dude who did porno soundtracks with his porno-actress girlfriend, people obviously not part of his circle . . . The Christian church makes a big deal out of the fallibility of man and that the ideal course is to be 'Christ-like.' In my humble opinion Larry was the most Christ-like person I ever met."[35]

Larry's funeral, held in Salem, Oregon, on March 1, 2008, had a festive air. Larry wanted a carnival atmosphere, and his family delivered. His life, after all, always did seem like a high-wire act, with certain disaster attending any wrong step. As family and friends gathered, they watched a video that began with somber organ music, which was, in due course, interrupted by a needle scratching across a record, and Larry singing at the top of his lungs, "I don't like none of them funeral marches, I ain't dead yet!" accompanied by his signature scream from "Why Should the Devil Have All the Good Music?" The flower registry was also of interest, the list of well-wishers including names like Phil Mangano, Ray Ware, and Holly Benyousky from the Street Level days; Gene Mason, Larry's co–lead singer from People!; David Crowder, the popular worship music artist; Bill Morrison, the illustrator from *The Simpsons* television show; and Bono, who attached a card that simply read: "Eternal singer, still eternal."[36] Gene Mason attended and spoke at the memorial.

In the year before Larry died, he repeatedly told Kristin Blix that he wanted to be buried on a hillside, underneath a tree. Kristin found what he wanted, at the City View Cemetery in Salem, Oregon. Larry's final resting place would lie on a hillside and under a tree. Going through papers in Larry's bedroom after he died, Kristin also found a notebook with a hand-drawn tombstone that read:

LARRY NORMAN
Evangelist Without Portfolio
1947–2008
Bloodstained Israelite

Without portfolio indeed. He was not authorized by any church or ministry, nor was he ever rewarded by the rock-'n'-roll industry for talking about belief. To the end, he stood in the public square, with a Flamenco guitar strapped to his chest, singing about Jesus, unapologetic about both his faith and his failures until the very end.

EPILOGUE

IN 2013 THE LIBRARY OF CONGRESS ADDED *ONLY VISITING THIS Planet* to the National Registry. It was an "American musical treasure," according to comments released by the library at the time. "Many earlier efforts in this genre concentrated on joyful affirmations of faith, but Norman also commented on the world as he saw it from his position as a passionate, idiosyncratic outsider to mainstream churches."[1] Christian magazines somewhat grudgingly rated it "the greatest Christian record ever recorded" even before the federal government did.[2]

It is tempting to dwell on these highlights when speaking of Larry—his artistic heights, the brushes with fame, the ways in which he inspired. He drew people in, held them in his thrall, and helped them believe that God still spoke in this world, and that he, Larry Norman, was the oracle. He did this for fans, friends, even family. I should know. I was one of those fans. When I was in college, I found myself thrown into management at a small radio station on our campus, which unfortunately, in my view, played adult contemporary Christian music. I hated virtually everything I heard. I asked myself why anyone would listen to artists who, according to the Christian record labels, "sound like James Taylor or Billy Joel" when I could listen to the real thing—not to mention more artistically adventurous acts. The only possible reason for doing so would have been to bolster my faith. But I was already reading philosophers and theologians like Søren Kierkegaard, G. K. Chesterton, and Carl F. H. Henry.

I didn't need a mildly talented singer standing behind a synthesizer to help me think more expansively about God. One such "artist" who particularly bothered me was a popular singer at the time named Carman, who had just released a song entitled, and I am not making this up, "Satan, Bite the Dust." On air I joked with my co-host that not only were we not going to play the new Carman song, we were conducting a weekend-long "no Carman, none of the time" marathon. I fielded angry calls from the few listeners we had at the time.

Then, one day, one of the DJs who was in his thirties and was a semi-professional broadcaster, said, "Hey, I do think there's one album you would like." We walked over to the wall that housed the station's dusty vinyl collection. He thumbed through a stack of LPs and plucked out *Only Visiting This Planet*. On the album cover, Larry Norman looked strange and confused—not very Christian. I sat down in the production room, pulled on the large studio headphones, and gently lowered the needle down. From the first lonely piano chords of "I've Got to Learn to Live Without You," to the last line ("What a mess the world is in, I wonder who began it, don't ask me, I'm only visiting this planet"), I was intrigued. In a pre-Internet world, I set about trying to find out if Larry Norman was still active. Somehow, I found out Larry was playing at the Ichthus Festival in Wilmore, Kentucky, 750 miles away. Virtually penniless college students, my friend Gary and I made the trek to see him.

Larry Norman did not disappoint. Standing alone onstage with just a guitar, he held me spellbound as I sat on the grass among several thousand other listeners. While I recognized some of the songs, the show had a more mysterious effect upon me. I couldn't quite put my finger on it. Maybe it was the lilting affect of Larry's voice, or his open-ended questions about our relationship with God, but somehow, in that moment, I felt like God was saying something to me. Up until then, my understanding of Christianity had been largely intellectual. I had faith as long as it was supported by the "facts," or at least the facts as I understood them. But Larry spoke of his life as though God really were a daily part of it. He raised a lot of questions in my mind that he never resolved in his recordings or onstage, but I have found them to be the same questions that so many of my friends and fellow travelers deal with to this day. They include, but are not limited to, the following:

> Is God real? If so, does God speak to us personally, or are we here alone?
>
> Do faith and art mix? Is combining them destined for failure?
>
> Will I be able to keep the faith despite my doubts and the private sufferings I experience in this life?

Larry Norman gave us the impression that he was a fellow traveler along these lines, even if he seemed more confident and self-assured than the rest of us did. He was a man who went through private pain and personal suffering, and that gave his music a wide appeal. Somehow, you felt that if Larry Norman was going to make it, you just might. If his faith was strong enough, yours just might suffice too.

Sometimes, however, that inspiration went sideways or even haywire. Fans like "Roger" from Ontario, Canada, obsessively wrote letter after letter to Norman over a long period, letters decorated with Christian symbols and Larry's lyrics on the envelopes. Larry never replied. Roger wanted to inform Larry about every facet of his life. To wit: "I'm an artist, a repressed one. I'm also an academic . . . a mature thinker lives inside. . . . I should have gone to art school." Sometimes Roger sounded deranged, relating in one letter how one night he destroyed Larry's albums in a fit of rage. In other missives, he sheepishly admitted to liking the Eurythmics, but that Annie Lennox and David Stewart "need prayer, they need Jesus." Other fans felt so personally involved in Larry's story that they became obsessed. Women became infatuated and sent him boxes of gifts, crafts, and locks of their hair. Others camped outside the US Post Office for days in Salem, Oregon, hoping against hope that Larry would show up in person to pick up his mail from the post office box where they sent their checks for his CDs and merchandise.

Other admirers seemed more, well, significant. Upon return from a European tour with Larry in 1992, his brother, Charles, took a separate flight back to L.A. Clearing customs at LAX, Charles recalls entering the arrivals area and noticing a man with a hoodie pulled up over his head seated on a bench near the door, apparently waiting for his driver to pull up. When the man raised his head to look up, Charles knew immediately who it was. He greeted Bob Dylan and struck up a conversation. When Dylan asked him where he had just come from, Charles told Bob he had just been on tour with his brother, Larry Norman. "Larry Norman . . ." Dylan replied. "Tell your brother I'm a fan." That encounter could explain the phenomenon that scholars Jeff Taylor and Chad Israelson describe in *The Political World of Bob Dylan*: the sometimes uncanny overlap between the music of Larry Norman and the post-1979 recording output of Bob Dylan.[3]

In time, even Christians playing rock, if not Christian rock, wound up having their artistic heyday. By the 1990s, some of the work was actually excellent, with bands like Chagall Guevara, fronted by former Christian artist Steve Taylor, landing a record deal with Geffen Records. Bill Mallonee and the Vigilantes of Love teamed up variously with Mark Heard, R.E.M. guitarist Peter Buck, and production legend Buddy Miller to release several noteworthy albums. Tooth and Nail Records, an alternative Christian rock label founded in 1993, seemed to succeed where Solid Rock had failed, producing artists that went on to be both critically and commercially successful. Finally, Switchfoot, originally produced by Christian music veteran Charlie Peacock, broke through to mainstream success on a national level. Many of these artists would regard Larry Norman's work as a forerunner to their own.

The truth is, Larry courted fame and famous people. He pursued these connections with the zeal of a new convert. He preached and practiced care for the poor but spent untold sums on entertainment, tabloids, and, well, junk. He claimed he never wanted to be a star, but photographed himself with the passion of a paparazzo. But any portrait of Larry that paints him simply one part musical maven, one part ecclesiastical gadfly, and one part rascal would miss the fact that he at least aspired to be something more noble. He sought to be a cultivator of people, an empath, a guide. Despite his troubled relationship with his first wife, Pam, Larry admired his mother- and father-in-law greatly and kept up with the Ahlquists long after the marriage ended. And in addition to the darker mysteries of his life, some of Larry Norman's secrets were more admirable. After his death, his family discovered that Larry had given thousands of dollars of monthly support to various artists, poets, and homeless people. One musician, a former professional wrestler turned blues guitarist, called to offer his condolences after learning about Larry's death. He also wondered, by the by, would his monthly check of assistance still be coming? The family was shocked. Larry also sponsored more than two dozen children through Compassion International, a faith-based world relief agency. When late in life, his medical expenses mounting, he queried family members as to whether he should stop supporting the Compassion children, his sister-in-law, Kristin, replied that Larry's decline was not the children's fault, and they'd find a way to do the right thing. She later found out Larry was probing the character of the people who surrounded him; she had passed the test.

Larry Norman believed in a world of objective truth and religious meaning and a strict code of ethics, but died of a heart attack before his sins could find him out. He lived in a world where Jesus loved him, and this he knew. But he loved himself too, which, in the final analysis, turns out to be the hardest thing for the rest of us left here on planet Earth to do.

NOTES

PROLOGUE: JESUS AND LARRY NORMAN

1. William Ayers, "Historical Chrono-spective," in CD booklet for *Stranded in Babylon*, Spark Music, CD-SK 7017, 1991, accessed April 14, 2017, http://www.onlyvisiting.com/larry/about/babylon_ayers.html.
2. Mark Joseph, "RIP: Larry Norman, the Most Amazing Artist You've Never Heard Of," *The Huffington Post*, February 26, 2008, accessed April 14, 2017, http://www.huffingtonpost.com/mark-joseph/rip-larry-norman -the-most_b_88451.html.
3. Unnamed reporter, quoted in Alan Gibson, *Larry Norman: Thirty-Five Years in Europe*, unpublished manuscript, Leeds, England, 2008.
4. Michael Lipka, "Why America's 'Nones' Left Religion Behind," Pew Research Center, August 24, 2016, accessed April 14, 2017, http://www .pewresearch.org/fact-tank/2016/08/24/why-americas-nones-left-religion -behind/.
5. Joseph M. Scriven and Charles C. Converse, "What a Friend We Have In Jesus," in *The Lutheran Hymnal* (St. Louis: Concordia Publishing House, 1941), hymn 457. The text to the hymn was written in 1855 but credited to Scriven in the 1880s, when the text was set to music. See also https:// www.en.wikipedia.org/wiki/What_a_Friend_We_Have_in_Jesus.

CHAPTER 1: JESUS VERSUS SUPERMAN

1. Larry Norman, unpublished handwritten promotional autobiography, 1973, Larry Norman Papers, Salem, OR, 2.
2. Margaret Norman, unpublished interview, 2008, Larry Norman Papers, Salem, OR.
3. Gaby Wood, "Who Killed Superman? The Sinister True Story Behind the Death of George Reeves," *Telegraph*, April 25, 2016, accessed

April 14, 2017, http://www.telegraph.co.uk/films/2016/04/14/who-killed
-superman-the-sinister-true-story-behind-the-death-of/.

4. Larry Norman, "Stress Point: Rebel Poet, Jukebox Balladeer," 1975, Larry
   Norman Papers, Salem, OR.
5. Larry Norman, promotional autobiography, 8.
6. Ibid., 3.
7. Ibid., 7.
8. Larry Norman, *The Long Road Home: Vaudeville, Dancing and How My
   Mother Met My Father* (Salem, OR: Solid Rock Publications, 2007), 9.
9. Burl helped in the construction of a rural church that Larry would immor-
   talize in a song he wrote at the age of twelve, "Country Church, Country
   People." Margaret remembered "all day sings and dinner on the ground" before "Decoration Day" became "Memorial Day." She would gather with the
   local folks at the cemetery to lay crepe-paper flowers on the gravestones—
   which became one of Larry's favorite images of his mother's childhood.
10. Norman, *Long Road Home,* 2.
11. Throughout his career, Larry referred repeatedly to growing up in what
    he referred to as an "all black neighborhood." When challenged on this
    characterization, Larry's sister Nancy conceded that "there were some
    Hispanic children there too."
12. Norman, *Long Road Home,* n.p.
13. Norman, promotional autobiography, 3.
14. Ibid., 2.
15. Margaret Norman to Larry Norman, undated c. 2002, Larry Norman Pa-
    pers, Salem, OR, 1.
16. Allen Flemming, "Interview with Margaret, Nancy, Kristy Beth, and
    Charles Norman," February 1, 2012.
17. Joanne E. Passet, "Itinerating Libraries," in Wayne A. Wiegand and Don-
    ald G. Davis, Jr., eds., *Encyclopedia of Library History* (New York: Rout-
    ledge, 1994), 315–17.
18. Norman, promotional autobiography, 25.
19. Larry Norman, "Down Under but Not Out," *On Being* (1986), 6.
20. Larry Norman, "The Streets," Larry Norman Papers, Salem, OR.
21. Norman, *Long Road Home*, 8.
22. Larry Norman, "Face the Wind," on *Magnetic Real: The Living Room
    Tapes*, vol. 1, Solid Rock Productions, 2011, CD.
23. Larry Norman, "Darkness and Light," school essay, May 6, 1966, undated
    c. 2007, Larry Norman Papers, Salem, OR, 1.
24. Larry Norman, "I Am Afraid to Die," on *Magnetic Real: The Living Room
    Tapes*, vol. 2, 1963, Solid Rock Productions, 2011, CD.

25. The Martin Luther King Jr. Center for Nonviolent Social Change, "The King Philosophy," accessed April 17, 2017, www.thekingcenter.org/king -philosophy. See also Charles Marsh, *Beloved Community* (New York: Basic Books, 2008).

26. Roger E. Olson et al., "The Work of Faith," ChristianityToday.com, February 23, 2005, accessed April 17, 2017, http://www.christianitytoday.com/ct/2005/februaryweb-only/32.0c.html.

27. Norman, promotional autobiography, 13.

28. Ibid.

29. Norman, *Long Road Home*, 5.

30. *Larry Norman Live* (fan recorded concert), Hawaii, 1973, Sunrise Concert, Track 10.

31. Larry Norman, "The Beatles and I," school essay, May 6, 1966, undated c. 2007, Larry Norman Papers, Salem, OR, 2.

CHAPTER 2: JESUS VERSUS L. RON HUBBARD

1. Darren Dochuk, *From Bible Belt to Sunbelt: Plain Folk Religion, Grassroots Politics, and the Rise of Evangelical Conservatism* (New York: W. W. Norton & Co., 2011).

2. David Frum, *How We Got Here: The '70s: The Decade That Brought You Modern Life (For Better or Worse)* (New York: Basic Books, 2000), xxiv.

3. Larry Norman, *The Long Road Home: Vaudeville, Dancing and How My Mother Met My Father* (Salem, OR: Solid Rock Publications, 2007), 4.

4. Ibid., 3.

5. John Riolo, "John Riolo," WikiVisually.com, accessed April 17, 2017, http://wikivisually.com/wiki/User:Jriolo.

6. Tony Cummings, "People!: Drummer and Songwriter Denny Fridkin Recounts His Life in Music," *Cross Rhythms*, August–September 2007, accessed April 18, 2017, http://www.crossrhythms.co.uk/articles/music/People_Drummer_and_songwriter_Denny_Fridkin_recounts_his_life _in_music/28810/p1/.

7. Larry Norman, *Why Should the Devil Have All the Good Music Songbook* (Hollywood, CA: One Way Publications), 1974.

8. Larry Norman, "Only Visiting This Planet," unpublished manuscript, Larry Norman Papers, Salem, OR, 14.

9. Ibid., 15.

10. Annie Sutter, "Sausalito Historical Society: Where Are Sausalito's Old Ferryboats Now?," *Marinscope Sausalito*, September 15, 2010, accessed April 18, 2017, http://www.marinscope.com/sausalito_marin_scope/

opinion/sausalito-historical-society-where-are-sausalito-s-old-ferryboats
-now/article_ca75bbbd-29d8-5156-9186-b2122bddfed6.html.

11. The Citizens for Love-Pageant Rally to Willie Brown, September 27, 1966, accessed May 30, 2017, http://s91990482.onlinehome.us/allencohen/images/Be-In_docs2.pdf.

12. Sheila Weller, "Suddenly That Summer," *Vanity Fair*, June 14, 2017, http://www.vanityfair.com/culture/2012/07/lsd-drugs-summer-of-love-sixties, accessed April 18, 2017.

13. Norman, *Only Visiting This Planet*, 18.

14. Ibid.

15. Larry Norman, *Four Track Motorola '66 Corolla*, CD booklet (Salem, OR: Solid Rock Productions, 2005), 10.

16. "People!," San Jose Rocks, accessed April 24, 2017, http://www.sanjoserocks.org/i_people.htm. See also David W. Stowe, *No Sympathy for the Devil: Christian Pop Music and the Transformation of American Evangelicalism* (Chapel Hill: University of North Carolina Press, 2011), 44–45.

17. Larry Norman, *The Best of People! Songbook, Vol. 2* (Salem, OR: Solid Rock Productions, 2006), 43.

18. Woody Allen, *The Third Woody Allen Album*, 1968, Capitol, CD.

19. Incidentally, that view of Norman seemed not to be shared by John Riolo, People's! original drummer before Fridkin. Riolo came to see Larry perform solo several years later and wrote Larry to reconnect with him, expressing nothing but positive memories. The correspondence between the pair shows mutual enjoyment in recalling their time in People!

20. Lawrence Wright, *Going Clear: Scientology, Hollywood & the Prison of Belief* (New York: Alfred A. Knopf, 2013).

21. Larry Norman, *Four Track Motorola '66 Corolla*, CD booklet (Salem, OR: Solid Rock Productions, 2005), 13.

22. Ibid., 14.

23. Denny Fridkin, "People!: Drummer and songwriter Denny Fridkin recounts his life in music—People!," Cross Rhythms. Accessed June 16, 2017. http://www.crossrhythms.co.uk/articles/music/People_Drummer_and_songwriter_Denny_Fridkin_recounts_his_life_in_music/28810/p1/.

24. As cited in *Fallen Angel: The Outlaw Larry Norman*, dir. David Di Sabatino, perf. Randy Stonehill, Pamela Newman, Philip Mangano, 2009.

25. Stowe, *No Sympathy for the Devil*, 37.

26. Andy Hermann, "The 20 Best Songs Ever Written About L.A. (VIDEO)," *L.A. Weekly*, February 22, 2017, accessed April 24, 2017, http://www.laweekly.com/music/the-20-best-songs-ever-written-about-la-video-5145826.

27. Larry became friends with Ted Neeley when he became a star on Broad-

way, and photos of the two and their wives were among Larry's personal memorabilia. "Ted Neeley," IMDb, accessed April 24, 2017, http://www .imdb.com/name/nm0624189/.

28. Elliot Tiegel, "Cap in New B'Way Try Via Beechwood," *Billboard*, November 23, 1968, 8. See also "Young Tunesmiths Rock Broadway Scene," *Variety*, vol. 253, no. 1, 1968.

29. "New Rock Musical Due," *Cashbox*, November 23, 1968.

30. Emmett Grogan and Frank Reichert, *Ringolevio* (Paris: L'Échappée, 2015). Bob Dylan also dedicated "Street Legal" to Emmett, after Grogan had passed away from a heroin overdose.

31. According to the original scores from Capitol, Norman wrote most of the songs alone, although occasionally Hendler added himself as co-author. *Alison: The Musical.* Los Angeles: Beechwood Music Group: Original Unpublished Scores, 1969.

32. Larry Norman, "Blow in My Ear and I'll Follow You Anywhere," performed by the Flies, Capitol Records, 1969. Larry Norman was in this group and sang lead vocals on both sides of the single. The B side included the song "I Got a Letter Today from the President."

33. Becca Maclaren, "The Seedy, Funky, and Fabulous Hollywood Boulevard of the 1970s," *The Getty Iris*, April 6, 2017, accessed April 24, 2017, http:// blogs.getty.edu/iris/the-seedy-funky-and-fabulous-hollywood-boulevard -1970s/.

34. "Susan Perlman," Jews for Jesus Staff Page, accessed April 24, 2017, https:// jewsforjesus.org/staff-page/?firstname=susan&lastname=perlman.

35. Larry Norman, "Sweet Song of Salvation," Capitol Records, 1969, CD, https://www.discogs.com/Larry-Norman-Sweet-Sweet-Song-Of-Salvation -Walking-Backwards-Down-The-Stairs/release/3428240.

36. "The Source Family," accessed April 24, 2017, http://www.thesourcedoc .com/#about. http://www.imdb.com/title/tt2245223.

37. Norman, *Only Visiting This Planet*, 17.

38. The Wrecking Crew have been the subject of a recent award-winning documentary. Denny Tedesco, Suzie Greene Tedesco, Carol Kaye, Plas Johnson, Tommy Tedesco, and Hal Blaine, 2015, *The Wrecking Crew!*

39. J. S. Robbens, "Jam Session," *Screen Stars* (Los Angeles: Official Magazine Coporation, 1969), 66.

40. Huntington Hartford, "Review of Larry Norman, 'Upon This Rock,'" *Entertainment World: The Trade Weekly for the Entertainment Industry*, vol. 2, part 2, 1970, 5.

CHAPTER 3: JESUS VERSUS ORGANIZED RELIGION

1. Larry Norman, *Live at the Way Inn*, amateur audiorecording, Hollywood, CA, 1970.

2. Larry Eskridge, *God's Forever Family* (New York: Oxford University Press, 2013), 60–61.

3. A., Lary, et al., "George Harrison Visits Haight-Ashbury in San Francisco." *The Beatles Bible*. Accessed June 18, 2017. https://www.beatlesbible .com/1967/08/07/george-harrison-visits-haight-ashbury-san-francisco/.

4. Ibid., 69ff.

5. Paul Baker, *Contemporary Christian Music: Where It Came From, What It Is, Where It's Going* (Westchester, IL: Crossway Books, 1985).

6. David W. Stowe, *No Sympathy for the Devil: Christian Pop Music and the Transformation of American Evangelicalism* (Chapel Hill: University of North Carolina Press, 2011), 103–4.

7. David A. Noebel, *Rhythm, Riots, and Revolution: An Analysis of the Communist Use of Music, the Communist Master Music Plan* (Tulsa, OK: Christian Crusade Publications, 1966).

8. Defaced Larry Norman Concert Poster, September 1972, Larry Norman Papers, Salem, OR.

9. James L. Patterson. "The Liberator Is Coming: Images of Jesus in the Jesus Movement," paper presented to the Evangelical Theological Society, Atlanta, GA, November 20, 2003, *Reclaiming the Mind*, accessed May 30, 2017, http://www.reclaimingthemind.org/papers/ets/2003/Patterson/ Patterson.pdf.

10. Larry Norman, diary entry, undated, Larry Norman Papers, Salem, OR.

11. Gordon Bailey was known as a Christian Beat Poet. He compiled a collection of the best poems of the evangelical movement in *100 Contemporary Christian Poets* (Tring, Hertfordshire: Lion Publishing, 1983).

12. Letter from Randy Stonehill to Larry Norman, June 4, 1970, Larry Norman Papers, Salem, OR.

13. Kristy Beth Norman, email to Charles Norman, June 10, 2012, Larry Norman Archives, Salem, Oregon.

14. John J. Thompson, "Still Runnin': The Saga of Norman and Stonehill," draft manuscript with edits and corrections made by Larry Norman, 2000, Larry Norman Papers, Salem, OR.

15. Class K application for Registration of a Claim to Copyright for the "One Way Poster" filed by Larry Norman on behalf of J. C. Love Publishing Company and Author Lance Bowen, Hollywood, CA, December 2, 1969.

16. Larry Norman and the Street Level Artists Agency to the editors of the New Bay Psalter, undated c. 1973, Larry Norman Papers, Salem, OR.

17. A film chronicling the Jesus movement was released in 1971 entitled *The Son Worshippers*, reference, YouTube, September 10, 2012, accessed April 25, 2017, https://www.youtube.com/watch?v=sunr6RvLgwM.

18. Larry Norman, "Right Here in America," on *Street Level*, One Way Records, JC7317, 1971, vinyl recording.

19. Richard Ostling, "The Jesus Revolution," *Time*, June 12, 1971, 61.

20. Billy Graham, *The Jesus Generation* (London: Hodder & Stoughton, 1972).

21. Ostling, "Jesus Revolution," 61.

22. George P. Hunt, ed. "Rallying for Jesus," *LIFE*, June 30, 1972, 43.

23. "Born Again! The Evangelicals," *Newsweek*, October 25, 1976.

24. Larry Norman, *Bootleg*, One Way Records, 1972, vinyl recording.

25. Historian Carl Trueman coined this term.

26. Eskridge, *God's Forever Family*, 139.

27. Pamela Norman, unpublished notebook, c. 1971, Larry Norman Papers, Salem, OR.

28. Larry Norman to Pamela Norman, October 14, 1971, Larry Norman Papers, Salem, OR.

29. Ibid., 4.

30. Wedding Invitation for Pamela Ahlquist and Larry Norman, Larry Norman Papers, Salem, OR.

31. Larry Norman, *Restless in Manhattan '72*, Solid Rock Productions, 2004, CD.

32. Ibid.

CHAPTER 4: JESUS VERSUS THE JESUS MOVEMENT

1. Larry Norman, "Only Visiting This Planet," unpublished manuscript, Larry Norman Papers, Salem, OR, 24.

2. "The Man Behind the One Way Sign—Larry Norman," *Buzz*, February 1972.

3. Larry Norman, quoted in Alan Gibson, *Larry Norman: Thirty-Five Years in Europe*, unpublished manuscript, Leeds, England, 2008.

4. Unidentified British reporter, cited in Alan Gibson, *The Larry Norman Biography: Thirty-Five Years in Europe*, unpublished manuscript, 2.

5. "No Place for 'Rock' Gospel," *West Lothian Courier*, February 1972.

6. Claude Eton, "Larry Norman Impresses," *Evangelism Today*, February 1972.

7. Martha Rogers to Larry Norman, February 23, 1972, Larry Norman Papers, Salem, OR.

8. Larry Norman to Pamela Norman, December 11, 1972, Larry Norman Papers, Salem, OR.

9. Jon Miller, as cited in Gibson, *Larry Norman,* 12.

10. Norman, *Only Visiting This Planet,* n.p.

11. Jon Miller, as cited in Gibson, *Larry Norman,* 12.

12. Russell Hall, "Band on the Run: The Harrowing Story Behind Wings' Classic Album," Gibson Guitar, December 14, 2013, accessed April 26, 2017, http://www.gibson.com/News-Lifestyle/Features/en-us/band-on -the-run-1213-2011.aspx.

13. Larry Norman to Charles Macpheeters, undated c. 1973, Larry Norman Papers, Salem, OR, 1.

14. Larry Norman, "The Great American Novel," on *Only Visiting This Planet,* MGM/Verve, 1972, CD.

15. *A Thief in the Night,* dir. Donald W. Thompson, released March 1973.

16. Larry Norman, "Reader's Digest," on *Only Visiting This Planet,* MGM/Verve, 1972, CD.

17. Larry Norman, "Pardon Me," on *Only Visiting This Planet,* MGM/Verve, 1972, CD.

18. Larry Norman, notebook entry, undated, c. 1973, Larry Norman Papers, Salem, OR.

19. Larry Norman, quoted in "New Music Interview 1980 Part 3," http:// www.larrynorman.uk.com/word24.htm.

20. MGM/Verve, Record Release Party Invitation for *Only Visiting This Planet,* January 29, 1973, Larry Norman Papers, Salem, OR.

21. *Billboard,* February 10, 1973.

22. *Cashbox,* January 6, 1973.

23. Wire service transmission, Larry Norman Papers, Salem, OR.

24. Rhodesia tour coverage, Larry Norman Papers, Salem, OR.

25. Letter regarding Stonehill tour, Larry Norman Papers, Salem, OR.

26. Alwyn Wall to Larry Norman, Larry Norman Papers, Salem, OR.

27. John R. Rice to Pamela Norman, Larry Norman Papers, Salem, OR.

28. Larry Borman to Gary Anderson, Larry Norman Papers, Salem, OR, 1972.

29. Cyril Shane to Gary Anderson, February 15, 1973, Larry Norman Papers, Salem, OR.

30. Larry Norman to Pamela Norman, December 11, 1972, Larry Norman Papers, Salem, OR.

31. Larry Norman to Dr. Ekke Schnabel, February 7, 1975, Larry Norman Papers, Salem, OR.

32. C. S. Lewis and Walter Hooper, *God in the Dock: Essays on Theology and Ethics* (Grand Rapids, MI: William B. Eerdmans Publishing Company, 2014), 93.

33. C. S. Lewis, "Christian Apologetics," in ibid., 93.

34. Larry Norman to Jarrell McCracken, April 3, 1974, Larry Norman Papers, Salem, OR.

35. *Larry Norman Live at The Royal Albert Hall,* January 6, 1973, Solid Rock Productions, CD, 2011.

36. Ibid.

37. AIR Studios Invoice, July 30, 1973, Larry Norman Papers, Salem, OR.

38. Larry Norman, "She's a Dancer," on *So Long Ago the Garden*, MGM Records, 1973.

39. Larry Norman, "Nightmare #71," on *So Long Ago the Garden*, MGM Records, 1973.

40. Derek Church to Larry Norman, August 16, 1973, Larry Norman Papers, Salem, OR.

41. The back cover of *So Long Ago the Garden* was shot in England, where Larry could find only green apples. He painted the one depicted on the back cover with red fingernail polish.

42. Review of Larry Norman, *So Long Ago the Garden*, cited in *The Lion's Roar*, MGM Records' internal trade publication, December 24, 1973, Larry Norman Papers, Salem, OR, 3.

43. "Tender Deadline Near on AM & Robbins, Feist," *Billboard,* October 7, 1972, retrieved July 29, 2010.

44. Larry Norman, "Larry Norman Isn't For Everybody: He Doesn't Try to Be," promotional biography, c. 1975, p. 4, Larry Norman Papers, Salem, OR.

45. Ibid.

46. Letter from George Martin to Larry Norman, March 12, 1974, Larry Norman Papers, Salem, OR.

CHAPTER 5: JESUS VERSUS *PLAYBOY*

1. Francis Schaeffer, *Art and the Bible* (Downers Grove, IL: Intervarsity Press, 1973).

2. Jeff Sharlet, "Holy Fools," *New Statesman*, October 25, 2007, accessed April 27, 2017, http://www.newstatesman.com/books/2007/10/francis-schaeffer-frank-art.

3. Francis Schaeffer to Larry Norman, January 16, 1974, Larry Norman Papers, Salem, OR.

4. Larry Norman to Francis Schaeffer, January 28,1975, Larry Norman Papers, Salem, OR.

5. Ibid.

6. Robert Thoreaux, "Whatever Happened to Larry Norman?" Interview, c. 1975, Larry Norman Papers, Salem, OR. It is entirely probable that Rob-

ert Thoreaux is a fictional reporter that Larry constructed to disseminate his views.

7. Michael Leo Gossett for Salvation Air Force, "Interview with Larry Norman for the *Lodestone Festival Paper* (Vancouver, BC)," transcript for audiorecording, September 1, 1974, Larry Norman Papers, Salem, OR.

8. Phil Keaggy, *What a Day*, New Song Records, 1973, vinyl recording.

9. "Philips U.S. Series," Microgroove, accessed April 27, 2017, https://micro groove.jp/mercury/Philips.shtml.

10. Devlin Donaldson, "Randy Stonehill: Life Between the Glory and the Flame," *CCM Magazine*, October 1981.

11. Jon Miller to Norman Miller, July 15, 1981, Larry Norman Papers, Salem, OR.

12. Larry Norman, handwritten summary of the history of Stonehill's recording contracts, management agreements, Larry Norman Papers, Salem, OR.

13. Unidentified woman to Randy Stonehill, January 7, 1974, Larry Norman Papers, Salem, OR.

14. Norman, handwritten summary of Stonehill agreements.

15. Stonehill retained legal counsel in the persons of Douglas D. Graham in Los Angeles, and subsequently Andrew J. Stern in the law firm of Michael R. Shapiro, in Beverly Hills, to extricate himself from his production agreement with Triumvirate, and by extension, Phonogram. After a volley of letters outlining how Stonehill's career had been adversely affected by the Triumvirate agreement, Miller shot back to Stonehill and his team of lawyers with a firm response. First, he said, Stonehill's album had not been released for a number of reasons, not the least of which was the economic crisis in England at the time. Second, that while in principle they were willing to release and hold harmless Stonehill from his contract, the songs he had written under the terms of the contract would remain under their control for publishing and licensing. (When Christian British record executive Norman Miller later inquired of the material under Triumvirate's control, Jon Miller quipped that most of these songs weren't very good fodder for a faith-oriented album.) Third, Miller rejected the idea that Stonehill had been summoned to England for a record release. In fact, Miller maintained, "I advised Mr. Anderson that Mr. Stonehill should not travel to England in the autumn of 1973 to promote the release of his album. This advice was ignored." Fourth, Miller responded to the charge that he had not paid session fees to Stonehill for playing on the record, as stipulated by the British Musicians' Union. Since Randy had not earned back the advance he had already received, it was doubtful in Miller's mind he owed any-

thing else. Still, he submitted the matter to the union, and offered to pay if they found any discrepancy. Finally, Miller wanted to be on the record that having Randy Stonehill under contract had not done much for his side of the equation either. They had spent a considerable amount of money recording *Get Me Out of Hollywood*, which had gone nowhere. Further, Miller put Stern on notice that Stonehill was in breach of his current contract; Miller had volunteered to proceed with his obligations under the contract and record further Stonehill songs, but Stonehill had refused. "I consider that by his action Mr. Stonehill is in breach of his agreement with us," Miller concluded, "and I maintain all of our rights under this agreement until the breach of this contract is repaired." Jon Miller to Andrew Stern regarding Randy Stonehill, October 18, 1974. Larry Norman Papers, Salem, OR.

16. Deborah Evans Price, *Word: The Story, Celebrating Six Decades of Hits* (Waco, TX: Word Incorporated, 2011).

17. Letter from Larry Norman to Jarrell McCracken, April 3, 1974, Larry Norman Papers, Salem, OR.

18. Gossett, "Interview with Larry Norman," 5.

19. A quick Google search turns up multiple tribute sites to the cringeworthy Christian album covers of the 1970s and 1980s. See, for example, "Bizarre and Hilarious Christian Album Covers," Beliefnet, accessed April 27, 2017, http://www.beliefnet.com/ilovejesus/features/bizarre -and-hilarious-christian-album-covers.aspx?p=2; "Awkward Christian Music Album Covers," *Sad and Useless*, accessed May 30, 2017, http:// www.sadanduseless.com/2016/01/awkward-christian-albums/; and Jesse Carey, "The Definitive Ranking of Insanely Awesome Christian Album Covers," *Relevant*, October 7, 2015, accessed May 30, 2017, http://archives .relevantmagazine.com/culture/definitive-ranking-insanely-awesome -christian-album-covers.

20. Letter from Larry Norman to Jarrell McCracken, April 3, 1974, Larry Norman Papers, Salem, OR.

21. Larry Norman, liner notes to *In Another Land*, Solid Rock Records, 1975.

22. Larry Norman, Solid Rock diary entry, c. 1975, Larry Norman Papers, Salem, OR.

23. Larry Norman, "New Music Interview 1980, Part Two," accessed April 27, 2017. http://www.larrynorman.uk.com/word24.htm.

24. Larry Norman to Steve Camp, July 28, 1975, Larry Norman Papers, Salem, OR.

25. Larry Norman, *Only Visiting This Planet,* unpublished manuscript, Larry Norman Papers, Salem, OR, 27.

26. Steve Camp to Larry Norman, April 4, 1974, Larry Norman Papers, Salem, OR.

27. Larry Norman, "As I See It No. 66—Christianity Real and Fake in the Music Business," *Hollywood Free Paper*, c. 1974.

28. Ibid.

29. Steve Turner, "The Rolling Stone Interview: Eric Clapton," *Rolling Stone*, July 18, 1974.

30. Turner released a book about the series of correspondences he had with Clapton. Steve Turner, *Conversations with Clapton* (London: Abacus Press, 1976).

31. Larry Norman Papers, Salem, OR.

32. Single-leaf newspaper clipping, 1980, Larry Norman Papers, Salem, OR.

33. Handwritten letter from Larry Norman to Pamela Norman, c. 1974, Larry Norman Papers, Salem, OR.

34. Letter to Pamela Norman, February 24, 1974, Larry Norman Papers, Salem, OR.

35. Cover Photo: Dennis Newell and Pamela Norman, *Playgirl* (March 1974).

36. Pam appeared twice on the cover of *True Secrets*, in 1977.

37. Letters from a suitor to Pamela Norman. (His name has been removed for privacy reasons.) Larry Norman Papers, Salem, OR.

38. Pamela Norman, handwritten entry, invitation to party at the Playboy Mansion West, dated July 13, 1979, Larry Norman Papers, Salem, OR.

39. Marcy Hanson was *Playboy*'s "Playmate of the Month" in October 1978.

40. Pamela Norman Notebook, undated c. 1978, Larry Norman Papers, Salem, OR.

41. Steve Turner to Larry Norman, July 10, 1975, Larry Norman Papers, Salem, OR.

42. There seems to be some dispute as to whether there was any basis to Larry's claims with respect to Turner. But in their correspondence, Larry was upset that Turner didn't deliver on deadlines or meet his expectations. Larry Norman to Steve Turner, date unknown, Larry Norman Papers, Salem, OR.

43. Larry Eskridge, *God's Forever Family* (New York: Oxford University Press, 2013), 62.

44. "Tony Alamo, Apocalyptic Ministry Leader Convicted of Sex Abuse, Dies at 82," *New York Times*, May 3, 2017, accessed July 24, 2017, https://www.nytimes.com/2017/05/03/us/obituary-tony-alamo-minister-sexual-abuse.html.

45. Ibid.

46. Robert K. Oermann, "LifeNotes: Evangelist, Costumer, Record Maker Tony Alamo Dies," *MusicRow—Nashville's Music Industry Publication—*

News, Songs from Music City, May 05, 2017, accessed July 24, 2017, https://musicrow.com/2017/05/lifenotes-evangelist-costumer-record-maker-tony-alamo-dies/.

47. Sieon Roux, "Inside the Arkansas Compound: Tales of Abuse and Neglect," ORLive.com, September 22, 2008, accessed April 27, 2017, http://www.OR live.com/news/index.ssf/2008/09/inside_the_arkansas_compound_t.html. See also: Guy Lancaster, "Tony Alamo," *Encyclopedia of Arkansas History & Culture,* last updated May 13, 2017, accessed May 30, 2017, http://www .encyclopediaofarkansas.net/encyclopedia/entry-detail.aspx?entryID=4224.

CHAPTER 6: JESUS VERSUS THE CRITICS

1. Randy claimed in concert to have begun writing the song on the way to his first studio recording session with Larry Norman in March of 2014. https://www.youtube.com/watch?v=-gk-3F2akJI, accessed April 17, 2017.

2. Larry Norman, *In Another Land,* Solid Rock Records, 1976, SRA 2001, vinyl.

3. Larry Norman, liner notes to *In Another Land.*

4. Douglas McGray, "The Abolitionist," *The Atlantic,* June 1, 2004, accessed April 27, 2017, http://www.theatlantic.com/magazine/archive/2004/06/the-abolitionist/302969/.

5. Larry recounts meeting Sarah in the following video: "Larry Norman 1987, Part 1," uploaded by D.Rex, June 4, 2009, accessed April 27, 2017, https://www.youtube.com/watch?v=4RwI2AxbrZk. The camp was Los Angeles First Congregational Church Cedar Lake Camp at Big Bear, California, in 1969. The school was the Marlborough School in Los Angeles. Australian historian Steve Walsh established the triangulation of these facts in an epic Wikipedia article, since removed.

6. Noel Halsey, "Dr. Meg Patterson, Her Life, Her Legacy, NET Drug Treament," DrMeg.net, accessed April 27, 2017, http://www.drmeg.net/Home.htm.

7. Margaret A. Patterson Medical Practice Brochure, Larry Norman Papers, Salem, OR.

8. Dan Wooding, "Meet the Rock 'n' Roll Missionary," *Worldnet Daily,* August 11, 1999, accessed April 27, 2017, http://www.wnd.com/1999/08/3778/#!.

9. George N. Patterson, *Patterson of Tibet* (n.p.: Long Riders Guild Press, 2006).

10. "George Patterson 1920–2012," GeorgePatterson.net, accessed April 27, 2017, http://www.georgepatterson.net/.

11. Alan Gibson, *The Larry Norman Biography: Thirty-Five Years in Europe,* unpublished manuscript, 50.

12. Ibid., 49.

13. Josh Jones, "Jimi Hendrix Opens for The Monkees on a 1967 Tour; Then After 8 Shows, Flips Off the Crowd and Quits," Open Culture, January 5, 2016, accessed April 27, 2017, http://www.openculture.com/2016/01/jimi-hendrix-opens-for-the-monkees-on-a-1967-tour.html. See also: Dave Swanson, "That Time Jimi Hendrix Joined the Monkees Tour," *Ultimate Classic Rock*, July 8, 2015, accessed May 30, 2017, http://ultimateclassic rock.com/jimi-hendrix-joins-monkees-tour/.

14. Gibson, *Larry Norman*, 49.

15. Mark Moring, "Remembering Mark Heard," *Christianity Today*, August 14, 2012, accessed April 27, 2017, http://www.christianitytoday.com/ct/2012/august-web-only/remembering-mark-heard.html.

16. Larry Norman, *Only Visiting This Planet,* unpublished manuscript, Larry Norman Papers, Salem, OR, 20.

17. Bill Jackson, *The Quest for the Radical Middle: The History of the Vineyard* (Sugar Land, TX: Vineyard International Publishing, 1999), 7.

18. Norman, *Only Visiting This Planet*, 25.

19. Alison Martino, "The Daisy in Beverly Hills," *Alison Martino's "Vintage Los Angeles"* (blog), August 29, 2014, accessed April 27, 2017, http://martinostimemachine.blogspot.com/2014/08/the-daisy-in-beverly-hills-daisy-which.html.

20. Larry Norman daily planner fragment, January 1977, Larry Norman Papers, Salem, OR.

21. Larry Norman, *Only Visiting This Planet*, 20.

22. Pamela Norman to Wendell Burton, January 23, 1976. He was a pretty well-known actor and his Wikipedia page confirms he was attending the Vineyard Church at this time. https://en.wikipedia.org/wiki/Wendell_Burton.

CHAPTER 7: JESUS LOVES THE LITTLE CHILDREN OF THE WORLD

1. Turner is abundantly clear on this throughout his many years of correspondence with Larry Norman. Larry Norman Papers, Salem, OR.

2. "Norman Barratt 1949–2011," *Cross Rhythms*, August 1, 2011, accessed April 27, 2017, http://www.crossrhythms.co.uk/articles/news/Norman_Barratt_19492011/44122/p1/.

3. "Duet for a Solo Singer," *Sydney Daily Telegraph*, Wednesday, August 31, 1977, 3.

4. The London *Daily Mirror*, September 22, 1977, 3.

5. Steve Turner, *Larry Norman: World Tour Biography*, unpublished manuscript, 44.

6. "1977 Tour Report," Solid Rock Press Release, Larry Norman Papers, Salem, OR.

7. Larry Blue Simplex Record notebook. C. 1977. Larry Norman Papers, Salem, OR.

8. Turner, *World Tour Biography*, 30.

9. Dr. Martin Melaugh, "Chronology of the Conflict 1977," CAIN, accessed April 27, 2017, http://cain.ulst.ac.uk/othelem/chron/ch77.htm.

10. Martin Dillon, *The Shankill Butchers: A Case Study of Mass Murder* (London: Arrow Books, 1990).

11. Turner, *World Tour Biography*, 11.

12. Ibid., 60.

13. Ibid., 71.

14. Ibid., 125.

15. Ibid., 138.

16. Ibid., 102.

17. Friedrich Nietzsche, *Daybreak: Thoughts on the Prejudices of Morality,* trans. R. J. Hollingdale, eds. Maudemaire Clark and Brian Leiter (Cambridge: Cambridge University Press, 1997); Friedrich Nietzsche, *On the Genealogy of Morals*, trans. and ed., Maudemarie Clark and Alan J. Swensen (Cambridge: Hackett Publishing Company, Inc., 1998); Friedrich Nietzsche, *The Gay Science,* trans. and ed. Walter Kaufmann (New York: Vintage Books, 1974); Friedrich Nietzsche, *The Twilight of the Idols,* trans. Duncan Large (Oxford: Oxford University Press, 1998); Friedrich Nietzsche, *The Will to Power,* trans. Walter Kaufmann and R. J. Hollingdale, ed. Walter Kaufmann (New York: Vintage Books, 1968).

18. Steve Turner to Larry Norman, April 21, 1978.

19. Letter to Steve Turner, from Larry Norman, May 25, 1978.

20. Steve Turner, *A Hard Day's Write: The Story Behind Every Beatles Song* (London: MJF Books, 2009).

21. "Musician's Workshop," Auckland, New Zealand, 1982, bootleg recording submitted by Doug Peterson, Larry Norman Papers, Salem, OR.

22. Ibid.

23. Ibid.

24. Alan Gibson, *The Larry Norman Biography: Thirty-Five Years in Europe*, unpublished manuscript, 59.

CHAPTER 8: JESUS VERSUS PAMELA

1. Jimmy Carter, "Address to the Nation on Energy and National Goals," July 15, 1979, The American Presidency Project, accessed April 27, 2017, http://www.presidency.ucsb.edu/ws/?pid=32596.

2. President Carter, *The Old Fashioned Gospel Singin'*, date unknown, film recording, National Archives at College Park, College Park, MD.

3. Larry Norman to United Airlines, April 15, 1978, Larry Norman Papers, Salem, OR.

4. N. F. Reeder of United Airlines to Larry Norman, June 8, 1978, Larry Norman Papers, Salem, OR.

5. Elsa Ronningstam, *Disorders of Narcissism: Diagnostic, Clinical, and Empirical Implications* (Lanham, MD: Jason Aronson, 2000), 96.

6. Mike Rimmer, "The [*sic*] David Di Sabatino's Fallen Angel Documentary," *Cross Rhythms*, March 28, 2010, accessed April 27, 2017, http://www.crossrhythms.co.uk/articles/music/Larry_Norman_The_David_Di_Sabatinos_Fallen_Angel_documentary/39066/p4/.

7. Marcelo Schwarzbold et al., "Psychiatric Disorders and Traumatic Brain Injury," *Neuropsychiatric Disease and Treatment*, August 2008, accessed April 27, 2017, http://www.ncbi.nlm.nih.gov/pmc/articles/PMC2536546/.

8. Larry Norman, *Only Visiting This Planet,* unpublished manuscript, Larry Norman Papers, Salem, OR, 29.

9. Mike Curb, "Biography," Mike Curb: Music, Motorsports, Public Service and Philanthropy, accessed April 27, 2017, http://www.mikecurb.com/about/bio.cfm.

10. John Kifner, "Eldridge Cleaver, Black Panther Who Became G.O.P. Conservative, Is Dead at 62," *New York Times,* May 2, 1998, accessed May 30, 2017, http://www.nytimes.com/1998/05/02/us/eldridge-cleaver-black-panther-who-became-gop-conservative-is-dead-at-62.html?pagewanted=all.

11. Ibid.

12. John A. Oliver, *Eldridge Cleaver Reborn* (Plainfield, NJ: Logos International, 1977).

13. Kate Coleman, "Souled Out: Eldridge Cleaver Admits He Ambushed Those Cops," in *New West*, May 19, 1980.

14. Buddy Huey to Larry Norman, February 28, 1978, Larry Norman Papers, Salem, OR.

15. Larry Norman to Buddy Huey, September 5, 1978, Larry Norman Papers, Salem, OR.

16. Ibid.

17. Larry Norman to Mark Heard, c. 1980, Larry Norman Papers, Salem, OR.

18. Mentioned in letter from Larry Norman to Mark Heard, September 10, 1980; also mentioned in Norman, *Only Visiting This Planet*, n.p.

19. Larry Norman to Stan Moser, September 5, 1978, Larry Norman Papers, Salem, OR.

20. Ibid.

21. Larry Norman to Steve Scott, November 28, 1983, Larry Norman Papers, Salem, OR.

22. Steve Scott to Larry Norman, January 19, 1984, Larry Norman Papers, Salem, OR.

23. Letter to Stan Moser, November 28, 1983.

24. "Pamela Norman Confession to Larry Norman of Check Forgery," audio recording, cited in Allen Flemming, *The Truth About Larry Norman* (blog), accessed April 27, 2017, http://www.thetruthaboutlarrynorman.com/shot-down/pam-newman/pam-and-larry-recordings-excerpt-7/.

25. Signed Letter from Pamela Norman to Larry Norman, July 2, 1980, Larry Norman Papers, Salem, OR.

26. "Loose Files: Pam," Larry Norman Papers, Salem, OR.

27. Pamela Norman to "B.J.," date unknown, Larry Norman Papers, Salem, OR.

28. Pamela Norman to unknown friend, date unknown, Larry Norman Papers, Salem, OR.

29. Phillip W. to Pamela Norman, October 27, 1979, 2, Larry Norman Papers, Salem, OR.

30. Phillip W. to Pamela Norman, c. 1979, Larry Norman Papers, Salem, OR.

31. Larry Norman to Mark Heard, December 12, 1980, Larry Norman Papers, Salem, OR.

32. Official White House invitation from President and Mrs. Carter, mailed August 12, 1979, Larry Norman Papers, Salem, OR.

33. Eleanor Blau, "Gretchen Householder Poston, 59, Ex–White House Social Secretary," *New York Times,* January 7, 1992, accessed April 27, 2017, http://www.nytimes.com/1992/01/08/us/gretchen-householder-poston-59-ex-white-house-social-secretary.html.

34. Larry Norman at the White House Old Fashioned Gospel Singin', September 9, 1980, audio recording, Jimmy Carter Library and Museum, transfer made April 24, 2002.

35. Ibid.

36. Larry Norman to Jimmy Carter, September 13, 1979, Larry Norman Papers, Salem, OR.

37. Gretchen Poston to Larry Norman, January 12, 1981, Larry Norman Papers, Salem, OR.

38. Larry Norman to Pamela Norman, December 23, 1979, Larry Norman Papers, Salem, OR.

39. Ibid.

40. James Haymer, *Silverspoon (The Greatest Band Nobody Ever Heard), plus Book 2 "Life After Silverspoon,"* "Chapter 7: BJ Taylor," January 1, 1970,

accessed April 27, 2017, http://jwhaymer.blogspot.com/2013/01/chapter-7-bj-taylor.html.

41. So enamored was Dale Ahlquist with the author of *Orthodoxy* that he converted to Catholicism and in 1996 founded the American Chesterton Society. In subsequent interviews, Ahlquist never shied away from giving Larry credit for the encouragement to read Chesterton. Dale Ahlquist, "Upon This Rock That Doesn't Roll," Coming Home Network, October 31, 2012, http://www.chnetwork.org/story/upon-this-rock-that-doesnt-roll-conversion-story-of-dale-ahlquist/.

42. Os Guinness to Larry and Pamela Norman, July 7, 1980, Larry Norman Papers, Salem, OR, available at: http://www.thetruthaboutlarrynorman.com/wp-content/uploads/OsGuinness.pdf.

43. Larry Norman to Os Guinness, September 8, 1980. Larry Norman Papers, Salem, OR.

44. Larry Norman to Clare Maclean, New Zealand, December 6, 1979, Larry Norman Papers, Salem, OR.

CHAPTER 9: JESUS VERSUS FRENEMIES

1. "Daniel Amos: TimeLine, 1977," DanielAmos.com, accessed April 27, 2017, http://www.danielamos.com/timeline77.html.

2. Terry Taylor maintains that DA had turned down the deal with Curb/Warner, although Larry claimed to have been the broker, and decided not to pursue Warner once DA was signed to Solid Rock, "Daniel Amos: TimeLine, 1978," DanielAmos.com, accessed April 27, 2017, http://www.danielamos.com/timeline78.html.

3. Larry Norman to Mark Heard, December 12, 1980, Larry Norman Papers, Salem, OR.

4. "Daniel Amos: TimeLine, 1978."

5. Daniel Amos Management Contract, Larry Norman Papers, Salem, OR.

6. Beverly Leasing Company Automobile Lease Agreement, October 4, 1979, Larry Norman Papers, Salem, OR.

7. "Daniel Amos: TimeLine, 1979," DanielAmos.com, accessed April 27, 2017, http://www.danielamos.com/timeline79.html.

8. Total receipts came to $122.26. Daniel Amos receipts, first week of September 1979, Larry Norman Papers, Salem, OR.

9. Ibid.

10. DA tour honorariums and expenses, October 1979. Larry Norman Papers, Salem, OR.

11. Larry Norman to Daniel Amos, April 24, 1980. Larry Norman Papers, Salem, OR.

12. Alex MacDougall to Larry Norman, May 13, 1980, Larry Norman Papers, Salem, OR.

13. Larry Norman to Phil Mangano, April 15, 1980, Larry Norman Papers, Salem, OR.

14. Ibid.

15. Larry Norman to Phil Mangano, May 1, 1980, 1, Larry Norman Papers, Salem, OR.

16. Ibid., 11.

17. Ibid., 17.

18. Ibid., 6.

19. Solid Rock Management and Artists Meeting, audio recording, June 17, 1980, Larry Norman Papers, Salem, OR.

20. Larry Norman to Daniel Amos, July 7, 1980, Larry Norman Papers, Salem, OR.

21. Larry Norman to Alex MacDougall, July 23, 1980, Larry Norman Papers, Salem, OR.

22. Pamela Norman diary, 1975–1979, 132–209, Larry Norman Papers, Salem, OR.

23. Larry Norman to Pamela Norman, March 6, 1973, Larry Norman Papers, Salem, OR.

24. Randy Stonehill to Sarah Finch, March 25, 1981. Her reply was undated, but was sent a few days later, as it involved tax-related questions that would need to be answered by mid-April. Larry Norman Papers, Salem, OR.

25. Kevin Fagan, "Homelessness Czar Mangano Now with Nonprofit," *San Francisco Chronicle*, December 1, 2009, accessed April 27, 2017, http://www.sfgate.com/bayarea/article/Homelessness-czar-Mangano-now-with-nonprofit-3208706.php.

26. David Seay, "Daniel Amos: Christian Music's Angry Young Men?," *CCM Magazine*, January 8, 1980, reproduced online at http://www.danielamos.com/articles/angry.html.

27. Blake Goble et al., "How Often Should Artists Release Albums?," *Consequence of Sound*, December 10, 2015, accessed April 28, 2017, https://consequenceofsound.net/2015/10/how-often-should-artists-release-albums/.

28. Karen Marie Platt, "Whatever Happened to Horrendous Disc?" *CCM Magazine*, March 1981, reproduced online at http://www.danielamos.com/articles/whatever.html.

29. Mark Allender, "Daniel Amos: Biography & History," AllMusic.com, accessed April 28, 2017, http://www.allmusic.com/artist/daniel-amos-mn0000673762/biography.

30. Larry Norman to Richard Schulenberg, January 30, 1981, 2, Larry Norman Papers, Salem, OR.

31. Richard Schulenberg to Larry Norman, February 12, 1981, 2, Larry Norman Papers, Salem, OR.

32. Larry Norman to Richard Schulenberg, February 20, 1981, 4, Larry Norman Papers, Salem, OR.

33. "Mutual Release and Termination," April 15, 1981, signed by Larry Norman, Terry Taylor, Jerry Chamberlain, Marty Dieckmeyer, and Ed McTaggart, Larry Norman Papers, Salem, OR.

CHAPTER 10: JESUS VERSUS THE SOVIETS

1. Greenbelt bootleg, disc 2, unreleased recording, Larry Norman Papers, Salem, OR.

2. Larry to Pastor Chuck Smith, August 25, 1981, Larry Norman Papers, Salem, OR.

3. Ibid., 3.

4. Don Gillespie, "Interview with Larry Norman," *New Music Magazine* (January–July 1980), reproduced online at Larry Norman UK, accessed April 28, 2017, http://www.larrynorman.uk.com/word24.htm.

5. Larry Norman, "A Special Solid Rock Interview," *The Blue Book* (Solid Rock Records, 1986), 10.

6. Larry's new group of British artist friends included Sheila Walsh, Mark Williamson, Bryn Hayworth, Lyrics, Alwyn Wall, and the Mark Barratt Band.

7. Steve Goddard and Roger Green, "The Tape Keeps Rolling," *Buzz* (May 1981), reproduced online at Larry Norman UK, accessed April 28, 2017, http://www.larrynorman.uk.com/word28.htm.

8. *Greenbelt at 40: The Film*, dir. Pip Piper, prods. Rob Taylor and Sarah Green, Blue Hippo Media, accessed April 28, 2017, http://bluehippomedia.com/greenbelt-at-40-the-film/.

9. Larry Norman to Randy Stonehill, September 2, 1981, Larry Norman Papers, Salem, OR.

10. Ibid., 2.

11. Devlin Donaldson, "Randy Stonehill, Life Between the Glory and the Flame," *CCM Magazine* (October 1981).

12. The rumor was mentioned in David Di Sabatino's film *Fallen Angel: The Outlaw Larry Norman*, 2009.

13. Norman tried and failed to correct Brad's impression in correspondence, Larry Norman Papers, Salem, OR.

14. Sandi Stonehill to Sarah Finch, October 28, 1982, 1, Larry Norman Papers, Salem, OR.

15. Postscript from Randy Stonehill, ibid., Larry Norman Papers, Salem, OR.

16. Ibid.

17. The song "He Really Loves You" appeared on Larry's records *Home at Last* (1989) and *Live at Flevo* (1989), respectively.

18. Mxv, "Executioner—Hellbound," *The Punk Vault* (blog), July 22, 2010, accessed April 28, 2017, http://www.punkvinyl.com/2010/07/22/executioner -hellbound/.

19. Louis Carlozo, *"I Have Big Plans for the World*, by Beki Hemingway: Review," *The Christian Century*, June 12, 2013, accessed April 28, 2017, https://www.christiancentury.org/reviews/2013-06/i-have-big-plans -worldby-beki-hemingway.

20. Jason Ankeny, "Hoodoo Gurus: Biography & History," AllMusic.com, accessed April 28, 2017, http://www.allmusic.com/artist/hoodoo-gurus -mn0000261106/biography.

21. Bob Pool, "Calabasas Colony, Once a Mecca for Artists, Now a Cause for Historians," *Los Angeles Times*, July 6, 1986, accessed April 28, 2017, http://articles.latimes.com/1986-07-06/news/we-22939_1_artists-colony. See also "Rudolph M. Schindler," MAK Center for Art and Architecture, accessed May 31, 2017, https://makcenter.org/rm-schindler-bio/.

22. Jimmy Swaggart and Robert Paul Lamb, *Religious Rock 'N' Roll: A Wolf in Sheep's Clothing* (Baton Rouge, LA: Jimmy Swaggart Ministries, 1987).

23. Nina Strochlic, "The KGB Welcomes You to Estonia's Hotel Viru. Please Mind the Hidden Bugs," *The Daily Beast*, January 30, 2017, accessed April 28, 2017, http://www.thedailybeast.com/articles/2014/07/31/the -kgb-welcomes-you-to-estonia-s-hotel-viru-please-mind-the-hidden-bugs .html.

24. An entire documentary was made on the Singing Revolution. *The Singing Revolution*, dir. Tusty and Maureen Castle Tusty, Sky Films, released December 1, 2006, http://www.singingrevolution.com/cgi-local/content .cgi?pg=1.

25. See Toivo Miljan, *Historical Dictionary of Estonia* (Lanham, MD: Scarecrow Press, 2004).

26. Larry's passport puts him in Helsinki the day before the concert, November 15, 1988.

27. Robert Royal, *The Catholic Martyrs of the Twentieth Century: A Comprehensive World History* (New York: The Crossroad Publishing Company, 2006).

28. "Nadezhda Tylik, the grieving mother of a *Kursk* sailor who was forcibly

injected in the shoulder, through her coat, while challenging a senior Putin official, tells a Western reporter the injection wasn't a sedative but was medicine for her 'heart condition.' Mrs. Tylik makes the statement to the *Times of London* after Putin met with her and other *Kursk* families and promised them cash equivalent to years of Navy salaries. Days before as the victim, Mrs. Tylik, was shouting at Deputy Prime Minister Ilya Klebanov, Russian TV showed a uniformed navy officer grab her from the front while a plainclothes 'medic' or 'nurse' approaches from behind and stabs her in the shoulder with a syringe. Mrs. Tylik then collapses and the video goes blank. Now, Mrs. Tylik tells the *Times* that the shot was not a sedative, but 'a heart medication' because she has 'a heart condition.'" *Russia Reform Monitor,* No. 792, September 13, 2000, American Foreign Policy Council, Washington, D.C., 1.

29. Receipt, Medical Reception Centre, Forumin Laakariasema, Oy, Mannerheimintie B, 00100, Helsinki, Finland, November 11, 1988, Larry Norman Papers, Salem, OR.

CHAPTER 11: JESUS VERSUS LARRY NORMAN?

1. Lyndsey Parker, "Martha, Martha, Martha! 35 Years Later, Original VJ Quinn Remembers MTV's Early Days," Yahoo!, August 1, 2016, accessed April 28, 2017, https://www.yahoo.com/music/martha-martha-martha-35 -years-later-original-vj-quinn-remembers-mtvs-early-days-042906236 .html.

2. Larry Norman, *Only Visiting This Planet,* unpublished manuscript, Larry Norman Papers, Salem, OR, 30.

3. William Ayers, "Historical Chrono-spective," in CD booklet for *Stranded in Babylon,* 1991, Netherlands, Spark Records, accessed April 14, 2017, http://www.onlyvisiting.com/larry/about/babylon_ayers.html.

4. "*Stranded in Babylon* (1991)," LiquiSearch, accessed May 31, 2017, http:// www.liquisearch.com/larry_norman/career/spark_music/stranded_in_ babylon_1991.

5. Michael Cash and Steve Mason, "Is Larry Norman Through?" Only Visiting (blog), accessed May 31, 2017, http://www.onlyvisiting.com/larry/ interviews/VOG/larry.html.

6. Cedars Sinai Medical Center Physician's Order Sheet Special, February 28, 1992, Larry Norman Papers, Salem, OR.

7. Ibid.

8. Larry Norman notebook entry, undated, Larry Norman Papers, Salem, OR.

9. See "Excerpt from the *Drew Marshall Show,*" posted by Paul Sparks, Face-

book, accessed May 31, 2017, https://www.facebook.com/paul.sparks .3956/videos/1708074102787318/?fallback=1.

10. Norman lost $10,000 in appearance fees due to the hospitalization, Larry Norman Papers, Salem, OR.

11. See "Larry Norman from His Hospital Bed in Drachten, Holland, 1993," uploaded by larrydavidnormanfan, August 22, 2009, accessed May 31, 2017, https://www.youtube.com/watch?v=_r8GvCIsTek.

12. Steve Rabey, "Troubled Troubadour," *CCM Magazine* (October 1995).

13. Email from Mike Roe to Larry Norman, December 16, 2004, Larry Norman Papers, Salem, OR.

14. Randy Stonehill to Larry Norman, January 12, 2001, handwritten letter sent via fax, Larry Norman Papers, Salem, OR.

15. Randy Stonehill to Larry Norman, April 3, 2001, handwritten letter sent via fax, Larry Norman Papers, Salem, OR.

16. Randy Stonehill as quoted in John J. Thompson, "Still Runnin': The Saga of Norman, Stonehill, Jesus Music, and Grace," in *Christian Music* 8, no. 3 (May/June 2003).

17. See *Fallen Angel: The Outlaw Larry Norman*, dir. David Di Sabatino, 2009.

18. Cornerstone Festival program guide, Larry Norman Papers, Salem, OR.

19. *Larry Norman Live at the Cornerstone Festival*, audio recording, July 7, 2001, Larry Norman Papers, Salem, OR.

20. Program, Gospel Music Association, Gospel Music Hall of Fame Induction Ceremony, November 27, 2001, Larry Norman Papers, Salem, OR.

21. 2003 interview notes with John J. Thompson, Larry Norman Papers, Salem, OR.

22. David Sanford, "Farewell, Larry Norman," *Christianity Today*, June 27, 2005, accessed April 28, 2017, http://www.christianitytoday.com/ct/2005/ juneweb-only/larrynorman.html.

23. "2007 Inductees," San Jose Rocks, accessed April 28, 2017, http://www .sanjoserocks.org/inductees.htm.

24. See "Larry Norman: Finale—Live in NYC 2007," uploaded by Greg Murray, October 17, 2012, accessed May 31, 2017, https://www.youtube.com/ watch?v=6Z4EmZWvalo.

25. Jennifer McCallum, "To Whom It May Concern," *From a Mother's Heart . . . by Jennifer McCallum* (blog), April 28, 2008, accessed April 28, 2017, http://jennifermccallum.blogspot.com/.

26. www.theresurgence.com/the-weird-story-about-three-dudes.

27. https://world.wng.org/2008/07/larry_normans_tragic_post_mortem.

28. On May 9, 2008, "the Daniel J. Robinson family" in Australia contracted with a lawyer in Salem, Oregon, who wrote the Normans in order to obtain a peek inside Larry's will. In response, the Norman family lawyer

asked for Daniel's birth certificate. Jennifer sent it along, and explained that it listed no father because Larry was unwilling to sign his name on the birth certificate since he wasn't present at the birth. Nevertheless, Australian law allows the mother to put her last name, the father's last name, or a combination of the two on the birth certificate (not to mention that birth certificates are not signed).

After Wallace went public with her story, she further engaged a lawyer to request a DNA test from Charles that might be able to establish a link between Daniel and Larry through an avuncular DNA test, which matches the sibling of a proposed parent to a child. An avuncular test does not carry the same weight as having a DNA sample from the parent, and in any event, Charles refused. Larry was gone, and why hadn't the family been contacted by Jennifer and Daniel before she went public with the request for DNA? Why was there an additional request to examine the contents of the will to determine the scope of Larry's remaining assets? Why couldn't there have been a time for them to see how Daniel might be involved with the family, even in Larry's absence? Charles preferred for Daniel to come get to know the family first. Any tests could be done once some trust was established—after all, Larry's life had been filled with rumors that turned out to be false. The Norman family's involvement in the case ended when a judge blocked the DNA request. As far as Charles was concerned, this was no longer his problem. See Mike Rimmer, "Talking About Larry Norman," *Cross Rhythms*, June 1, 2012, accessed May 31, 2017, http://www.crossrhythms.co.uk/articles/music/Charles_Norman__Talking_about_Larry_Norman_and_the_Fallen_Angel_documentary_/48678/p3/.

29. Larry Norman, "Love and Sex," Larry Norman Papers, Salem, OR.

30. "'Father of Christian Rock' Dies," NPR, February 27, 2008, accessed April 28, 2017, http://www.npr.org/templates/story/story.php?storyId=64442288.

31. Lars Gottrich, "Larry Norman: Rebellious, Reborn, and Reissued," June 5, 2008, accessed May 31, 2017, http://www.npr.org/templates/story/story.php?storyId=91146302.

32. Obituaries, "Larry Norman," *The Times of London,* March 7, 2008, reproduced online at http://www.larrynorman.com/uploads/7/0/9/5/7095730/london-the_times.pdf.

33. Dennis Hevesi, "Larry Norman, Singer of Christian Rock Music, Dies at 60," *New York Times,* March 4, 2008, http://www.nytimes.com/2008/03/04/arts/music/04norman.html?_r=0.

34. Chris Willman, "Remembering Christian Rock Maverick Larry Nor-

man," *Entertainment Weekly*, February 26, 2008, accessed April 28, 2017, http://ew.com/article/2008/02/26/remembering-chr/.

35. Andrew Beaujon, "God Only Knows: The Legacy of Larry Norman, Who Inspired Bob Dylan, U2, and the Pixies," *Spin* (May 2008), 120.

36. Virgil T. Golden Funeral Service Floral Record, Larry Norman Papers, Salem, OR.

EPILOGUE

1. "Christian Rock Pioneer's Album Added to National Recording Registry," *Washington Post,* April 2, 2014; Mike Barnes, "Everly Brothers, Linda Ronstadt, U2 Recordings Added to Library of Congress," *Hollywood Reporter,* April 2, 2014, accessed April 29, 2017, http://www.hollywood reporter.com/news/library-congress-everly-brothers-u2-692078.

2. CCM Staff, "The Best Contemporary Christian Album of All Time," Today's Christian Music, accessed April 29, 2017, http://www.todays christianmusic.com/artists/larry-norman/features/the-best-contemporary -christian-album-of-all-time/.

3. Jeff Taylor and Chad Israelson, *The Political World of Bob Dylan: Freedom and Justice, Power and Sin* (New York: Palgrave Macmillan, 2017), 179–89.

ACKNOWLEDGMENTS

I WOULD LIKE TO THANK my in-laws, Jack and Carolyn Carmichael, for their generosity in helping underwrite research assistance and travel for this project. I also owe a debt of gratitude to my family, Kimberly, Kate, and Carolyn, who have put up with boxes of Larry's correspondence and paraphernalia stacked up in our apartment in Manhattan for years. They've been long-suffering with me when I had to find time to write on weekends and holidays.

I would not have been able to write this book in the way that I had hoped if the Norman family did not give me access to Larry's extensive archives—an embarrassment of riches for a biographer. Nothing was held back. It allowed me to examine the life of my subject through a neutral lens (as much as was possible) without having to rely upon the distant memories of the friends and foes of the father of Jesus rock, memories that can twist over time. Yes, I reconstructed the story through Larry's letters, diaries, files, and tapes. Since he is dead, his private views needed to be heard. But I hope I have said, "Not so fast," when warranted. Larry's mother, Margaret, and sisters, Kristy and Nancy, gave invaluable help in reconstructing Larry's early childhood years. Derek Robertson, a Norman family friend, gave invaluable help along the way.

Larry's brother and sister-in-law, Charles and Kristin, worked to fulfill every request I had for documentary evidence. Charles went through countless boxes of unopened archival material, and separated the wheat from the chaff. I am deeply grateful for them.

Other friends who cheered me on throughout the work include Jeff and Shelly Colvin, Skip and Timshel Matheny, Joe "The Kernal" Garner, Kirby Brown, Rev. Thomas Vito Aiuto, and Eric Metaxas. My agent and editor, Megan Hustad, has been an invaluable interlocutor and help, who, along with my editor at Penguin Random House, Derek Reed, have had the patience of Job with a busy college president who tried to find time to complete a biography.

And finally, to the many Larry Norman fans who have written their own accounts, and offered their own remembrances online and elsewhere, thank you. This book is for you.

INDEX